To Sara
with love from
Bebta ♥
Leanna ×× ×
2011

COME AWAY WITH
THE FAIRIES

COME AWAY WITH THE FAIRIES

By

Leanna Greenaway
&
Beleta Greenaway

Edited by Karol Kowalczyk

ISBN

Dedication

I would like to dedicate this book to my dear and trusted friend Karol Kowalczyk who has worked relentlessly with me for six months editing this book. Thank you so much for all of your help and support this past year. I can think of no one else I would rather work with than you.

Leanna

Contents

Introduction

Dearest Reader,

Before we begin, I would like to introduce myself to you. My name is Hester and I'm a fairy. I know what you're thinking, why is a fairy introducing the opening chapters of this book? Well you see, this book is all about our species and because I happen to be related to the two main characters (through an excellent bloodline, I might add) the authors saw it fitting to give me the job!

We fairies dwell in a magical place called 'The Enchanted Hollow' in Bluebell Forest. This secret location is, probably by far, the most beautiful of all the fae realms, of which there are as many as your own human countries. The flowers there offer everlasting colour with aromas that you could only dream about. We live happily and in unison with all the animals and insects but also have creatures that are totally unique and not seen in your world. One of our most treasured varieties is the swannikin; they resemble your swans but are periwinkle blue with bright red beaks. To own one of their feathers is indeed a privilege as they are only given to the pure of heart.

Fairy children are also fond of the dodibells, who are both a blessing and a curse. They are small and furry with pointed ears and kitten-like faces and come in a variety of colours. When stroked they sing in a high pitch vibration and giggle non-stop. They will entertain a child for hours but they breed at the drop of a hat and will build nests in the attic and roofs of our dwellings and then we cannot get rid of them. When in their hundreds, the noise is overpowering and sleep is impossible. They are also immune to any kind of spellcraft and they love to snuggle up in a fairy bed.

Now, although many of you human folk regularly walk your canine creatures through Bluebell Forest, the Enchanted Hollow is a much deeper place in an isolated part, and has lain quietly undisturbed for thousands of years beneath a thick canopy of trees. Because of this, we only ever see you walkers from time to time and mostly from a suitable distance. Of course, on the odd occasion, a rambler might get lost and stumble accidentally into our area, or every few years a gamekeeper might make a random check; but thankfully most of the time we are left to go about our business without interruption.

There are thousands of Hollows like ours throughout the world, which house generations of little people. These portals of magic and mystery are suspended in time, enabling humans and fae to live in a parallel existence.

I know you earthly people have studied our breed to a fashion and on occasion have perhaps been a little mendacious about spotting one or two of us at the bottom of your gardens, but what many of you don't realise is that whilst fairies are in fact still a mystery to you, we can quite easily see you humans going about your day to day activities. Over the past few decades, our younger generation of fairies has taken to observing human beings in much more detail. I suppose we have always been fascinated by you, and of course, the entertainment and amusement you give us with your quirky behaviours and deep-set traditions is, at times, quite hilarious! However, what we fairies didn't take into account was that whilst examining you in the way that we have, these studies have led to the rapid evolution of our world. Would you believe it if I told you that we are now *copying you*? Oh yes, gone are the days when things were straightforward and simple; we are now adapting to your ways and beginning to get more up to date, racing into 21st century fairyland, with all of the latest technology and new-found gadgets.

There is no doubt that we have, and always will maintain, equilibrium with the Earth Realm. We have the same life problems: the same spirited teenagers; equivalent marriages - good and bad; identical joys and comparable sadness; so apart from the obvious difference in our size and a little magical know-how here and there, our way of life is much the same. To give you an example, it is not uncommon for elfin folk to eavesdrop on your kind when we are bored or have nothing in particular to do. During these times, we often hear the older humans complaining about the state of the youth today and like you, we sometimes sit around a table with the neighbours, grumbling endlessly about our youngsters.

In my day, one would never have been allowed to back chat or say something rude to an older, wiser soul. It was a case of being seen and not heard. Should we have been so bold as to speak out of turn, our parents and grandparents would have had no hesitation in silencing us with the flick of a wand. Nowadays, it's a sad story; good manners have slipped away like treacle from a spoon and just as you have your yobbish louts, hoods are now beginning to cover the heads of many a young elf man here! I suppose the only difference is we fairies can cast our spells, whereas you poor people are resigned to using the law!

Anyway, I'm droning on - I know that it's one of my faults. I have lived here for approximately seventy-five years and folk still tease me about it! Some say my great niece, Spellbound, has inherited the 'droning imperfection' from me, which of course is utter nonsense! As I mentioned at the beginning, I happen to be related to the two main characters in this book and because of this fact I would delight in making it my mission to give you a peek into their world.

Leticia Zamforia, who you will come to know later, is really quite a sweet fairy, if somewhat wilful and disruptive at times! She has been my niece for thirty-three years and although she is loved and revered by all, woe betides any one who crosses her! Her remarkable transformation spells are feared in all our realms, so most are careful not to upset her. However, she is also widely admired for her potent magic and potions, and many fae folk come to her with their problems. She is always kind enough to mix up the odd concoction for them and cure them of their illnesses or broken hearts.

Trying to guide her has been somewhat of a challenge for me over the years and although I have succeeded in some areas, I have failed miserably in others. Since the age of three, she has had a strong proclivity to swear, so I feel I must apologise for this before we delve any deeper into the book; and with this in mind, it may come as no surprise that her teenage daughter, Spellbound Zamforia, has inherited the very same trait.

Even though she is my great niece, which some would say leaves me a tad biased, Spellbound is probably one of the dearest and most beautiful fairies I know. In your earthly terms, she stands around four centimetres high, with a wingspan similar to that of a blue tit. She has elfin features, with long dark silken hair, a small retrousse nose and light green sparkling eyes, which she inherited from her handsome father Zamforia. Her faults? Let me think … she can be somewhat brash at times … oh, and loud. Oh yes, very loud!

Although absolutely delightful, her other 'down side' is that she takes after her mother and is known for her irascible nature. But if I'm being honest, Spellbound is not such a bad little thing. Of course, she can be unduly disobedient and stay out rather late with her girl friends, but over the years, Leticia has thankfully displayed a stern approach and is not averse to reprimanding her should she step too far out of line. This takes nothing away from the fact that their relationship is a very solid one.

It was cemented into a strong bond when Spellbound's father, the great magical Zamforia, mysteriously vanished from the forest three years ago. Oh, my heart went out to Spellbound, the poor little mite, who cried and waited unwearyingly for him every day. It got so bad at one point that Leticia had to devise and cast a spell to remove her from the pain she was feeling. As the years rolled by with still no news of his homecoming, she eventually began to accept that she might never see him again. This doesn't stop her thinking about him, though. Each day she reflects on her father's memory and every night, if you peek through her bedroom window, you will see her kneeling at the foot of her bed praying to the great goddess in the sky for his return.

Being the daughter of probably the most powerful fairy in the realm, it may come as no surprise that Spellbound was initiated into the art of fairy magic from an early age. Regrettably, Spellbound doesn't seem to have her mother's flare for these things and on the rare occasions she has tried to perform magic, Leticia has had to prepare a series of additional spells to undo the damage. It really is quite sad and puzzling! There is a rumour that her sadness at her father's disappearance is actually the cause of her rather unfortunate lack of magical talents, but it is my belief that Spellbound does not pay attention, does not concentrate hard enough, and her inability to focus results in her making these catastrophic mistakes!

I had stiff words with my niece last year and since then Leticia has put her foot down with a firm hand and allowed her daughter only to perform harmless rituals at the weekends. I did suggest that she limit her wand practise to once or twice a week; that way, the cottage where they both reside may stay intact and not have to be continually repaired. Eventually, we sat down and decided to break her in gently and get her some extra tuition. Neither Leticia nor Spellbound liked this idea very much, but my theory was that the two fairies were too close and familiar with one another. It was possible that Spellbound's lack of progression in the magical arts could have also had something to do with Leticia being a little over-bearing and exacting.

In the end, and after much persuasion, we agreed that she should take three lessons a week with a spell mistress called Faerydae Sorbet, and since then Spellbound has actually managed to change the colour of a badger from black and white to pink and green! (That reminds me, we really do need to return him back to his former glory at some stage!) Had her father been around, she would have probably got more of her own way and skipped the lessons altogether!

Now don't get me wrong: although Leticia is stern with her daughter, Spellbound is, in fact, her pride and joy. Unlike in the human world, female fairies actually choose when they want a baby and will only get pregnant if they wish to, so there are no unplanned births here in the fae realms; it is all very sophisticated and civilized. With a quick pre-ordered potion from the Elders, one can be 'with child' and cradling the infant within three months. Leticia had always been the maternal type and from being very young had dreamed of having a daughter. So very soon after she married Zamforia, little Spellbound made her entrance into the world and since then Leticia has had her hands rather full so to speak!

I would now like to switch to the subject of the book's content. You must realise that this read, although enchanting at times, is not for the faint hearted and I certainly wouldn't leave it lying around where *little* hands could pick it up. Believe me; if I had written the book myself then it would be far more upstanding and acceptable! The characters express themselves a little too freely for my liking and so I ask you to turn a deaf ear to the vulgar language that often leaps from the pages. To be honest, I am still trying to get to grips with why I agreed to be a part of this project at all! Anyway, let's not dwell on the negative aspects of this manuscript and try to focus on the more positive and encouraging elements of the book. At which point, I advise you to take a seat and make yourself comfortable. Pour yourself some iced tea or whatever it is you human people drink and we'll settle down and begin our tale.

Your Magical Friend,

Hester

Chapter 1

Eddie the Elf

Once upon a time, one Thursday afternoon, Leticia Zamforia's voice could be heard calling her daughter from the bottom of the stairs, in their small cottage on the outskirts of the Enchanted Hollow.

"Spellbound, there's a phone call for you. It's Eddie the elf again!" Leticia had been calling her for at least thirty seconds and was fast becoming impatient. "SPELLBOUND!" she screeched again at the top of her voice, tapping her foot hard on the floor.

Spellbound was lying face down on the bed, snuggled under yards of lavender satin covers, with one tiny hand resting under her chin. A copy of one of Mamma's slushy *Spells and Swoon* novels lay open in front of her and she nonchalantly flicked through the pages, not paying much attention to the content.

"Tell him I'm out," she yelled back, sulkily. "Drat Eddie the elf, drippy little elf," she muttered again under her breath. Her whispered ranting did not go unnoticed as she heard her Mamma climbing purposefully up the worn wooden staircase.

"Spellbound," Leticia said icily as she entered her room, "I know you're in one of your strops again dear, but poor Edward has phoned six times this week, not to mention half a dozen times on your spell-phone. You really can't keep ignoring his calls. You will appear to be rude, and no daughter of mine will disgrace this family with impolite manners." Spellbound mimicked her Mamma's nagging, her top lip curling as she copied her facial expressions exactly.

Leticia stood with both hands on her ample hips and her violet eyes flicked coolly over her defiant child. She was about to remonstrate with her when her attention was distracted by the untidiness of the bedroom. She sniffed disdainfully as she rescued a shoe from the top of the lampshade and then with the tip of her fingers, she picked up a forgotten lilac bra, which had been unceremoniously thrown over the back of the chair.

"Keep your temper, Leticia," she chided herself under her breath, and then decided to try and appease her daughter rather than scold her. "With Edward's mother being a Lady, dear, and his father a Lord, he is virtually royalty in this forest," she continued. Spellbound stuck both fingers in her ears and pulled an un-fairylike face.

Leticia's patience was beginning to wear thin; she was at the end of her tether as far as her daughter was concerned. This girl could be so stubborn when she wanted to be. Where she got it from she would never know! She stopped in her thoughts for a few short moments. Actually, she did know: her grunt-futtock father, Zamforia!

"I do have a certain reputation in this wood for being a decent and friendly fairy, Spellbound!" She drew in her breath importantly and pushed her ample chest forward. "And you know that I've played fairy Zingo with Lady Elf now five Fridays on the trot."

Spellbound still wasn't listening and her fingers remained firmly plugged into her ears. In exasperation, Leticia threw her hands in the air and approached the side of her bed.

"What will they all think, eh? I'll tell you what they'll think, shall I?" she said, biting out in frustration. "They'll all chit-chat and gossip behind our backs and say that I haven't raised you right and proper, that's what they'll say, and we both know that isn't the case. You are an insolent little baggage and you need to learn some etiquette and respect girl, especially since you will be turning sixteen in two days time!"

Spellbound now had her head firmly buried under the silky pillow so she couldn't hear her Mamma's constant raving.

"Come out from there, this minute," Leticia said in her sternest voice.

"I don't want to talk to him and I shan't, and *you* can't make me. I wish my Papa was here, he would understand!"

Leticia rolled her eyes. "Well, he's not here, so get used to it." She gave a huge sigh and counted to ten. "Dear Eddie is such a decent and charming young elf. If only you would give him a chance and not to be so obstinate all of the time."

"I don't like him and I never will!" Spellbound spat out petulantly. "He's nerdy and so *not* cool. Just talk to the hand, Mamma." Spellbound raised her arm from under the covers and thrust her palm towards her Mother.

"Oh futtle-shuck," Leticia said aloud, "I see you are still far too immature to recognise breeding when you see it. And YOU, a

Zamforian fairy and not a scrap of natural, psychic intuition, it's scandalous!"

"Awww MAMMA!" wailed Spellbound, as she tossed the covers back in a belligerent fashion, "I just wanna be able to see any elf I want." Tears began to spill down her cheeks, "You just want to spoil things. You always want to spoil things!"

Leticia bent forwards and stroked the top of Spellbound's head. "Oh sweet child, look, you are all hormonal, that's what it is, darling. It's your fairy hormones kicking in. I just think Eddie is a much nicer proposition than some of the other riff-raff in this realm. He has *breeding,* dear girl, and that is hard to find, even in fairyland. Now clean up this wasp's nest of a bedroom; we are eating supper shortly."

Spellbound sobbed into her pillow, slamming her fists into the feather cushions. She had used up all her energy on her dramatic performance but it wasn't long before she calmed down and then the image of Eddie came into her mind again. For as long as she could remember, her Mamma had preoccupied herself with thoughts of a coupling with Eddie, the 'soon to be' Lord. She supposed some of her fairy gal pals would find him handsome in a greasy sort of way.

Eddie had inherited his tousled blond hair from his great-uncle Basil, who was thought to be a bit of a rake in his day. Unfortunately, he hadn't inherited the dazzling charm of his uncle and came over as a bit of a weed. Thrusting out his nether regions, he would wiggle his lanky pelvis in a bid to get her attention, and then agree annoyingly with every word she said.

She decided she wasn't hanging around for another moment to listen to her Mamma's constant nagging and flitted out of the bedroom and down to the kitchen. Leticia was standing by the stove arranging some newts' legs creatively onto two plates. Her fringe blew back at the sheer speed of her daughter's flight.

"Erm ... excuse me!" she exclaimed frostily, "just where do you think you are going?"

"I'm off to meet Pumpkin," Spellbound snapped back with little care.

"And what about your supper?"

"Leave it on the table. I'll have it later!" and with that Spellbound was gone. Angrily Leticia untied her apron and threw it onto the back of the chair, her wings flapping in irritation.

***

Spellbound sat moodily by the edge of the lily pond with Pumpkin and Taffeta, listening to them happily chit chatting about the latest girly things and the hottest new elf band, The Backwood Boys.

"Ya look like ya licked fly piss off a lemon, Spelly! Try and cheer up hun," said Pumpkin. "Let's all go get something nice to eat at the new fly-through restaurant that's just opened."

Spellbound's ears pricked up at the thought of food. Being a true Taurean fairy, she just loved to sample any delicious delicacies she could get her hands on. Her one weakness was food. Mamma's recipes left a lot to be desired; they contained elfy ingredients like gilly flowers and stuff that was supposedly good for you. But the fast food that had become rather popular in the last few years was just so yummy, it was impossible to just walk past a diner without grabbing a bite.

"Who's paying?" she asked, quickly jumping to her feet.

"I am," replied Pumpkin, "so smile, will ya, and try not to think too much about Eddie. I'm sure there are a few fairies that would be happy to take him off ya hands in a few years from now."

Spellbound pulled a face and Pumpkin and Taffeta fell about giggling. "He's nothing but a spaddy-wacker, that's what he is," she groaned dejectedly. The squeals of laughter could be heard for a mile and a half.

"Language, Spelly! You don't wanna let ya Mamma hear you saying that!" Taffeta said, laughing again. "Aww, come on, Spell, let's try out this new diner. It's called *McFlys R Us,* and they sell something called a Waspy Whopper. I just have to try one."

Whizzing through the bluebells, past a family of foxes, the three fairies darted as fast as their little wings could take them.

***

Spellbound launched into Broomsticks Cottage. She was seriously out of breath, but nothing could stop her wanting to get home. Three Hoppy meals, a McCricket sandwich and a Snadderfly salad with extra mayo had left her tummy in a very delicate state. With only one thing on her mind, she barged through the old oak door, almost knocking it off its hinges, then clattered up the stairs two at a time, swinging the bathroom door closed with a resounding crash.

"Spellbound!" Leticia shrieked, "SPELLBOUND! You infuriating child! Will you please try and be a little more restrained, you frightened the very life out of me, girl!"

Leticia was seriously high tech and quite up to date as far as fairies went. She had the latest Alchemist 2012 glitter gold computer, which she used on a daily basis. For three years, she had been under a punishing contract to write ten romantic novels a year for *Spells and Swoon*. The best techniques for producing her books she had found were a lit pink candle, lavender smelling incense sticks and complete and utter silence.

She also had a stash of fairy porno books to give her stories a bit of passion and clout when her inspiration was running low. They had arrived in a plain brown envelope from the famous *Anne Winters* catalogue. She had prayed no one would suspect what was in the brown paper parcel, especially as they had thrown in a free vibrator, *Afro Boy*, jumbo sized. She had cast a spell and made it invisible, just in case Spellbound stumbled upon it. Oh the chances she took, she berated herself uneasily.

Her daughter's noisy intrusion had entirely disrupted her thought process, causing the worst writer's block she had experienced for months. "SPELLBOUND, GET DOWN THESE STAIRS THIS MINUTE!" she shrieked.

"You'll have to wait a minute, Mamma. I'm on the tootle-hole, nature is calling."

Leticia tapped her foot impatiently. "Don't forget to wash your hands and then get down here PRONTO!"

"Won't be long, Mamma," she called sweetly.

At the bottom of the stairs, Leticia was furious, her hands on her generous hips, her wings flickering in a sinister fashion, backwards and forwards. Spellbound realised she'd gone a bit too far but nonetheless, her rebellious nature kept her smile firmly in place. Defiantly she stopped three stairs from the bottom, kicking the stair rod over and over again.

"What have you been eating, Spellbound?" Leticia asked with a quizzical look.

"Nothing, Mamma," she replied with a pained expression.

"Don't try and patronise me, my girl, and wipe that sickly smile off your face this instant. Oh just look at you, your bladderbart father all over again," she grated, looking directly into her daughter's eyes. "Now you know Mamma's psychic, Spellbound. I have been telling the fortunes of fairies for more years than I care to remember, so give me the intelligence to know when my own daughter leaves a perfectly good plate of newts' legs for … wait. … it's coming, I am seeing the full picture." Her expression became intense while she concentrated. "Two waspy whoppers, a bug burger *and* a snadderfly sandwich! Oh futtle-shucks! You know what all that high fat food does to your figure and now your innards are aching. Oh! But am I surprised? Maybe I should have called you gutso at birth!"

And then, as if Spellbound's Fairy Godmother had answered her prayers, there was a loud rapping knock on the door. Leticia turned and glared at Spellbound. "I'll be back young lady; don't you dare move!"

Lady Elf stood at the door, smiling broadly and bearing a basket full of cherries and a box of hearty fairy biscuits in a package with *Horrids* emblazoned on the lid. Leticia seemed to forget her daughter's gluttony as she welcomed her newest and most prestigious friend. The two fairies launched straight away into the local gossip whilst Spellbound breathed a big sigh of relief and unnoticed, tiptoed back up the stairs.

Her bedroom was a typical teenager's haven, the fuchsia pink walls plastered with pictures of her favourite idols, Elfish Pressme and the all-famous fairy boy band, Witch Life, who, Mamma said, sang like a bunch of comatose caterwaulers. And then there was her 'ever loving' Lionel Witchy, who Mamma sort of tolerated.

Spellbound was not particularly tidy. Her tiny pointy ballet shoes were thrown on the floor; her bed looked like an explosion and gossamer dresses littered the bottom of her wardrobe. Leticia despaired of her, but Spellbound could never quite get used to being orderly and took the constant nagging as a part of her daily life.

She stepped over the mess and furtively closed the door, pressing her ear against it to make sure her Mamma and Lady Elf were still chatting. At last, when she had heard the two fairies saying goodbye, she skulked downstairs, biting on her bottom lip nervously. Mamma may have put off the interrogation for the moment but knowing her like she did, it would be far from forgotten. As Spellbound approached the door to the kitchen she was amazed to find Leticia fluttering around the kitchen cupboards, singing merrily to herself.

"Hello sweet fairy child," she sang joyously.

"Hello Mamma," Spellbound replied apprehensively. "Erm, you sound happy?" She squirmed uneasily and started to fold a length of her dark, glossy hair behind her ear.

"Oh, I am, Spellbound, I am!" Leticia exclaimed. "Lady Elf kindly came to inform me that Zingo has been called off tomorrow, so

I took the opportunity of inviting her and Eddie over for supper instead. She holds such a prominent position in the forest and is on all of the local community projects. She's also invited us both to her place, Elf Hall. I have never seen it, but it's rumoured to be stunning. They've even got two pixie pools and a sauna, not to mention the three dragonflies in the faerodrome ..." She babbled on and on, her excitement plain to see.

"Now Spellbound, I will want you to wear something special and put your pretty hair in a bow. You really will have to make a good impression; you're such an attractive little thing when you make the effort and Lady Elf is just dying to meet you."

"Oh great," fumed Spellbound under her breath, this was worse than she had feared. She didn't know whether to demonstrate her hormonal age by flapping her wings frantically and disappearing in a sulk to her room for a week, or blissfully appearing comfortable with the situation in order to stop her Mamma prattling on about fast food again! Either way, she promised herself, if Eddie tried any funny business, she would definitely zap him in the mushrooms with her birch twig wand and if need be, she would have no compulsion in doing so in front of the noble Lady Elf herself! So there!

Chapter 2

A Recipe for Success

Leticia paced the kitchen floor. It was Spellbound's birthday the next day and she was getting extremely nervous. On inviting Lady Elf and Eddie to supper, she had totally forgotten that she had planned to spend most of the day finalizing the plans for her daughter's birthday ball, and the rest of it designing and making her daughter a dress. There were so many matters to attend to concerning the ball, it was all beginning to make her head spin, and now she would have to put off creating Spellbound's spectacular, head-turning gown until tomorrow.

She wasted the morning and most of the afternoon consulting her many books of spells to find the most appetizing, not to mention impressive meal to magic up for her prestigious guests. Finding nothing to please her in the books, in desperation she decided to call her cousin Larissa on her spell-phone. Her cousin reassured her everything would turn out fine and suggested a dish that seemed to have all the qualities she was looking for: simple and quick to make, delicious, and above all elegant and sophisticated enough to impress Lady Elf and her son. She was sure Lady Elf would be very impressed. Cousin Larissa always gave her the best advice at times like these!

It was now almost 6 p.m. and her guests were expected soon. She paused and turned towards the impressive open fireplace, which had always been the focal point of her kitchen. Her eyes flicked over the bundles of herbs and some of the more ancient jars that cousin Larissa had kindly given to her some years before. Then, peering inside the hearth, she viewed the magnificent black cauldron, which for centuries had been used for casting the most powerful spells by her ancestors. Not only did it produce the most tremendous potions, it also created the best boil-in-the-bag fish dish one had ever tasted. However, this time, she needed something extra special to work her magic with.

Her eyes finally rested on a gift from her cousin. Being more of a traditional sorceress, she had placed it on a cupboard in the corner of her kitchen and simply forgotten about it. "Thank goodness for cousin Larissa and the micro-gnome oven!" she said aloud.

Trying to memorise the recipe Larissa had dictated to her over the spell-phone, Leticia spun on her heel and went to the walk-in larder to gather the ingredients. Without too much hesitation, she quickly hurled three baby potatoes, a shallot, a knob of butter and the wings from a Snadderfly into a bowl. She sniffed disdainfully as she continued to spoon a black concoction of fermented meadow weed and heel scrapings into the mixture. If Larissa said it would work, then it would, she told herself firmly, even though the stench was making her eyes water a bit. Drat, she would have to do her eyeliner again now. She paused briefly, holding her nose as she held two bat's toes over the steaming potion, before dropping them in too. Then she placed the bowl inside the contraption and closed the door.

With a quick spell and a final zap, the wondrous meal for the evening would finally be ready. Speaking very fast, she recited an invocation with fingers crossed behind her back.

> *Take this high tech bit of plastic,*
> *Make the contents taste fantastic.*

With a double whap of her spoon and a flick of her wand, it was done. The door let out a soft *ping*, opened by itself, and she peered inside. The meal looked delicious. Leticia silently congratulated herself on her latest efforts as she tasted the amazing concoction. Larissa was one hell of a cousin! She must be sure to thank her when next she saw her.

***

Spellbound glared sullenly over the table at Eddie. She was sure her mother would consider this to be a scene of perfect domestic bliss: Mamma to her left, Lady Elf to her right and puke face Eddie opposite her. The meal tasted okay but it was nowhere near as appetizing as the cuisine she had tasted at *Mc Fly's R Us*. She sat for a moment pushing the food around her plate, occasionally letting out the odd sigh.

"So, Spellbound," Lady Elf said, trying hard to make conversation. "Your mother tells me that you would like to be a tooth fairy some day, how wonderfully exciting!"

Spellbound slowly lifted her eyes from her plate and smiled politely.

"Oh yes!" interrupted Leticia. "She has always talked of it - for years even. The head of Molars Incorporated will be sure to want her once they catch a glimpse of how special she is." She smiled proudly at her daughter. "You see, Esmee," she said, reaching out to touch Lady Elf's hand, "you don't mind me calling you Esmee, do you, dear? It's just that I have a feeling you and I are to become firm friends," she winked ever so slightly. "Maybe even family one day," she tittered under her breath, pausing at the thought. "Where was I? Oh yes, you see Molars Incorporated only employ the slimmest and sylph-like of fairies and my Spellbound, well … she'll have no trouble squeezing through the cracks of any window, and image is *so* important these days, don't you think?"

"And have you applied for the position yet?" Lady Elf enquired in a genteel kindly manner. Spellbound opened her mouth to speak.

"Oh yes she has, haven't you, dear?" said Leticia, replying before her daughter could say a word. "She filled out all the forms last week. I handed them in at reception only yesterday. It won't be long now before we hear from them."

"Actually, Mamma," Spellbound interrupted in a jaded tone, "I never wanted to be a blewdy tooth fairy in the first place! That was your idea. You know I always wanted to be a nurse like Papa's sister, Aunty Histamine."

Leticia darted her eyes from side to side in embarrassment. "Now, now, dear," she said, a little irritated. "No daughter of mine is slogging herself stupid wiping the bottoms of ancient pixies and leaving herself open to all manner of bugs and infections, which, dearest, you could even bring home to Mamma. Never, Spellbound … do you hear me? Never, never, never!"

Leticia was fast becoming red in the face and she turned to Lady Elf. "I do apologise," she said trying to calm her temper. "Teenagers, eh! They think they know it all!"

Eddie sat captivated, looking adoringly at Spellbound. "I think you would make a super-duper tooth fairy, Spelly, and if you like I could always accompany you on ya first mission." His periwinkle blue eyes glazed over as he ran his hand through his tousled blond hair, hoping she would notice him. "I could hold all of those little toofy pegs for you, sweet Spellbound; in fact, I would follow you to the ends of the earth if you would let me," he lisped, staring dreamily at her little rose bud mouth.

"Listen, cloth ears, if I do have to be a tooth fairy, I'm quite sure that I'll be quite capable of holding my own toofy pegs thank you," she replied haughtily. "I'd rather not allow the likes of you to accompany me, Eddie. And if I do go travelling, you can bet your life it won't be with you. I do have some brain cells y'know!"

Eddie didn't seem at all phased by Spellbound's rudeness and reached across the table in her direction. "Every word you ever say, Spelly, stays imprinted in my head. Just having you speak to me or see you glance in my direction is enough to raise my spirits and when I go home to my little bed at night, I keep a diary of all of our conversations, sweet fae."

Spellbound glared over at him and rolled her eyes dramatically. Just for a second, she wished that she were a million miles away from this drippy elf and his mother.

"Awww, don't they make a lovely couple?" Leticia whispered to Lady Elf. Eddie continued to sport a sickly grin as he blew imaginary kisses at Spellbound.

"Dearest Spellbound, whether you think it proper or not, I will be there by your fairy pretty side to assist you in all you do!"

Spellbound had just about enough of this simpering idiot. "Oh stop being such a pathetic grunt-futtock, Eddie, or I swear I'll vomit."

Leticia's expression turned from a proud polite smile to one of horror. "Spellbound, language child!" she chastised under her breath, "that is no way to speak to our guest!" She gave a nervous laugh, rising quickly to her feet. "Anyone for a slice of twinkle pudding and custard? Eddie, surely you will have some; you must have a huge elfy appetite?" she chuckled, trying to hide her embarrassment.

"Yes, I do have an appetite, Madam Zamforia, but mainly for your lickle wickle daughter." He swung back on his chair, and his laughing eyes fastened on the furious face of Spellbound.

Leticia groaned under her breath and went off to the kitchen to get the pudding plates with Lady Elf hastily following her, glaring at the two teenagers as she went.

Spellbound's eyes remained transfixed on the pink paper napkin that she was systematically shredding to pieces under the table. She knew that Eddie was looking longingly at her and this way she could avoid making any eye contact with him. She reached out and deftly took another napkin and began folding, creasing it one way and then folding it another, then creasing it again. Slowly she opened out some ears and began shaping the head. Bit by bit the napkin finally turned into the form of a cat, a trick her Father had shown her when she was little. Eddie gazed in admiration at her origami abilities.

As Leticia and Lady Elf returned to the room with the dessert, Spellbound immediately snatched the napkin and hid it in her lap. Anything that reminded Mamma of her father would put her in the sourest mood for weeks!

Leticia started to serve out the pudding and stopped when she noticed Eddie crouching down, peering beneath the tablecloth. Lady Elf had also noticed the absence of her son's head and peered over at her host, smiling weakly. They both shrugged and looked at Spellbound for an explanation. Fidgeting slightly, Eddie bent even further down, adjusting his bottom as he went.

"What *are* you doing, Edward?" asked Lady Elf stiffly. He shuffled and bumped his head slightly as he tried to emerge from under the cloth.

"I'm just looking at Spelly's little pink pussy under the table, Mammy," he replied nonchalantly. Eddie glanced upwards and saw everyone's shocked, frozen expressions, not to mention the custard being poured over the teapot!

"Edward!" Leticia remonstrated," I really thought you were a nice boy!"

Lady Elf blushed a furious crimson. "Edward, when I get you home, your father will kick your elfin butt right into next week!"

She stood up and cuffed him hard around his ear. Spellbound collapsed into peals of laughter, holding her stomach as the tears ran down her face.

Leticia was mortified. "Spellbound, get to your room and stay there until I say you can come down," she shouted.

Lady Elf walloped her son across the head again and then frog-marched him to the door. "HOME THIS INSTANT ... RIGHT NOW ... AND MOVE IT!"

Chapter 3

A Fairy Happy Birthday

As the sun began to rise over Broomstick Cottage, Leticia was busily preparing for the day ahead. Today was Spellbound's sixteenth birthday and tonight she would be coming out into society and attending her very first birthday ball. It was a fairy tradition that once a fae child reached the age of ten and six, a ball would be held in her honour to celebrate at Lord and Lady Wizard's Grand Forest Hall. It was possible that almost every pixie, fairy and elf in the realm would arrive and be welcomed, usually laden with gifts. It was widely known with events such as these, that no invitations were sent out; the more guests that arrived, the more status was given to the fairy.

Leticia raced through the cottage, whizzing in and out of rooms with armfuls of sequins, glitter and lace. She quickly but carefully arranged them on the old wooden table, hunting frantically in her belt for her wand.

Sitting quietly nearby, Spellbound was watching her Mamma as she equipped the table with the necessary items needed for her spell. Leticia took eleven silver pins, a full size human bodkin, four oyster shells and six blue tit feathers, which the birds had devotedly given that morning.

She zapped the wand over her head and closed her eyes in intense concentration. For a moment the cottage fell into eerie silence before she took a long deep breath and chanted,

> *Oh Wand so great, Oh Wand so fine,*
> *Make this ball gown look divine!*

Sparks of magic flew from the tip of the wand. Spellbound was genuinely impressed; she was always wide eyed whenever her Mamma conducted a spell. How she wished she could be as powerful a fairy as her. Everyone told her that one day she could possibly follow in her Mamma's footsteps but as always, whenever she tried to perform any magic it would go disastrously wrong.

She cast her mind back to her fourteenth birthday, the day when her powers were unbound and she unwrapped her first wand. Mamma had stood proudly watching, with an excited look on her face. It was a special moment in every mother's life. At this age, a child was considered ready to learn the dynamics of magic and so went to magic school five mornings a week. Leticia had stood at the school gates on Spellbound's first day, with a little tear glinting in her eye as she waved her white chiffon scarf at her daughter.

By the end of the week, it was a very different story. It seemed that every other fairy who attended the school was casting spells left, right and centre, but Spellbound? Well, she just couldn't get the hang of it. Her teacher had set a very simple task for her to focus on three white daisies and turn them red.

"Now concentrate, Spellbound," she had said. "Think red in your mind … the power of the mind, Spellbound … think hard."

Spellbound didn't much care for her teacher. She was tall and wrinkly and thought nothing of punishing her students by turning them into a stick insect for few hours.

"CONCENTRATE, SPELLBOUND!" she bellowed, and so, biting her bottom lip, Spellbound zapped the wretched daisies. With a bolt of fire they burnt to a crisp!

It didn't get much better from that day on. Leticia even returned her wand to the maker calling it an 'old warped baton', but still the replacement staff failed to cast the perfect spell. Leticia had been so distraught. How could *her daughter*, the offspring of the ever so magnificent magical Leticia Zamforia, be cursed with such inferior powers? She immediately blamed her inabilities on the inherited genes of her 'bladderbart father' and proceeded to spend at least four hours a day wand-training her child herself.

Within two years Spellbound had managed to master the odd bit of magic but was far better at cursing than casting. Somehow, when Spellbound got angry or giddy, a rush of emotion would engulf her and suddenly her spells might just work.

"I don't know how many times I have to tell you this, Spellbound," Mamma had said, wagging a straight finger at her, "never work your magic when you are mad or excitable. Awful things can happen and the spells can be irreversible, I tell you, irreversible!"

The air in the cottage became very cold and soon an icy wind began circling in the room, as Leticia's spell began to work. Her wand started to crackle and spin, while puffs of green smoke began to emerge before their eyes. Like a tornado it whirled and swirled around the items she had prepared, until finally it stopped, leaving behind the most glorious sight.

Spellbound coughed and wafted the air a little as she walked over to the table. There before her was the most incredible gown she had seen in her life. Dewdrops of pearls fell romantically from the silken lavender skirt and silver glitter encrusted the heart shaped bodice. She gazed at her mother, open-mouthed. Leticia stood looking quite self-satisfied with her magical creation.

"Mamma," she gasped, "it's super fantastic. It's stupendous!"

"Well, my dear, you are only ten and six once in your life and with this being your first ball you have to look sensational. We can't have you over-shadowed, can we? Now pay attention, dear," Leticia said smiling, and scooped the creation into her arms. "Twirl the dress this way and it turns silvery pink, then twirl back and it's iridescent turquoise. You will be a cascade of captivating colour, my dear."

Spellbound turned and ran into Leticia's arms and the two fairies embraced. "Thank you, Mamma," she said. "You're the best, you really are!"

Leticia patted her on the head and with an affectionate smile she murmured, "Ah, sweet child. You are so much like your Mamma. Now run along to the store and fetch me an ounce of hogweed. I need it for something *very* special."

***

Leticia stood in front of the full-length mirror. Her ample bosom spilled over the top of her finest blue chiffon ball gown. The dress was a little tighter since she had last worn it. She turned around to view the back of the gown and gazed at the reflection of her plump derriere.

"It's just no good," she said aloud. "My daughter's sixteenth birthday and look at me! I look just like an over sized butter ball!"

She sidled up to the mirror again, this time peering closely at her face. Tiny lines had started to emerge around her eyes and spider trails encircled her mouth.

"Shall I do it?" she wondered. "No I mustn't, it's against the rules. I'm not old enough." She peered again, this time with more scrutiny. "Oh blewdy hell, I shall do it anyway."

Without another thought, she went over to the large oak dresser and reached into the secret compartment to retrieve the magical potion. She gazed at the blue glass bottle, inlaid with gold, and remembered what her Grandmamma had said: "Only use this for a special occasion and don't forget to add the fresh hogweed."

"Well," she muttered again. "It's my daughter's birthday ball and I shall be mixing with the whole of the fairy kingdom, and anyway, my magic is great enough to be able to reproduce this potion in the future, I'm sure of it! It's just a little bit of this and a little bit of that!"

She carefully unscrewed the lid and greedily drank the contents of the bottle. A strange fizzy feeling started to permeate her body and then suddenly, her wings wilted.

***

The ballroom was a flurry of activity. Fairies of all shapes and sizes had gathered together; some had even come from the further realms, dressed in dazzling gowns and looking their best. A sixty-piece dance band was on the stage playing some lively, joyful tunes and Lord and Lady Wizard, known and respected elite socialites of the Wood, were greeting everyone who arrived and engaging them in light conversation.

There was an air of anticipation amongst the guests. Spellbound's beauty was often talked about and many of the guests had never seen her. Leticia was also known for her youthful good looks but her daughter's reputation was spreading fast.

Eddie was dressed in his finest brocade doublet and hose, his blond hair gelled immaculately back into a stiff little quiff. Smiling a toothy grin, he felt very stylish indeed, although one ear had become rather swollen and red from the bashing his mother had given him after the paper napkin incident the evening before. Many of the younger female fairies tried to catch his eye. He was, after all, going to be a Lord one day, they simpered amongst themselves.

Lady Esmee Elf stood by his side, resplendent in deep purple and wearing the famed Tregora diamonds clasped around her aging neck. On her other side was Lord Elf, a tall, striking individual who stood a good head and shoulders above the rest. Eddie's gaze frantically searched the huge golden ballroom to see if Spellbound was in sight. Just then, the ballroom fell quiet as the doorman made his announcement. "Lords, ladies, fae folk, pixies and elves. May I introduce our Guests of Honour, Spellbound Elspeth Zamforia, and the respected Madam Leticia Zamforia!"

"I still don't get it, Mamma," Spellbound whispered out of the corner of her mouth as both fairies stood side by side, awaiting their introductions. "This morning when we embraced, I nearly drowned in your boobies and now, well, where have they gone?"

"Shush, dear child," Leticia said, colouring slightly whilst scanning the crowds, "this is your big moment. I promise, I will tell you all later."

"Another thing, Mamma," Spellbound persisted. "Your hips are kinda tiny and your face looks, well … younger. It's like you just went and got a make over!"

"Spellbound," Leticia said through gritted teeth, trying to change the subject, "I don't know what you mean, dear. Now focus on your entrance, come, come!"

The band started to play the Happy Birthday song and all the guests started to clap and cheer at their entrance. Spellbound was standing at the top of the grand staircase with her Mamma at her side, her beautiful gown glistening under the lights. She was a total picture of perfection with her hair carefully entwined with freesias, orchids and cowslips, woven into a perfect floral wreath that sat neatly on the top of her head. Her dress was the colour of a rainbow and all the fairies gasped in astonishment at the most magnificent outfit they had ever seen.

Leticia had decided that following her magically aided instant face-lift, breast reconstruction and painless lippo-suction; she would abandon the blue chiffon as it was now far too big and opt for a cascading silver sheath instead. Both fairies looked towards one another and Leticia squeezed her daughter's arm reassuringly before they descended the staircase together.

Eddie eyed Spellbound and began fanning himself. "What a sight! What a gal!" he muttered under his breath.

Spellbound tried very hard to recall the advice her Mamma had given her before they had left the cottage. "When you enter the ballroom, my dear," her mother had insisted, "just look up and don't stop smiling. You must collect your skirts in a dainty fashion, always looking up, never down, do you hear? Up, up and up. When the music begins, take the stairs in time with the rhythm and don't stomp. Remember, you are Spellbound Zamforia, daughter of Leticia Zamforia. Fae folk will travel miles and miles to get a glimpse of you, you know. You are your mother's daughter and the image of me at your age!"

Spellbound was so absorbed by her mother's instructions that she hardly noticed the five hundred or so fairies below her.

"Keep your back straight at all times, Spellbound, and remember dear, smile!"

Gracefully, Spellbound gathered her skirts up, exposing two little golden slippers. Very steadily she tiptoed down, one step at a time, trying to keep up with her mother. Suddenly, it dawned on her how many folk had actually turned out to witness her birthday. Mamma was right, there must be a zillion people here, she thought, as she continued to glide gracefully down the marbled flight of stairs.

In the midst and splendour of the occasion and the gasps of admiration, a tiny fragment of lace hung like a demon from the bottom of Spellbound's silken skirt. Leticia graciously began waving and smiling as she descended the staircase, oblivious to everything other than savouring the moment. With the next move forward Spellbound's golden shoe buckle lightly brushed this piece of rogue lace and with each step downwards, it continued to graze the jewel-encrusted metal. Spellbound glanced over at Leticia again and saw her nodding in recognition at some of the fae folk she saw in the crowd.

The lace was now suspended directly over the buckle and Spellbound, completely unaware of it, fixed her eyes straight ahead of her, smiled sweetly and proceeded to take one more step down the stairs. At that moment, the filigree material caught the buckle and she immediately lost her balance. With her arms outstretched, she plummeted downwards, her wings fluttering madly, to loud cries of horror from her guests.

Eddie rushed forward, colliding with a footman at the bottom of the staircase. Leticia watching in horror, as her daughter made the biggest entrance of her life.

"Well isn't that typical?" she spat under her breath, "just like her futtle-shuck of a father, always making an exhibition of herself!"

Spellbound tumbled down the last five steps, before landing in Eddie's arms.

"I knew you would fall for me eventually, sweet Spelly," he said triumphantly as he caught her. The guests cried out with cheers of "Hurray!" and "Well saved, Eddie!"

Under her breath, Spellbound hissed at Eddie. "Fooooweeee ... You sure need to use some Minty Mouf, elf boy, your breath smells like a turdwart fly!"

* * *

"Of course, I always felt a fondness towards Edward," said Leticia, and took another sip of bluebellade. She was enjoying a gossip with Lady Wizard. "Word in the Wood has it he is wonderful husband material and worth quite a tidy sum when he inherits. I have great hopes for them both." She clasped her hands in delight and then waved gaily to Lady Elf across the room.

The ball was in full swing, and pixies, elves and fairies were all happily dancing, drinking or chatting. As Leticia looked around the ballroom it seemed that everybody was having a marvellous time. She smiled to herself and found a seat. Oh, how good it felt to be young and thin again. Her neat little bottom perched high on the chair and her pert little breasts sat proud on her chest with just a tiny spillage in view. She gazed down and smiled at her feet. Been a while since I saw you from this angle, she thought gaily. If only this miracle could last. Still, as long as she impressed the masses this evening, tomorrow she could go back to her old self. She would stay in the cottage for a few weeks so as not to draw any attention to herself and if anyone commented on her appearance, she would simply explain that she had gained a little weight.

"Well, hello there, you enchanting creature?" said a voice next to her.

Looking up, Leticia espied a tall, dashing elf standing at the table, his handsome face smiling down at her. She shook her head a little as the poppy juice she had drunk earlier started to take effect.

"And who is this?" she said, turning her slim little body to face him. "Have we ... hic, oops ... met?" She was slurring ever so slightly but held out her dainty hand to greet the handsome stranger. "How fairy nice to meet you."

"The pleasure is most definitely all mine," he replied as he gently planted a kiss in the palm of her hand. "The name's Philip MacCavity, founder of Molars Incorporated," he said in a low, sexy drawl, "and you of course are, the ever so beautiful Leticia Zamforia." He stared deeply into her half closed violet eyes. "My goodness, they said you were a beauty but pray tell me, am I hallucinating?"

"You are too kind, Philip," Leticia tittered.

"May I ask if there is a space on your dance card?"

"Why, I am sure I can ... hic ... find a slot somewhere." She bent down to retrieve her card from the floor and her tiara fell off her head and rolled at his feet. "Ooops!"

"Allow me, fair madam." He gently placed the diamond tiara back on her head, adjusting it lovingly. "Would you be so kind as to have this dance with me?"

Leticia looked into his eyes feeling considerably squiffy but not so tipsy that she couldn't see an opening for manipulating the situation and securing her daughter a job as a top tooth fairy.

"I'd be delighted!" she twinkled up at him. The ballroom cleared as Leticia and Philip stepped onto the crystal sprung dance floor.

Spellbound looked frantically at her mother. "What's going on?" she mouthed, but Leticia just raised her eyebrows knowingly in her daughter's direction and gave a minuscule wink.

As the music came to an end she did a perfect pirouette towards Philip, but the poppy punch got the upper hand. On her final twirl, she lost her balance and fell against him and they landed in an ungainly heap on the floor. Howling with laughter, they clung on to each other as they lurched to their feet.

"Oh, I haven't had so much fun in years!"

"Me neither," Philip added as they made their way back to the table.

"We must do it again sometime, perhaps a little candlelit supper for two," she said demurely, and then with no further ado, she planted a peck on his cheek.

"Madam, you are enchanting," he whispered as he kissed her hand again.

***

The birthday ball had begun to wind down. The guests were still chatting and laughing loudly, but most were definitely feeling the effects of the poppy punch. Spellbound was relaxing on a huge purple cushion with her friends Pumpkin and Taffeta. She had expertly managed to duck and weave Eddie for most of the evening, although on the four or five occasions she did catch sight of him, he was secretly blowing onto the palm of his hand and smelling his breath quizzically. This made her feel a little ashamed; after all, he had caught her with such skilled precision at the bottom of the grand staircase and his breath really wasn't that bad. Maybe next time he cornered her she would apologise, but for now, she was happy being the belle of the ball.

Finally, she was growing up and although she had made one hell of an entrance, only one other thing could have made the evening more perfect and that would have been to have her Papa share her special day. Her mood suddenly changed from being contented to feeling slightly sombre but the sound of her mother's voice snapped her out of it in an instant.

"Spellbound darling, do come over here. I have some exciting news, child."

Spellbound lifted herself off the cushion and sauntered over to her Mamma and Philip MacCavity, who were sitting happily at a nasturtium leaf table drinking more poppy punch. Leticia turned to Philip and patted his hand conspiratorially.

"Mr. MacCavity has agreed to give you that job as a trainee tooth fairy, dear. You're to start next week. Isn't that wonderful, dear? Aren't you pleased?"

"Oh blewdy hell," Spellbound muttered miserably under her breath. "That's just great that is, fooking great!"

Chapter 4

Poor Clifford

Leticia Zamforia, on the whole, was a very caring parent but because she had an incredible knack for reading minds, it didn't take much for her to tap into her daughter's thoughts and put a stop to anything she saw as unfitting. Not wanting to appear too rigid and because she wasn't a total control freak, she let her daughter off the lead from time to time. The fact that Spellbound was now ten and six meant she was reaching maturity and could even be wed at this age if she wanted, with or without her permission. Unthinkable!

Sinking down into her favourite chair by the large stove, Leticia cast her mind back to the time when she herself had been ten and six and married that 'grunt-futtuck'. She silently scolded herself. No one could have been more foolish than she. Every god-damned female fairy in the Wood had tried to snare the great Zamforia and a few elves too! But oh no, Leticia *had* to make a point of completely captivating him, making sure that no one else had him.

She chewed on her bottom lip and sighed as her mind travelled back. She had used spellcraft unashamedly. Not only that, but she had gone one step further and had programmed him to love her for life! That was one hell of a big spell, she mused bitterly. It had taken her the best part of a month to prepare and put into action. She just *had* to have him and make him hers, and the fact that he was engaged to the 'ever so awful' Tinky Bonk at the time only made the challenge more thrilling!

Of course, his money and his Locust Three Convertible had clinched it for her too; it matched the colour of her eyes. Because Zamforia clearly adored his young and beautiful wife, he would often change the hues of the car to blend with her clothing. She sniffed disdainfully and flicked her raven locks over her shoulder. He should have known better than to try and hoodwink her, she seethed.

Although Zamforia was indeed a powerful elf in his own right, he was no match for her. Her magic was ten times more forceful than his and she delighted in reminding him of it. The only time she was not in control was when they made love. He was very clever at those sorts of things, she mused dreamily. He would look intensely into her eyes, which were the most unusual shade of green, just like Spellbound's, and he had this cute little dimple in the centre of his chin and his nose was a tiny bit ...

With a jolt she pulled herself up short. Okay, so he was more than good in bed but he'd had enough blewdy practice hadn't he? The bastard!

Yes, she quite enjoyed reading minds. Not only did she read Spellbound's on a regular basis but she would often tap in to Zamforia's thoughts too. Unfortunately, having a male brain, it did tend to be somewhat boring at times. He would frequently excite himself over the state of the Fairy Financial Times and ponder for hours over which dragon would win the annual Great Air Race. And then of course he would do the usual elf thing. Extremely racy thoughts would enter his head every three minutes or so, which frankly made Leticia's eyes water! The good part was that Leticia was always the centre of his fantasy, so this made her feel safe that he would never stray. But when all was said and done, she, the 'great' Leticia Zamforia had failed to read his mind on *that* fatal day. Oh yes, where were her extra sensory powers then, huh?

"Don't you dare think of that no-good bladderbart," she berated herself sternly. Her heart ached. Even after three years, the pain was still as acute as ever. The only way she could deal with the grief and heartache was to stay as mad as hell at him. She glanced at the corner of the room. Only one other soul in the whole of fairyland knew of the spell she had cast on Zamforia.

Clifford Eyesaurus was loyal to the hilt and had served her for all of her growing years. He was her eyes, her ears and most of all, an extremely necessary ally to have around if she ever needed to know what Spellbound was up to. Once again, she began to wonder just how Zamforia was coping in his 'faraway' place and, like many times before, she decided to unveil her comrade and obtain some answers.

On the rustic table in the corner of the kitchen sat a large crystal ball, covered in a sumptuous swathe of purple velvet. Leticia carefully removed the cloth and with a perfectly manicured nail, tapped lightly on the glass.

"Clifford," she whispered. "Clifford dear ... do wake up." The glass ball lay dormant with only a faint sound of snoring emanating from the depths. "Clifford," she said again, this time a little louder. It's no good, she thought, this just won't do. She picked up a silver spoon from the table and began banging loudly on the glass, her wings flapping in annoyance. "Blewdy wake up, Clifford!" she shouted, as a single eye appeared in the transparency of the ball. "Ah ... so ... you *are* in there then!" she spat sarcastically. Clifford's huge hazel eye blinked a couple of times and began looking around.

"Milady," he said, slightly startled, "I do apologise, I was just taking a nap."

"This is no time for napping," she sighed loudly, "I need you. I have to know if the wazzack is still suffering. Do come along dear and take a peek for me; put my mind at ease."

Although she was good at mind reading, Zamforia was simply too far away now for her to reach and she needed Clifford's help to find out what she wanted to know. Eyesaurus had been cursed some four hundred years ago by her Mamma's great, great, great something grandmother, the evil Morgana. Morgana had been a powerful sorceress, who tried relentlessly to bed the stunningly handsome and widely renowned warlock, but apparently his only interest at the time was for his magic and sorcery. He'd found nothing remotely attractive about her, so with venom and unrequited love in her black heart, she cast a powerful curse on him and encapsulated him inside her crystal ball.

For a hundred years, he served the wicked sorceress until she finally met her demise at a magical battle between two warring towns. With Morgana in fairy hell, he would never be free of his ball, and so accepted that he would no longer be the warlock he once was. For him, he must spend an eternity trapped inside a piece of glass and be handed down through the generations of Leticia's family line.

On her twenty-first birthday, Leticia had 'inherited' him from her Mamma, causing Spellbound no end of trouble! Spellbound disliked Clifford intensely. He had a habit of getting her into deep doo-doo and alerted her Mamma whenever she went off the rails. Much to his annoyance, she had refused to speak to him for a whole year when he had revealed her plans to get a tattoo and got her grounded with no wand privileges for two months. Her only consolation was that Clifford was imprisoned inside the crystal ball and that somehow made it more bearable.

Clifford let out a sigh as the glass inside the crystal ball became a smoky green. It was obvious that he was searching for his mistress's answers. She gazed at the ball intensely and after a few minutes of watching the smoky reflections unfold before her eyes, the image of Zamforia appeared. Her heart jumped a little, as it always did when she saw him. He was walking up and down a long stretch of beach, alone and obviously miserable as she watched him rake his fingers through his thick jet-black hair.

"Yes," said Clifford, "he's still depressed, just as you wished it, although why you still need to have this kind of sadistic satisfaction, my dear, I will never know!"

"I need it, Clifford, because … it makes me feel better. He was the complete and utter love of my life and he was stupid enough to cross the most powerful fairy in all the land. He deserves his punishment and, trust me, I will not be completely happy until I have made him feel as wretched as I am!"

"You know, I can understand you banishing him to some far away land in the beginning, but don't you think you've taken it a bit far? It's been three years now and you keep sending him magical sand messages which, frankly my dear, are just blasphemous and childish. It's really not good for your karma!" Clifford's ball began to clear, until only his eye was visible again.

"He shall remain in limbo until the day that I die," she hissed. "I am the only fairy that can reverse the spell and I shall never free him ... not ever!"

"Well, that may be true," Clifford spoke gently. "But despite the fact that she is young and skittish at the moment, Spellbound is a bright and clever little fae and although her powers are somewhat erratic, should she ever discover exactly what did happen to her father, I'm sure she could find out how to bring him back herself. She does have your magical genes after all!"

Leticia sniffed defiantly, going slightly pink. "Well, she will never find out! As far as she is concerned, her father Zamforia disappeared, abandoning his family, and is never coming back. And, lordy lord, Clifford," she continued in a raised voice, "if she ever did find out, I would know exactly who told her. For your sake, I wouldn't breathe a word. NOT A WORD, do you hear? Or I'll banish you to Morgana and her fairy hell pit!"

Clifford gulped ever so slightly. He secretly worshipped the ground his mistress walked on and in truth was more than a little bit in love with her. Her figure was womanly and deliciously plump, her skin milky white. In fact, she looked just like an older version of Snow White. He had seen her grow from being a baby fae to a child, who would tap his glass mischievously when her Mamma wasn't looking. Over the years, she had become the most stunning of all fairies and ever since then his heart had almost burst with the longing and love he felt for her. As a gallant and genteel warlock, he frequently had to shake off the lustful emotions that began to surface whenever she peered through the glass in her cleavage-spilling gowns. He would silently curse himself at his lack of self-control but thankfully, she had never guessed the passion inside the warlock, inside the ball, and only saw him as a faithful servant. If he could just get out of this glass prison, he vowed to show her what a real warlock was and make her forget Zamforia once and for all!

Chapter 5

The Bling Thing

"Aww, Mamma, why not? Why can't I have my belly button pierced? Every fairy in the wood has hers done and I'm the only one that has to be different. Do you want me to be a laughing stock?"

"I've told you before, Spellbound, and I will not tell you again," Leticia said sternly. "If the great Goddess above wanted you to have a diamante in your navel, you would have been born with one. Now stop harassing me child! I am trying to compose a really raunchy sex scene for my latest book. The publishers have specifically asked me to step the tempo up a bit. And as it's been years since I've had sex, I must really concentrate, child." She turned back to writing and began silently mouthing something erotic.

"What's sex like, Mamma? ... does it hurt and what's an orgasm like, Mamma? ... did you have an orgasm with Papa in the olden days?"

Leticia peered over her very, very tiny designer crystal spectacles and drummed her perfectly polished sugar pink nails on the desk top. "Enough! Spellbound ... you are infuriating me!"

"I should be able to know these things. Pumpkin said that she heard her Mamma and Papa moaning and groaning in the next room and the bed was creaking. It went creak ... creak ... creak ... and then very fast ... creak, creak, creak! She said they were screwing. What's screwing, Mamma? Did you screw in the olden days?"

"SPELLBOUND! Do you want to be grounded?"

Spellbound hung her head and prodded the chair repeatedly with her red satin ballet slipper. "No, Mamma. So... *can* I have my belly button pierced? ... *please, oh pleeease, pretty Mamma*?"

Leticia decided to ignore her daughter's whining and carried on. Maybe the girl would whoosh off somewhere and leave her in peace if she pretended not to hear.

Spellbound sauntered slowly over to the desk where Leticia was working, and peered over her shoulder to read the unfolding story. Sticking her fingers down her throat and rolling her eyes dramatically, she groaned.

"Ughhhhhh!!!!! Mamma!!! Gawd ... that is SO NOT cool ... yuk ... yuk ... yuk! I can't believe he sticks THAT in her pee-pee hole!" She turned on her heel and stomped upstairs to her fairy untidy bedroom. As she slammed the door with a resounding crash she muttered, "Drat Mamma and her silly *Spells and Swoon* book." It was all lies anyway, she thought, none of it was true and she would NEVER EVER do anything like that with a pixie or an elf. As soon as she could, she would leave home and look for her Papa.

Spellbound went over to the cream cupboard at the side of her bed and reached in the drawer for her wand. If Mamma wasn't going to whiz her up some belly bling, she would just have to do it herself. The wand was made of apple wood and had a petite little amethyst crystal glued firmly in the tip. She scrutinized it for a moment and then closed her eyes and circled it around her head three times.

This Magic I make with speed and haste,
Bring that bling before my face.

Ok, she thought, so she may not have the knack of rhyming her words like Mamma did but it should work all the same. There was an explosion of yellow and red sparks and murky looking smoke filled the bedroom. The cloudy mass was so thick that Spellbound choked and coughed on the fumes.

"WHAT THE FOOK WAS THAT, SPELLBOUND?" Leticia yelled up the stairs.

"GET DOWN HERE RIGHT NOW, GIRL! You are really getting out of hand. I just don't know what I am going to do with you!"

Spellbound stomped down the stairs two at a time, glowering under ridiculously long black eyelashes.

"Have you quite finished banging and clattering around the cottage? The noises you are making resemble that of a troll, not the dainty little fairy I am trying very hard to raise you to be." Leticia took one look at her daughter and stepped backwards, placing her hand to her throat. "Oh just look at you!" she said aghast. "What in heaven's name have you done to yourself, girl?"

Spellbound skulked over to the cheval mirror that was positioned in the corner of the room and nearly did a double take when she viewed her reflection. Her hair was stiff and stuck out in all directions, her face was as black as soot and a glittering emerald sat perfectly in the middle of her nose. She immediately began tugging at the jewel to try and remove it from her face and, when it wouldn't budge, the tears rolled like a river down her cheeks.

"I really just wanted my belly button pierced 'coz all the other fairy gals are doing it," she whimpered, half defiant, half snivelling. "I'm the only one in my gang that hasn't got it done. Everyone else is in crop tops with slashed jeans and what do I have, Mamma, eh, what do I have?" She finally broke out in a dramatic wail. "I HAVE GLITTERY 'COME PRANCING' FROCKS AND A NAKED NAVEL ... ARGH HA!"

It was getting late and Leticia had just about had enough of Spellbound's histrionics for one day. She had a seven day deadline to get her latest book *Whose Mushrooms are you Bouncing on Tonight?* on her editor's desk or she would be in breach of contract. Lately, with everything that was going on in fairyland, she just couldn't find the time to sit down and write and when she actually did get a minute's peace, the inspiration didn't quite flow like it should.

Her thoughts came back to the present situation. If Spellbound had what she wanted, just this once, she might get the chance to finish it. It wasn't often that Leticia gave in to her daughter's demands but this was important. She really did have to crack on.

"Okay, Spellbound," she said quietly.

Spellbound was still playing the drama queen, sobbing dramatically into a tea towel. She blew her nose loudly, fixing her tear-drenched eyes firmly on her Mamma.

"Well, well, my girl, it might be an idea to enter you into Fada Drama College, you would make a perfect actress. I think you get that skill from your bastard father! Now, stop this ear-splitting racket. You have just about given me the worst headache since I gave birth to you!"

Spellbound came down from her theatrical climax and twiddled with the emerald, still obviously stuck fast to her nose. Leticia winced and walked over to her, waving her dainty fingers ever so slightly in the air.

"I'll cast a spell, just this once for you to have the ... the ... what is it? ... belly button mutilation thing, IF, and ONLY IF you promise to behave and let me get on with this blasted book. I'll whiz you up a pair of slashed jeans and a ... what was it?" Her mind started to wander, "Oh yes, a crap top. But be warned, Spellbound," she continued with a steely expression, "this is just for tonight, do you hear? Just for tonight. Now then," Leticia said, rummaging around in the pocket of her green velvet gown for her wand, "have you any preference as to colour?"

Spellbound couldn't believe her luck. All that ranting and raving had actually worked! Her girlfriends had told her that parents normally gave in if you kicked off a bit, but this was soooo easy-peasy. Not wanting to change her Mamma's mind, she answered very sheepishly in a high pitched squeak.

"Um, err," she snivelled, "red would be quite good, Mamma."

"Red it is then ... and the belly bling ... what colour?"

"Um, err ..." she hesitated, before hiccupping loudly, "... a ruby ... um ... a real one if poss, Mamma ... with a diamond cluster, please?"

Leticia scratched her head with her wand for a second, scouring her brain for the correct ritual and then stood to face her daughter.

"Good grief, girl," she said, looking her straight in the face, "all that weeping and wailing has turned your eyes bright red. You look like something out of a goblin horror movie! I suppose I will have to fix that too." She gently touched each of Spellbound's shoulders with the tip of her wand before reciting her invocation.

> *Make a red-hot top that's cropped,*
> *Let the emerald from her nose be dropped.*
> *Wipe the tears from her face,*
> *And make sure the navel gem's in place.*
> *Finish off with jeans of red,*
> *And wipe that soot from off her head!*

The usual whirls and swirls of colour encircled the room, as they always did when Leticia made her magic. Before Spellbound knew what had hit her, a funny fizzy feeling erupted through her body and her appearance started to change. She quickly ran to the mirror again. The first thing she looked at was her nose. The emerald had gone. Then, glancing down, she saw a pair of the sexiest little red shredded jeans, which sat sweetly on her narrow hips. A good-sized sparkly ruby and diamond cluster was neatly ensconced in her navel and, casting her eyes upwards again, she noticed the fantastic deep red crop top that just about covered her chest.

To finish it off, Leticia had added a few extra touches. Spellbound found a pair of black suede booties, with killer heels, on her feet, a tiny tattoo of a unicorn on her lower back, and her hair was gathered up sexily into a high ponytail.

"WOW, MAMMA!" Spellbound cried in awe. "How do you do it? You are the *Most Wonderful Mamma in the Whole Fairy World* and you even got the wings to match! Oh Mamma, I love you, I REALLY love you!"

"Stop grovelling, child ... it doesn't become you."

Leticia was pleasantly surprised to see how well her spell had actually worked. She was a stickler for fairy tradition and liked nothing more than to see Spellbound in gowns with twinkles and tiny sequins, but she had to admit, for a teenager in fairyland, they would have to go a long way to beat this outfit. Perhaps she should have been a fashion designer instead of an author, she mused dreamily.

"Right, now go out and have some fun," she said, with a slight smile on her perfect lips, "and remember, the belly bling is just for tonight and tonight only. Off you go and make sure you're back by twelve."

Spellbound needed no further encouragement; with a flutter of fairy dust and a cheery goodbye, she was gone. Leticia breathed a big sigh of relief. "Blewdy peace at last!"

Chapter 6

Molars Inc.

It was Spellbound's first day at Molars Inc. and as she sat in the large marbled reception area she glanced around curiously at the other applicants, wondering if they were as apprehensive as she was. To her right was a little blonde freckled fairy nervously chewing on one of her already bitten down nails. She smiled shyly at Spellbound, who smiled back and then looked to her left. Sitting there was a voluptuous pale blue creature with two long forehead antennae, whose large boobs spilled over the tight bodice of her fairy frock; Spellbound knew her from the fairy club scene. She was flicking idly through a copy of *Ofay* magazine. On the front was a huge picture of Elfish Pressme with his jet-black hair greased back into a high quiff. Spellbound tried to get a better look at her idol. The snooty fairy sniffed disdainfully and rattled the magazine, glaring daggers at her for being so nosy. Spellbound raised her eyebrows haughtily, the way that Mamma always did, and settled back in the over-stuffed chair. Her mind returned to a few days ago.

With a lot of pleading and constant droning (something she was getting very, very good at), she had managed to keep the red slashed jeans and crop top, and also the spike-heeled booties. She hadn't taken the trendy ensemble off for two days, just in case Mamma changed her mind and spelled them away. Mamma said she might even wear something like it herself when she had the time to whiz up an outfit. Spellbound's mouth had dropped open at this remark; she could never have anything original of her own, and if Mamma did create her own outfit, you could bet yer bleedin' life it would be ten times better than hers!

Unfortunately, Mamma had kept to her word about the ruby and diamond cluster bling. This had disappeared when she got home, but Mamma being in a very good mood since she had managed to finish her new book on time, had replaced it with a jazzy *twinkle* belt. It was very *a la mode* and only just out in the shops. She had remarked she might quite like to borrow Spellbound's new outfit later as she was going to a 'Bad Taste Party'. Why Mamma didn't just act her age, after all, she was ancient at thirty-three years old. She ought to get a life and her own blewdy wardrobe!

Looking around the grand marbled reception area, Spellbound saw a large picture and plaque on the wall of Philip MacCavity, the President of Molars Inc. He was famous for being the only fairy in the history of Molars to ever bring back a gold tooth from the human realms. No one was ever quite sure how a human child ended up with a gold tooth in its mouth - perhaps its father had been a dentist! But nevertheless, it was now proudly displayed in a secure walnut cabinet, with a gold plaque inscribed with the words: *We get the tooth, the whole tooth, and nothing but the tooth.*

"Miss Spellbound Zamforia, please."

Spellbound stood up quickly.

"This way," said a slender blonde fairy, in a rather superior voice. She was in a no-nonsense navy pencil skirt and pristine white starched blouse. Spellbound nervously followed her into a large office, where she observed the great Philip MacCavity sitting behind a sumptuous oak desk. On the desk were a collection of spell-phones, a bright red laptop and one photograph of a rather dashing younger man, probably his son, she thought. Spellbound looked at MacCavity. He was an older fairy with huge brown eyes and dark hair with two white flashes at either side of his temples. On the whole, he looked very distinguished and Spellbound knew he was as shrewd as they came. On his hand, she noticed a large gold handfasting ring; she was surprised there was no picture of Mrs MacCavity.

"Miss Spellbound ... aahh ... do come in and take a seat." He gestured her over to a chair which directly faced his own. "My word, you certainly are a carbon copy of your wonderful Mamma. And how is that very beautiful fairy? Be sure and pass on my felicitations and remind her we never did go out for that candle-lit dinner she promised me."

He frowned, tapping his silver pen erratically on the highly polished desktop. Spellbound smiled nervously. Placing the tips of his fingers gently together, he continued in a more business-like manner. "Anyway, you may not know this, Spellbound, but teeth are *seriously* big business here in Fairyland."

Her gaze drifted over him and she tried to look captivated.

He went on, "Every tooth that is collected from a human child is precious, and once it's brought back to the fae realms, it is ground down for making things such as cement for building our houses, fairy expensive talcum powder and of course, the finest bone china. I myself have the very rare sixty-piece *Toofy Pegs* dinner service. There were only two ever made in all the realms. Ours was displayed on the *Fairy Ant-eeks Toadshow* last year. I believe your father, Zamforia, purchased the other dinner set if I remember correctly and he had the extra six soup tureens too…and ladles," he mused jealously.

Yeah right ... how interesting is that, she thought to herself. And what idiot didn't know that dinner plates and talcum powder came from human teeth? Did this guy think she was thick? And of course she knew about the *Toofy Pegs* dinner set and six extra tureens. Papa said he had bought it for her and her alone for when she was older, she sniffed proudly. Mamma had been really envious too, and scolded Zamforia for spoiling his daughter and splashing his vast fortune around as if he had money to burn. He had remonstrated with Mamma, and Spellbound could clearly remember him barking out, "Leticia ... mind your own business. What I do with my money is MY business, okay?"

Mamma had glared daggers at him and then she had laughed and purred like a little pussy cat and kissed him on the tip of his aquiline nose. It was no secret that Mamma loved strong men and Papa was nobody's fool. He knew just how to handle her, that was for sure. Suddenly she remembered where she was again.

"Anyway, every fairy starts out their missions with a work colleague, Spellbound," Philip MacCavity went on, lighting a rather large purple cheroot and blowing a cloud of pungent smoke right into her face. "After serious consideration, I have decided to partner you with my loyal and long standing employee, Steffan Hogsbeer."

Appearing from behind the curtain as if on cue, Steffan stepped out with a flourish. He was so much taller than her, at least six millimeters, with a tanned, fit, muscular body, a gold hoop earring in each lobe and a whiter-than-white smile. His dark brown hair was immaculately groomed with Slugga-Slug gel, and a tiny diamond was fixed to his front tooth so that every time he smiled his teeth dazzled. Spellbound's first impressions were, "WOW ... who is this powerful, fairy chunky hunk?" But it didn't take her long to realize that Steffan Hogsbeer was right up his own fairy hairy arse.

He may have the face and body of an elfin Adonis, but the compact mirror tucked neatly into the back pocket of his sexy tight-fitting jeans just didn't do it for her. He also spoke with an annoying lisp and could not pronounce his r's properly. Spellbound nearly peed herself when he said that he was a 'vewy pwoud faiwy' and that he 'impwessed people with 'aving such a wesponsible caweer, wepwesenting The Molar Tooth Wemoving Company'. But what really nailed it for her was that he also had the really annoying habit of saying the words 'Blinding! Hey, hey!' after nearly every sentence.

"No-one who works for Molars Inc. is expected to work alone, Miss Spellbound," said Philip MacCavity in a low drawl. "Your job will be to accompany Steffan four nights a week and liaise with the local 'spider intelligence web-work'. Do you have any idea how that operates?" he asked.

SPIDERS! thought Spellbound. Oh futtle-shucks! She wasn't the greatest lover of spiders. No one had told her that she would have to work with a team of sinister creepy crawlies. She gulped and shook her head.

"Ah, well, I will enlighten you, my dear," Philip MacCavity said, as he swung the swivel chair around and crossed his large feet on the oak desk. "We have a massive network of widder spiders that are constantly present in the human realms, purely there to spy on the state of children's teeth and inform us when one is about to drop out. They lurk in the deepest corners of the children's bedrooms, sometimes hanging on the ceilings above; but we do try to dissuade them from doing that, as they often lose their lives to those 'evil adult humans' who pulverize them. Not to mention the spray deterrents they use, which you must never have the misfortune of experiencing or having contact with, as they are lethal to spiders and fairies alike." He glanced at her.

Spellbound gulped again. Mamma had said nothing about it being like a fooking assault course.

"You will meet many spiders en-route, Spellbound," he continued, "so always be sure to be polite and try not to get caught in their cobwebs. You could be there for days ... nay ... weeks, if you are not careful. Rest assured that the spiders don't usually devour fairies."

He paused and then remarked quietly, "Umm ... but there again, Millicent was a little unfortunate. We gave her a fairy nice funeral ... at our expense, of course," he added quickly as he moved on. "You will enter the bedrooms after dark, through the spiders' entrance holes and for the first week your job will be to keep watch while Steffan here removes the teeth from under the children's pillows. He will then slip a silver coin in its place and because human coinage is extremely weighty, you won't be expected to do any heavy lifting. You see, dear, we employ him purely for his for strength and stamina."

Steffan grinned and flexed his muscles proudly.

"Looking at you, I'd say that you are ideal for this role." Philip MacCavity set his eyes firmly on Spellbound's hips and slowly worked his way up to her eyes. "I am very particular in employing only the finest fairies from the most elite families," he said with a slight letch. "My, my, you do so remind me of your Mamma and it was she that convinced me that you were exactly right for this role, and that's why you are here today, dear."

Steffan Hogsbeer was checking himself out again in the mirror, preening his hair and moulding it with some more of that strangely smelling slug gel. "What do you fink of me 'air colour, Spellbound?" he asked, tweaking the little spikes with the tips of his fingers. "It's all me own, not dyed or nuffink. I got it styled today at the 'air dwessers. Blinding init …? Hey, hey!"

Fook your fooking hair, she thought sulkily. She was going to have a very short life if those pesky spiders got hold of her. She hated her Mamma with a vengeance for arranging this job, and she hated spiders. She hated every goddamn person in fairyland right now. How she wished her Papa was here. He would never let her go anywhere near those evil widder spiders, let alone have her venture into the human world.

***

Later that evening, she was sitting in the Intelligence Room reading the work rosters, trying to sort out exactly where they were heading tonight. She looked at her fairy trendy Tumex watch. "We have to go at 7 p.m. according to this," she said, "which means in five minutes."

Steffan turned his attention away from his appearance and looked at his own huge silver and gold watch. "I make it fwee minutes on me twendy, top of the wange, Wolex wistwatch. Blinding! Hey, hey!"

Both of them were called on the internal sound system into the Molars main hangar. Waiting for them was a rusty coloured brown bat. Spellbound had never ridden a bat before, and was extremely apprehensive. "Why bats?" she gulped, as they mounted it.

"Cos bats work better at night. They use their wadar to get about, ficky; didn't you know that?" asked Steffan, "and they 'ang awound for us at the end … hey hey, blinding!"

He sat up front and punched the spider information into the Batnav system and within a mouse's squeak they were flying like the wind through the trees, dodging other bats, also with fairy fliers onboard.

"Tuck yer wings in, Spelly, we got dwatted wing dwag and it's dwaining me power."

Spellbound attempted to fold her silver wings into the back of her very tight trousers but wasn't having much luck. Thankfully, after a few minutes of struggling, she managed to fix them neatly into the sparkling belt Mamma had magicked up, making the speed of the bat much faster.

"That's better, we're making good headway now, Spelly. Blinding … hey, hey!"

It wasn't long before Spellbound could make out the human world fast approaching. Trouble was, it smelt fairy funny, sort of like rotten eggs, mould and a cheesy kind of stench she couldn't quite make out.

"Very sowwy 'bout the smell, Spell, must be the cuwwy I 'ad before I left. I'll shake the bat awound a bit to get wid of the pong."

The poor bat began to gag at the pungent odour, and weaved and heaved, swinging its passengers erratically this way then the other. Spellbound slithered, lost total hold of the saddle and fell straight off the back of the bat into the darkness. As she tumbled through the air, she instinctively tried to flap her wings but they would not budge from the sparkly belt. Worst of all, she had forgotten her wand!

"Fooking … twutting … ahhhhhhh!" she screamed as she spiralled downwards. She plummeted through some very prickly holly trees before finally bouncing off a plastic bottle lying on its side, into a small pool of some sticky pungent amber liquid on the ground.

Meanwhile, Steffan was unaware of Spellbound's plight. He was pleased with the new bat performance because they were actually ahead of the time schedule. As he reached his destination he steered the bat towards the house and looked for the aerial hole which the widder spiders had advised was the best point of entry. He brought the bat to a screeching halt and looked round furtively.

"Where's the fwiggin' faiwy gone?"

Spellbound managed to stand up, goo dripping all over her little body. The super tall grass was sticking in her thighs and she couldn't see a thing. Thinking quickly, she began rolling around and around in the grass. Grabbing a giant dock leaf, she wiped the gloop from her eyes so that she could see again. It was at this point she spied the label in bold red letters on the bottle she has just landed on.

"Oh no," she muttered, "blewdy self tanning lotion!" That must be the same as 'elf tan' in fairyland, she thought, and if this was the case, she would be a funny colour in less than an hour. How she hated this horrible, horrible job.

She could see she was in a garden, next to a massive sun recliner. She managed to unfasten her wings from her belt but they were so gungey and filthy she wondered if she would ever fly again!

In the distance, she heard a swish and a splatter of water and then it hit her full force. It was freezing cold and she caught her breath with a gasp. Splish, splash, gush … it knocked her backwards into an untidy heap. The water jet was spinning round and round watering the grass systematically. Why didn't they just order rain like they did at home? Stupid idiots! She ran towards the spray and dived under where it was less forceful. Spellbound started to rinse the lotion away, letting the spray bring her wings back to their former glory. Well, at least she could fly again now. How she wished she was at home in her little bedroom, all safe and sound with her hand held Game Girl!

Steffan decided to re-trace his journey and fly at low level. Fortunately, the *Batnav* was very accurate and kept to the same course. It was not long before he saw a weird trail of orange lotion. On closer inspection, all he could make out was a bedraggled moth-like creature in a sparkly belt, looking rather sorry for herself.

"Spelly, is that you? You pwat! What are you fwiggin' doing down there? You ain't a pwetty sight now, are yer gal?"

Spellbound scowled at him furiously as she climbed on the back of the bat.

"I fell off cos of your brainless antics, that's if you had a brain, and if you did you'd be very dangerous. And if you think I'm gonna tie me wings up again, you can think again. Are you sure you've got a bat license?"

Steffan had the grace to look guilty and offered her a weak smile. "Sowwy, Spell, I pwomise I will go a bit slower now."

At last, both fairies managed to get to the aerial hole where they could enter the appropriate house. As Spellbound held onto the flex, she noticed her hands were becoming much darker compared to the white cable.

"I'm friggin' bright orange!" she screeched at the top of her voice.

"Shoooosh, do be quiet, Spell!" warned Steffan. "You'll wake up the kid."

He pushed the now orange fairy through the hole into the bedroom. Spellbound fluttered around the room. This was awesome, she thought, as she spotted a huge plasma screened TV, much, much bigger than the one she had at home and then, wow, she thought. This kid has an XBOX 360. She had heard of these gadgets. Weren't they similar to the Buzzbox 120s? Oh how she would love to have a go, but alas, the primped up pussy fairy boy was deeply engrossed in finding the child's tooth, with his cute little backside sticking out from under the pillow. Somehow, she just managed to stop herself from kicking him right up it!

Flitting over to Steffan, she could see the hair and face of an angelic female child. This was one helluva big kid; what on earth did they feed them on, she wondered. She tried not to be fearful of this giant child. After all, this was her first glimpse of a human in her young life. She moved in for a closer look. Spellbound hovered over the child's face. It was a girl of about six years of age, she guessed. Her hair was golden and spread over the pillow in a fan. She was all peaches and cream and very pretty for a human. Spellbound was fascinated with her eyelashes, that were so long they resembled butterfly legs.

As she looked closer still, a little dewdrop of water, which must have been trapped in her wings, plopped onto the girl's face with a splash. Suddenly the child awoke, her blue eyes flying open in a panic. Quickly, she flipped on the light switch above her head and started to shout and scream for her mother at the top of her voice.

Spellbound made a mad dash and hid behind the curtains. Steffan Hogsbeer had managed to find the tooth and was struggling to push the huge silver coin under the child's pillow. "Sod it, no time for this, let's get outta here ... pwonto!"

He spotted Spellbound and grabbed her roughly by the arm, dragging her back through the aerial hole quickly. He pushed her clumsily onto the back of the bat and they leapt into the air with a loud whoosh.

Faintly they could hear the distraught mother trying hard to calm her daughter down.

"Look dear, I may as well tell you now," they heard her say. "There are really no such things as fairies, not even little orange ones!"

Chapter 7

Gone! Gone! Gone!

Two weeks had passed and Spellbound was sitting in the kitchen on one of her evenings off, while her mother was busy preparing their supper. Apart from the initial hiccup of her falling into the self-tan and turning bright orange for three whole days (to the great amusement of all her friends and co-workers), she had settled down well, and her supervisors seemed to be very satisfied with her progress. Leticia was fussing around in the larder, complaining because she had run out of bee-balm and sweet clover and it was clear that she was becoming crankier by the minute. Spellbound's mind drifted back to her father, who seemed to dominate her thoughts more and more these days.

Spellbound spoke apprehensively. "Mamma, why do you always call Papa a bastard?" she said in a quiet 'oh shit ... so there ... I finally asked her' kind of voice. She knew that in the past Leticia's mood would become very explosive at the mere mention of her Papa's name, but she was curious and needed answers.

"I have no wish to discuss your Papa, Spellbound," Leticia replied, turning away from her daughter and walking towards the cauldron in the hearth. The fire was burning fiercely, which was welcome, as winter had set in with a vengeance.

"Mamma, I do have a right to know why you hate him so much and ..."

"Quiet, Spellbound!"

Clifford's eye appeared hazily in the ball, as he had been roused by Leticia's sharp response. He quietly listened to the conversation between mother and daughter.

"All that you need to know is that your father is a complete and utter swine and that he always will be, child. Anyway, it is of no concern; he's away for a very long time in the Austrial Realm on business." Leticia's tone was terse and Spellbound sensed that her impatience could boil over at any minute.

"I'm not so sure he is in the Austrial Realm, Mamma, because if he was, he would call me like he did before when he went there on business. No, I don't believe it. I have a funny feeling in the tips of my wings. Wherever he is, I think he'll come back, Mamma, and say sorry for whatever it is that made you call him a bastard, I really do. Where is he, Mamma, do you know? We can ask Clifford ... he will know," Spellbound bravely droned on and on. "I can find him and bring him back, Mamma, if you'll let me, that is. I miss him so much. Please tell me where he is and I will talk to him. I know I can. I can talk to him and you and Papa can get back together and ... and we can all be happy like we used to be ..."

"Trust me, Spellbound," Leticia interrupted in a tight-lipped manner. "Your father will never come back. I'll see to that! He has gone, so get rid of this silly childish fantasy clear out of your head, girl. He has gone, do you hear me? Gone, gone, gone! He is never coming back. Never ever, coming back, do you hear?"

Something was different, Spellbound thought. Normally her Mamma would say things like 'Zamforia had abandoned them' or 'Zamforia had forsaken them' when describing her father. This time she had failed to use those expressions and seemed to favour the word 'gone'. She glanced over at Clifford and saw his huge hazel eye snap shut. She drew her knees up defensively and clasped her arms around her legs. No ... something was definitely not right here. Crappy Cyclops Clifford definitely knew something. Determined to get to the bottom of it, she courageously made up her mind to grind her Mamma down.

"Have you heard from him at all these past three years, Mamma? Has he been in contact, has he asked how I am? After all, I know he loved me. I always got the best toys at Yuletide Solstice and he would read me a goodnight human story every night without fail. And once he let me drive his Locust in the faerodrome. And he did buy me the whole *Toofy Pegs* china set. He must have at least asked about me, Mamma, he ..."

"SPELLBOUND, WILL YOU SHUT UP!" That was it, Leticia finally snapped. "Go to your room NOW," she said, pointing her wooden spoon at the staircase, "and don't come down until supper. I am sick to death of your constant droning, girl. Just go!"

Spellbound jumped to her feet and shot her Mamma a look that would kill a beetle. Her eyes filled with angry tears and she rushed out of the cottage and into the wood. "You'd better be careful, Mamma, very careful or I might not love you anymore," she tossed vehemently over her shoulder.

Leticia dropped onto the chair by the hearth and held her head in her hands despairingly. She started to cry heart-rending sobs, something she hadn't done since that fatal night. Why, oh why, were teenagers such hard work? Spellbound was as stubborn as her father at getting what she wanted; she was really wearing her down. What a mess it all was.

"Don't cry, Leticia dear. You know you can't keep lying to her," Clifford said respectfully. "This day was bound to come sooner or later. She is ten and six and classed as an adult now. You were wed at her age and after all, it's very natural for her to be curious about her father. They adored each other."

"I know, I know, Clifford," Leticia sniffed and dabbed her watery eyes with the edge of her snow-white pinafore. Suddenly her voice hardened again. "If that bastard had been the good and proper husband and father that he should have been, then none of this would have happened. It is his fault. All of this is HIS FOOKIN' FAULT ... NOT MINE!!"

***

Spellbound sat at a bright red mushroom table with a group of her friends in the Astral Diner, drinking a huge glass of Zimpto. As she swirled the straw around in the purple liquid she noticed that Pumpkin was all dewy eyed and dreamy. "What's up with you, Pump, you look miles away?"

Pumpkin continued to look dreamily into space. "Oooh, Spelly! ... I think I'm in love for the first time in me life."

"In love ... who with?" they all chorused together, giving Pumpkin their complete attention.

"Drillian MacCavity," she replied, "y'know, Philip MacCavity's only son. Oh my goodness, he's scrummy and gorgeous, not to mention incredibly rich."

Daffy looked at her friend in amazement. "Yeah I've heard about him. Doesn't he manage the northern branch of Molars Inc. in Toncaster for his Pa?"

Pumpkin turned to face Daffy and nodded.

"Oh my god, oh my god!" Taffeta started waving her napkin around in an excited fashion. "They say he's one of the wealthiest elves there is, nearly as rich as yer Papa, Spelly, and they say he can have any fairy gal in any realm that he wants … just with a snap of his fingers. Fairies just go all limp and fall at his feet."

"Well he had me good and proper last night … on the sun lounger at the Rainbow Club," Pumpkin confided quietly under her breath. "I shouldn't have had all that fooking poppy punch. After we had had rumpy pumpy," she added despairingly, "he cracked me on the botty and said he'd see me around sometime. Then he sauntered off without so much as a kiss on the cheek and started chatting to some other fairy gal."

"Well what did he say to this other fairy?" Spellbound asked.

"Dunno, not quite sure," Pumpkin replied, scratching her chin. "Sumink about being ready to rock and roll in twenty minutes. I guess he wanted to go dancing, but still, I feel such a fool!"

Spellbound frowned, leant over and touched Pumpkin's arm sympathetically. "He sounds such an un-cool, big headed git. Don't you be mooning over him, Pump … stay well away from him in future."

"I don't know if I can, Spell. I've never hit the sack with anyone quite like him before. He's the bestest one I've ever had and he's got a huge todger."

All the other fairies, apart from Spellbound, dissolved into a fit of giggles.

Spellbound worried about her friends. Everyone knew that sex was readily enjoyed in fairyland and was freely available, without the social stigma the human realm seemed to have. For fairies, a night of passion was just like enjoying a nice meal or a blueberry ice-cream. No fairy got pregnant unless she wanted to and there was no such thing as venereal disease. For Spellbound though, she had a completely different attitude to all her fae friends. She had never actually performed the sexual act and had absolutely no intention of doing it until she was married. That is what Mamma had always taught her. Somewhere hidden within the genetic make-up of Leticia's family tree, a little 'Victorian' gene, which belonged to Aunt Hester, had made its way into their DNA and this mother and daughter didn't share the same views as all the others.

"Oh my gawd, talk of the devil," Pumpkin gasped. "Look who's over there. Ooh shit, he's coming to our table RIGHT NOW … am I blushing?"

All four fairies stared at the hunky elf approaching them. He was tall, tanned, toned and drop-dead gorgeous. His thick black hair was longer than usual and his steel grey eyes swept over the group of girls lasciviously.

"Hi Pumpkin," he said, giving her direct eye contact. The slight smile that touched his lips and the sexy twinkle in his eyes told her in no uncertain terms that he would like to repeat the events of last night. "How ya doing, sweet cheeks?" he drawled, touching her face with the tip of his fingers, before turning away from her and fixing his attention on the rest of the group. "And are you going to introduce me to all your friends here?"

Pumpkin blushed and looked at him adoringly. "Yes of course, Drill." She cleared her throat nervously. "This is Daffodil, or Daffy as we call her, and then this is her sister Taffeta and, of course you will know of Spellbound, who works as a tooth fairy for yer Pa."

Each fairy looked and nodded respectfully in his direction. This elfin guy was so hot that he even gave Eddie a run for his money. He picked up Taffeta's hand and gently opened her palm, dropping a romantic kiss into the centre before repeating the gesture with Daffy.

Spellbound very slowly and firmly sat on her hands. He wasn't going to fooking well kiss her hand and that was for sure. What a big head!

He quickly glanced towards Spellbound and caught sight of her lifting her chin disdainfully, as if he wasn't there. He turned his attention back to Pumpkin. "So what are you doing tonight, baby doll?" he grinned down at her, showing perfect white dazzling teeth.

Pumpkin, once again, blushed the colour of crimson and replied, "N..n..nothing really, Drill."

"Well how would you like to go Elfpin bowling at Ziggies?" he asked, his eyes fixed on hers.

"Cool, yeah, oooh yeah, so cool!"

Spellbound looked up with disgust. Her friend seriously needed a reality check. This was so NOT cool, falling all over some guy like some kinda … her thoughts were distracted as she turned and saw that all three of her fairy friends were gazing admiringly at Drillian and all drooling like idiots!

"Anyway, my little rampant butterfly. Get your pretty self ready and I'll see you there in an hour… and if the rest of you want to tag along, that's fine by me. We'll hit a night club and pick up where we left off." He flashed a sexy smile and turned on his heel. Daffy's mouth hung open and Pumpkin and Taffeta sighed dreamily.

"Just look at the sight of you all!" Spellbound spat in disgust. They chose to ignore her.

"Just look at the arse on that … cor, I could really fancy a piece of that." Daffy said in a lusty voice.

Pumkin was in a daze. "I gotta go hunnies and find something sensational to wear!" In less than a nano-second she had whooshed off in a cloud of pink smoke.

"Well waddaya think of him, Spell?" Taffeta leant over. "What a hunk. They say he likes group sex as well, the more fairies the merrier. Perhaps we ought to take him up on his offer!"

"Well he won't be having me. I only just met him and I can't stand the smarmy git," Spellbound spat out.

"Just as well then, Spelly, all the more for us!" They began laughing again.

***

In her room later that night, Spellbound was thinking about Pumpkin and 'Driller the Killer', a nickname this smutty, smarmy guy had earned himself in the Wood; just how stupid Pumpkin was to be used in such a way. Surely she could see it was all going to end in tears.

Leticia's mood had softened somewhat by the time Spellbound returned home after racing out of the house earlier. She had even asked if her daughter was feeling all right and had tutted sympathetically about the black widder spiders. Then she suggested doing something she had never done before and brought out her Tarot cards from the pentagram-jewelled box to give Spellbound her very first reading.

Spellbound could sense this was her mother's way of apologizing about shouting at her earlier. She was excited and sat and watched the colourful cards being laid out. They were literally alive and the pictures kept changing like a TV screen.

"Umm!" Leticia sighed deeply and looked directly over the top of her tiny designer glasses. "Oh I say, I say! I see an elfin man here who's going to fall completely and madly in love with you, Spellbound." She glanced back down at the cards. "It's a stormy ride and full of emotion."

"What's he like, Mamma, and who is he? I bet it's that stupid Eddie."

"Shush child … I'm concentrating." Leticia peered even harder at the cards.

Spellbound wondered why her Mamma was being so kind to her, especially as they were talking about elves.

"And there I was thinking that Edward was the one for you, sweet child, but alas, it seems that he is in for some stiff competition. No, Spellbound, this elfin man is going to be a match for you, I'll say that." Leticia fell silent for a moment and squinted as she studied the cards further and then as if she had been hit by a reminder of the past, she mouthed the words under her breath, "Oh no, a second blewdy Zamforia!"

"Is he handsome, Mamma?"

Leticia peered closer and pulled another card from the deck, before losing a little of her rosy colour. "Umm … too good lookin' for his own good. Oh lordy lord, Spellbound, you are going to have to have your wits about you with this one! He looks like trouble with a capital T and he's … he's," she peered a little closer in to the cards, "he's into the sex thing … BIG STYLE! Perhaps I should cast a spell to protect you. I'm not sure you can handle this one, darling."

Spellbound's eyes were out on stalks as her Mamma leant over and pushed a lock of her daughter's hair affectionately out of her eyes.

"My sweet girl is so young and naive and Mamma is going to have to teach her all of the tricks of the trade, because this elf is going to play mind games with you, darling," she cooed. "Now you promise Mamma you won't go jumping into bed with him or anyone till you are at least ten and seven, or better still, married."

Spellbound looked aghast. Leticia shuffled the cards and spread them out in an array of colours over the table. "Pick one card for me."

Spellbound's hand trembled as she pointed to her choice." Leticia drew it out and sighed mysteriously. "This is all karma … not a thing can be done to change it, Spellbound."

"What's karma, Mamma?"

Leticia's gaze drifted over her daughter and then she smiled gently. "Karma is when fate and destiny is in charge of you, sweet child. It's what's planned for you and nothing can alter the course of time. Your Papa was my karma, you see."

She paused and looked into space. She had interfered with Zamforia's karma, she thought. She shuddered slightly, before wondering what her punishment would be. Quickly, she snapped out of her reverie. "Anyway ... we will cross the bridges as we come to them. Mamma is very clever about love wisdom, Spellbound, and I will teach you all you need to know, so don't fret and, lordy lord, you better learn quickly, girl. This guy is a ruthless bastard among bastards and he will do ANYTHING to get you!"

Chapter 8

Leticia Remembers

Leticia poured herself a drink of freshly squeezed cranberry and settled down in front of her new book. Her publisher, *Spells and Swoon,* had specifically asked her to put together the next bestseller, and as she had nosed fifty or so top writers out to win the job, she really had to get it right. They even had plans to televise it as a mini drama in the spring of next year. She was so excited, she could barely contain herself!

This time, she had been given carte blanche on the storyline and so after much deliberation and hours of pondering as to which way the plot should pan out, she decided that she would base the book on her own life story. After all, it was always better to write about something you were familiar with. With this in mind, Leticia had chosen to base the male role on Zamforia. Normally, she would angrily push the bastard out of her mind and completely forbid herself to think of the happier times she had had with him, but this career move was way too important. No, she would have to get on with it and do what she did best.

She slowly cast her mind back to the first time she had set eyes on him at the fairy ball. He was twenty and she wasn't quite ten and six, but from the very beginning the sexual chemistry was just so obvious. It was common knowledge that he was engaged to a horrid little fairy called Tinky Bonk and their marriage was to be the most glamorous event in the fairies' social calendar for the following year.

Tinky was quite pretty in a painted sort of way. She always wore the shortest 'ra ra' skirts and her tanned, shapely legs turned most elfin heads. Her hair was as silver as spun cobwebs and her wings resembled those of a dragonfly. It was safe to say that she was not popular by any account as she was renowned for her acid tongue. Throughout her years in spell school, she had slept her way through most of the elves, pixies and fairies, but that was nothing new in fairyland.

The free sex thing had always repulsed Leticia but no one else seemed to care. She was in a minority and was considered different from all the others. Some even teased her about her Victorian principles but she couldn't help the way she was and would only give herself to someone she loved. It was only when a marriage took place that you were expected to be monogamous; until that time, it was a free for all!

The couple were dancing dreamily to a waltz and Zamforia was laughing at something Tinky had whispered in his ear. His hand slowly caressed her back as they moved to the rhythm of the music. It was obvious to anyone watching that they were already lovers.

Leticia had heard of him, of course, who hadn't? But she had never had the pleasure of meeting him in person. He was as good looking as the gossips had said: thick black hair, green eyes and taller than most other elf men. His presence filled the room and it seemed every fairy had their eyes fixed on him.

She had spotted his Locust 2000 as she came up the drive earlier. It was the only one of its kind in all the realms. He could change its colour at any time and tonight it was bright red. Suddenly her hand was grabbed and her cousin Lennox whirled her onto the dance floor.

"Hi Tish, you looked all lost and alone. Come on, let's do the trogstomp, gal!"

She laughed and was swept along with her cousin's enthusiasm. He was a very good dancer with a terrific sense of rhythm. After a while the music drifted to a stop and the compere announced that the next dance was to be an 'excuse me'. Lennox winked. "I'm going to ask the stunning Tinky for a dance, okay?"

Leticia shrugged good-naturedly and started to walk off the dance floor. Tinky was handed over to Lennox and just as she was about to reach her seat, Zamforia approached her for the exchange. Her heart lurched and her knees went so weak, she felt as though she had lost all muscle power for a second. No other fairy had affected her like this and for the first time in her life, she felt terribly gauche. Before she knew it, she was in his arms, staring into those incredible green eyes. He smiled sexily and as she gazed at his pearly white teeth, she was dazzled. He was the first to speak. "The name's Zamforia, and you are?"

Get a grip girl, she remonstrated with herself as he tightened his arm around her waist and pulled her even closer. She cleared her throat slightly and smiled at him, her violet eyes misting over.

"Leticia," she answered with a whisper, and as the dreamy waltz started to play, it just seemed natural that they should move in time with the music.

"Well I must say, you're a very quiet fairy," he said with a glint of humour in his voice. "Are you enjoying the ball?"

"Yes, it's wonderful," she husked.

"I don't think we have met before, have we?" He smiled down at her, and this time his eyes rested intensely on her pink rosebud mouth. "Which part of the realm do you live in?"

"Br..Br..Broomsticks Cottage," she stuttered. "It's on the outer perimeters of the forest and ... er ... no ... we haven't met before." She cleared her throat a little.

"Well, trust me," he said, his fingers pressing firmly just below the base of her wings. "If we had, I would have remembered".

"I hear you are to be married soon to Tinky Bonk."

He continued to stare into her face, his gaze not faltering for a second. "Yes, we hope to set the date for sometime next year."

She smiled and nodded before he negotiated a swift move around another couple. All too soon, the dance was over and as the music came to an end, Tinky strolled over to them, her wings twitching menacingly. She had been watching Leticia in Zamforia's arms and her silvery blue eyes were cat-like with jealousy.

"Leticia, how nice to see you again," she purred. "How's your mother, Elspeth, and her toy boy, what's his name ... Brod Twit?"

Leticia controlled her temper. It had taken some time for the rumours of her mother's affair to die down. Brod was ten years younger and had swept her mother well and truly off her fairy pretty feet. She had fallen madly in love with the young elf and planned to start a new life with him in a different realm. Leticia had kicked off to such an extent that it was finally agreed that she would stay behind.

"They are married now and live in the Amerigus Realm," Leticia spat out icily.

"Ah, so that's where they ended up after the scandal then," said Tinky smugly. "So your parents divorced...and your Papa, what happened to him?"

Leticia flushed. Was any of this her goddamn business, she fumed. Through gritted teeth she answered, "He is also married and lives in the Austrial Realm with his new wife."

Tinky laughed scornfully as she clung onto Zamforia's arm. "Gawd … what a dysfunctional family you have! I'm surprised you don't need fairy therapy or a shrink to sort you all out."

"Shush, Tinky." Zamforia looked embarrassed.

Leticia picked up her swishing lavender skirts, and spinning around, she marched off the dance floor with as much dignity as she could muster. If she had had her wand with her, she seethed, that fooking fairy would be a heap of fox shit on Zamforia's shoe. Fook the pair of them!

Later that night she sat in bed going over the events in the ballroom. Tinky Bonk was so obnoxious; she'd better keep out of her way in the future. Her magic was far more potent when she was angry. Tinky was welcome to Zamforia. She punched the soft-feathered pillows with her fists and tried to settle down to sleep. Tomorrow, she had agreed to read the palms at a Fairy Fete for the charity PFTD, *Protection for the Dragonfly*, so she needed her rest.

***

The Fateful Fete

The next day was scorching hot and Leticia was taking a well-earned break from the palmistry readings. Her psychic gifts were already well known and the fairies were queuing up to see her. She took her wand and magicked cool perfumed air into the dome-shaped tent. Her gown was slightly dishevelled, so with another flick of her wand she changed it into a stunning turquoise creation. She heard the flap of the tent open. "Tea break time, please come back later!" she called out over her shoulder.

Zamforia took no notice of her instruction as he moved towards her. "I'm sorry Leticia. I didn't mean to disturb you but I had to come to say sorry for Tinky's behaviour last night. I don't know what came over her. I did try to get her to come to you in person but she wasn't having any of it."

For a moment, Leticia was speechless as she gazed at him.

He continued more earnestly, "I could see you were very upset and embarrassed."

"It's okay," she said, smiling, "I can look after myself. I was angry, very angry, and for a second, I had to stop myself from turning your precious soon-to-be bride into a beetle … or worse. But I am over it now."

"Please let me take you to lunch, Leticia, as an apology, and let's forget the whole sorry incident."

"No, no," answered Leticia sweetly. "There is really no need. We don't want to upset Tinky any further now, do we? Please don't worry, it is all forgotten." She gave him a slight smile and turned to her small table. "And I have another two hours of palm readings to do, so I'd better get on."

Zamforia hesitated. "I hear on the jungle drums that you are very good at that. Would you read my palms?"

"What, now?" Leticia sounded surprised.

"Yes, please."

As he sat down he held his open palms towards her and she lifted them in hers. His hands were beautiful and he had a very long life line. His heart line was true and faithful and it was clear to her that he would never cheat. She had no chance of snaring him then, from the dratted Tinky Bonk. The only way that would ever happen would be if she were to magically remove the obnoxious female.

She cleared her head. No, she could never resort to that, as it was extremely unethical as far as fairy-craft goes. Then she smiled to herself, but oh, what fun it would be to wipe the self-satisfied grin off that fairy's face.

Concentrating on his hands once again, she told him the events of his past, as he gazed at her in astonishment. "You are one very incredible fairy, Leticia, all that knowledge and from one so young."

She smiled shyly at the compliment and went on to tell him about the present; his business plans and investments. "Wow, what can I say. You're brilliant! Now for my future, Leticia, what's in my future?"

She stood up. "Sorry, you must go, Zamforia. My appointments are waiting. I'm doing this for charity today so I must crack on."

"Well, perhaps I can come another time for my future ... may I?"

"Perhaps," she smiled brightly.

He flicked open his wallet and dropped a huge bundle of bank notes on her fairy tablecloth. "Please put that towards whichever charity you are supporting today."

As he left she whistled through her teeth, counting the money. Hells fire, the guy was not only sex on legs, he was stonking rich as well! She picked up a stray Tarot card and began fanning herself madly.

***

Cooling off Hot Tempers

The heat wave continued. Leticia and a group of her friends decided to visit the river in Bluebell Forest. It was fast flowing and very cold, just what she needed. Her friends had hitched a lift on the back of her sparrow hawk, Stanley. She had mended his broken wing last year, and in return she would just call his name and he would be there in an instant.

The banks were covered with other fairies, sunning themselves and enjoying the coolness of the river. Leticia dropped her floaty sarong to the ground and dived like a blade into the sparkling waters. "Absolute bliss," she breathed, lying on her back.

Suddenly, there was a noise above the trees and a smart, ebony *Swirleybird* hovered over the grassy bank. It landed with a flourish and out stepped Zamforia and Tinky Bonk, all ready dressed in their suits for a swim.

"Ye Gods, not her again!" Leticia spat out under her breath. Her head bobbed above the water line as she spied Zamforia on the bank. He was in the tiniest little white bathing trunks, showing his elf-hood very nicely. His tan was perfect, his hair was perfect, his body was perfect. She groaned and looked up to the sky. "Drat him and his putrid fiancée!"

Tinky was in a bright scarlet spotted bikini, showing her tanned curves off to perfection. Leticia doggie paddled for a while, letting the water cool her heated skin.

"Come on, Tish, over here!" Caitlyn, her best friend, was waving on the other side of the river. "We've got some very potent poppy punch."

Leticia started to swim strongly against the current, passing Tinky on the way, who hissed, "If I were you, I'd stay in the water, dumpling. You wouldn't want anyone looking at a butter ball like you ... surely!"

"Fook that fairy ... always when I haven't got me fookin' wand!" Leticia thought angrily. Pulling herself up on the bank she spat out to Caitlyn, "I'll swing for that Tinky Bonk, I will, I swear it! Does my arse look fat in this costume? Come on now, be honest, Caitlyn!"

Caitlyn soothed, "Of course not, dearest. You know you have a perfect hour glass figure and please, dearest, try not to keep swearing so much."

Leticia frowned. Caitlyn had the most beautifully refined voice and was the most genteel of fairies in the Brittanic Realm and if she said her arse wasn't big, then it wasn't. She arranged her towel and took a big swig of the poppy punch, still fuming. Lying back, she closed her eyes, letting the sun warm her curvy creamy body. She and Caitlyn drifted off into a light sleep until she felt droplets of water being dribbled over her bare tummy. She opened one eye and saw Zamforia smiling down at her mischievously.

"Hi Leticia, are you enjoying the sun?"

She sat up like a jackrabbit and Caitlyn giggled girlishly.

"Um ... yes, thank you," she replied, looking frantically around for Tinky.

"Tinky has gone to get champagne and fickleberries from the tent. Would you like some?"

Leticia shook her head, trying not to look at the bulge in his trunks. Suddenly he flopped down next to her, causing every fairy to look over at them. Leticia felt very uncomfortable, especially as she could see Tinky stomping towards them with her hands full of goodies.

"Did you make lots of money for the charity the other day?" he asked pleasantly.

"Er ... I did, yes ... especially with what you donated."

"Good ... good ... and will you be doing any other charity events in the near future?"

"Not until the Primrose Ball at the end of the month."

Tinky was now within earshot of them and was clearly enraged. "Zammy, I could really do with some help with this lot," she glared at him.

"Sorry Tink," he said, rising to his feet. "Here, give me the bottle." He glanced at Leticia and Caitlyn. "Sure you two won't join us?" Both shook their heads in unison. "Well, see you at the Primrose Ball then ... bye!" His gaze lingered a little longer on Leticia and for a moment, their eyes locked.

"Wow, what an absolute hunk," Caitlyn breathed, as they walked away. "It's true what they say about him, isn't it? He really is drop dead gorgeous! Don't you fancy him just a little bit, Tish?"

Leticia pulled a face. "Nah ... not a bit! And he's as near as goddamn married anyway, so what's the point?"

***

The Primrose Ball

Three weeks had gone by since Leticia had last seen Zamforia and tonight it was the Primrose Ball. It wasn't all work, she thought, only the first two hours, and then she could relax and have some fun. She was determined not to let Tinky Bonk get the better of her and had her wand secured in a secret pocket in the folds of her stunning magenta and gold gown.

She had worked all week on the spell for her dress and she knew no one would be able to surpass it. The material had come from the Amerigus Realm. Her mother had sent it a few months ago and the fabric was not known in the Wood. As she moved, it changed colour and she was really pleased with the results.

On entering the ballroom, she spied Caitlyn and waved gaily to her. Looking at her fairy accurate Tumex watch, she pointed to it and mouthed, "See you in two hours."

As usual, there was a queue of eager fairies waiting to see her. Her fame really was spreading now and she was booked up for private readings well into the next year. It kept the wolf from the door and made her very self-sufficient. In fact, she was getting a nice little stash of money together. She might even be able to move out of Broomsticks for something bigger if it continued like this, or perhaps even visit her dear mother.

After a gruelling two hours, she headed for the drinks table. Caitlyn was waiting there with a tumbler of her favourite tipple.

"I really need this," she smiled at her friend and downed it in one go.

"Wow, be careful, dearest, you don't want to get squiffy too soon."

Leticia smiled and helped herself to another tumbler and drank half the contents.

"I've just seen that Tinky Bonk," she hissed to her friend. "I need some blewdy Dutch courage if I have to eyeball her again."

"Don't let her upset you, dearest, she's just not worth it."

The silver bombshell was eyeing Leticia's dress, and with a sense of satisfaction, Leticia knew she was envious. Zamforia waved a greeting before being pulled away to talk to some of their mutual friends. Within seconds, Caitlyn and Leticia were surrounded by young fairy suitors and spent the next hour on the dance floor enjoying all the attention.

Leticia was so thirsty she really needed another drink. Dodging the throng, she downed a huge glass of luminous green fairy-aide and tucked herself away in a quiet corner behind a huge fernious plant for a moment to ease her aching feet. She smiled as she saw Caitlyn doing the *Thrust* with a hunky elf she'd had a crush on for weeks.

"So there you are." Zamforia was smiling down at her and looked striking in a black and crimson doublet.

"Oh, hello there. Enjoying yourself?" She asked lamely.

"You certainly are the belle of the ball in that wonderful gown, aren't you, Leticia? Do you fancy a dance with me?"

She shook her head and her long black hair tumbled over the low bodice of her dress.

"Feet are killing me, so sorry, and besides, we don't want to go and get Tinky in a bad mood again!"

"Tinky's gone home. I'm afraid she got a bit tipsy. I had my chauffeur take her back. So," he held out his hand, "do we dance or not?"

Before she could answer, he pulled her forcefully out of the chair and onto the dance floor. Her heart leapt. Just what was his game, elf handling her in this way? Never one to hold back, she said bluntly, "Zamforia … you'll have every tongue wagging in the place. Why are you dancing with me when you are engaged to be wed?"

He pulled her a little nearer. "Umm … that's what I keep asking myself," he said in a low husky voice. "You captivate me, I guess."

She was just about to respond when there was a commotion at the far end of the ballroom. Tinky was back, worse for wear, swaying like a tree in a storm. She flew over to them, screaming at the top of her voice, "Get your fookin' hands off my fiancée, lard ass!"

The dancing throng stopped and all eyes turned upon them in the hushed silence. The band stopped playing and the guests circled around the three fairies.

"Tinky, will you shut up," Zamforia barked at her. "You've had far too much to drink, now apologise to Leticia!"

Without any warning, she lunged at Leticia. "You're a bloated cheap tart, just like your prozzie ma!"

Leticia became as cold as ice. Caitlyn was at her side in a flash. "Dearest, come away from them, they're both trouble. Please don't get mad, they're just not worth it."

"Call yourself a fairy?" Tinky continued, swaying. "Yeah, yer just like ya ma. Any elf man will do. You just try and steal a piece of my guy. Get an elf of your own so you don't have to prey on someone else's. That's if anyone would want a blubber ball like you!"

A white mist had descended over Leticia and she began chanting in elfish under her breath. She slowly took out her wand and pointed it at the jealous fairy. Tinky's goading fell silent as gasps of horror came from the crowd.

An icy wind blew Leticia's hair behind her as she circled the wand high into the air, taking Tinky with it. She tumbled her three times then sent her spinning around and around the ballroom. Plumes of red, green and yellow smoke crackled and lit up the huge room. Suddenly Tinky Bonk was changed dramatically into a huge slug, which landed with a squelch at Zamforia's feet.

"Your fiancée will need a little help to get home again; be sure to scrape her up carefully now. The spell will wear off at noon tomorrow," she spat out coldly. "Perhaps you will remind her to keep well out of my way in the future and if she doesn't, then I will make sure she stays like this until some troll or goblin conveniently treads on her, or even better, eats her."

As she left, with her head held high, there was a hushed silence and a pathway opened up hastily for her. She already commanded a deep respect because of the magic she had just demonstrated in front of the crowd but she was ten and six in twelve days and then her powers would be increased thrice fold.

***

As the door slammed shut in her little cottage, Leticia ran upstairs and threw herself on the bed. She cried for an hour, which turned her eyes red and made them smart like hell. She wished her Mamma and Papa were here to kiss her better. Once the tears had subsided, she started to reflect on the recent events, and anger began to surge through her fairy veins.

"At least that jumped up fairy will never come near me again," she said aloud with a vengeance, "and I'm going to have Zamforia for myself just to punish her. When I'm ten and six I can spell for whatever I like, and I really like him. I want him ... and oh, I shall have him and you, Tinky Bonk, you can rot in a fairy hell pit!"

***

As if by Magic

The following day she gathered every spell book she could lay her hands on. She emailed cousin Larissa, her guardian until she was sixteen, for advice. Larissa was phenomenal with her spell craft and Leticia had been her apprentice for as long as she could remember.

Zamforia tried to get in touch with her many times in the ten days that followed, but she ignored him, staying in her Broomsticks Cottage, feverishly swotting and learning the biggest spell she had ever concocted in her young life. One day he had knocked on her door for so long that she had had to resort to using her wand to cast a powerful force field of protection around the cottage so that he couldn't get in.

Tomorrow was her sixteenth birthday and every single person in the realm was welcome to attend her party. She wondered if Zamforia would come. Larissa had planned the event with skill and oodles of magic and thrown money at it like it was going out of fashion. Her parents and their spouses had already flown in for the party and she was so excited.

Her silver gossamer gown was her mother's gift and the sapphire tiara, necklace and earrings were gifted from Aunt Hester. She twirled in front of the cheval mirror and knew she had never looked more beautiful.

As was traditional, her birthday ball was to be held at Lord and Lady Wizard's Grand Forest Hall. The ballroom was outside, in a small forest glade, surrounded by multi-coloured mushrooms, along with three grand marquees, each themed with exotic speciality dishes from various realms. These huge tents were cleverly lit with thousands of glow worms and fire flies and already they were packed to the brim with fairy guests. Leticia's parents, reunited just for the party, were delighted as the considerable number of guests that had decided to put in an appearance surely attested to their daughter's high prestige among them. The orchestra was in full swing and many couples were already dancing. The whole event was stunning, thanks to Larissa.

With her mother on one side and her Papa on the other, Leticia greeted each of the guests, thanking them for attending. As she looked up, Zamforia came striding towards them. Her heart flipped as he gave a neat little bow and kissed her open palm. His green eyes drifted over her in amazement. He chatted for a while with her parents.

Caitlyn drew her into a small alcove. "Wow, you look stunning, Tish … what a gown! What a party! There are hundreds of fairies here.

They must have heard of your spell when you zapped Tinky Bonk. I noticed she hasn't turned up here tonight, dearest. Bet she wouldn't dare show her face. Oops! Here comes prince charming: the one and only Zamforia. I'm off, see you later, dearest."

Leticia turned to meet him and he smiled.

"You are always running away from me," he scolded, with a grin. She frowned and he held his hands up in mock horror. "Promise you won't zap me with your wand now!"

She giggled and he took her hand and led her to the ballroom. As they glided over the floor she asked, "Your fiancée isn't going to turn up here, is she, and spoil my party?"

He coughed, slightly embarrassed, "Um, no, she won't be doing that, so relax. I seem to spend my life apologising for her."

"You would do better to get rid of her, she's a social embarrassment." Leticia tossed her head.

"She is a little hot headed but I think she may settle down now, after you …um … changed her into a slug!"

Leticia sniffed irritably; he still thought he was going to wed the stupid fairy. She must be really red hot in bed to have this devotion, because she had nothing in between her ears! She would show Tinky Bonk! She was more determined than ever to marry Zamforia and have his love, status and money. Throughout the evening, he never left her side and they danced until the early hours before he sped her home in his Lotus 2000.

The next morning she gathered everything together for the spell. The table was loaded with different herbs, potions and crystals. A golden platter held the most sumptuous fruits that her mother had brought from Amerigus. Three huge books were open and the cauldron was nearly at boiling point. She quickly threw the ingredients in and sang in a long forgotten fairy elfish tongue. Her sweet voice rang out as the room disappeared and a magical portal opened.

Witches rising from the East,
I summon you now to this magical feast.
Witches from the North give power,
Awaken the spell in this sorcerous hour.
Witches from the South bring light,
Quench my desire, burning bright.
Witches from the West I need,
To take my offerings and do this deed:

From now and for eternity,
Make Zamforia love only me.

Stepping out of the portal, the four male witches approached and encircled her, spinning her around and around until she was dizzy. She felt her body fizz and crackle and then she passed out.

Opening her eyes, she saw she was neatly tucked up in bed. Her parents were leaning over her, most concerned.

"Ah, at last she is awake. What a fright you gave us, child. We thought you were dead. Have you been visiting the outer astral, dear?" Elspeth remonstrated. "You know that is forbidden until you are ten and eight."

Leticia smiled weakly and nodded, "Something like that, mother."

"Bad, bad girl," her father said with a twinkle in his eyes.

Two hours later, she had fully recovered and with the protection spell neutralised, Zamforia was knocking furiously on her door. She opened it tentatively and wondered if the magic had worked. Without invitation, he marched into her modest abode and gazed longingly down at her.

"Leticia, I have been such a fool. I have told Tinky that the wedding is off and it's you I love. How dense was I not to know this before. I must have been blind. Please, say you could love me too, sweetest fairy." He dropped down on one knee. "Can you ever love me, Leticia?"

"Ye gods!" she said to herself. That was one powerful spell and it had certainly worked big style!

"Zamforia, please get up. I don't like to see you on your knees."

"I will stay here forever until you say you will marry me."

Leticia giggled. "In that case I have no other option but to accept."

He stumbled to his feet and took her into his arms. As their lips met for the very first time, her head reeled. He was so sexy and he was going to be *her* husband. Very soon she would be Leticia … she stopped for a moment, trying to think of what her new surname would be. How in the heavens could she agree to marry an elf without knowing his last name?

"Zamforia," she said quietly, "it seems I have agreed to be your bride without even knowing what your family name is!"

He threw his head back and laughed. "Why, it is Zamforia!" he chuckled again. Leticia looked confused and scratched her head.

"I know what you're thinking," he said, highly amused, "but at the age of ten I decided to be known by only my last name, you see."

"Oh, and why in the goddess's name would you do that?" she asked, amazed.

"I'll let you into a little secret. I have the worst birth name in all of the realms. I hated it so much, I banished it."

Leticia's eyes were wide with curiosity and her voice gentle, "And that is?"

"Ivorboil," he replied, under his breath.

She contemplated his newly discovered name for a few seconds … Ivorboil Zamforia … and grinned up at him. Then, at exactly the same moment, they both began laughing uncontrollably.

***

When Fate Strikes

Their new house was finished at last and was stunning. It sat in splendid isolation on an island in the middle of Bluebell Forest. The land had belonged to the Zamforia family for countless generations and Zamforia wanted her to have the best of everything. He had built the house for her as a token of his devotion.

They had been married for twelve wonderful years and their daughter was soon to be eleven. Spellbound was beautiful and Zamforia lavished his money and love on his only child. Leticia often felt guilty at the way she had snared her husband. He was a powerful elf and the richest in all the realms but he could not hold a wand to her magic and she had used hers unashamedly to get him. He was the love of her life and she wanted no other but him.

Tinky Bonk had fled the shame by moving to the northern end of the wood and no one had seen her for years. It was rumoured that she feared Leticia's magic so much that she would never show her face in public circles again.

Tonight many guests were expected at their house-warming event. The bowers and gardens were a delight and the caterers from *Horrids* had provided the finest foods and wines. Spellbound was allowed to have four of her closest friends for a sleepover and she was zipping around the grounds laughing and enjoying herself. Leticia had magicked a larger pair of wings for her, especially for the party, and Spellbound was having great fun experimenting with them.

Life was so wonderful, Leticia mused. Zamforia's arms were wrapped around her from behind as he nuzzled hot kisses into her neck. She still found him heady and turned to kiss his chiselled mouth.

"You look stunning tonight, darling ... so ... so very beautiful," he whispered. She peeped up at him and laughed at his compliments. Spellbound swooped over them and she and her friends all yelled, "Yuk, they're kissing, how uncool is that?!"

Zamforia gave her one last kiss. "Sweetheart, our guests are arriving. Shall we...?" He held his hand out and they walked slowly towards the entrance.

Several hours later, Leticia was on the balcony getting some fresh air; the party was over and had been a huge success. Spellbound and her friends had been in bed for some time now and at last they had all gone to sleep, their wands exhausted and out of power. The noise they made had been horrendous and it took a stern visit from Zamforia to calm them all down. He had such a way with children, she smiled.

Whilst he was away seeing to the last of the caterers, Leticia decided to explore the grounds of her new home. With having to organise the party, she hadn't had the time to take a peep at the gardens. For more speed, she used her wings to get to the large glittering pond and looked around there for ten minutes before she went in search of her husband. Zamforia was nowhere to be seen. She frowned and continued to search for him.

She swooped into a part of the vast grounds she had not seen before and saw the most beautiful building. It was domed, Grecian and made of pale pink alabaster, with marble with gold embellishments. Two angels guarded either side of the door. Inscribed above the arch were the words, *'Dedicated to the love of my life'.* She gulped back the tears and stared mistily at his message. He had secretly had this made but even though she could usually read his mind, she had not tuned into it, probably because she had been so busy with the arrangements for the house warming party. She pushed the door open and gazed in amazement at the hundreds of lit candles. The rooms were elegantly furnished and ablaze with soft light, a romantic and passionate boudoir of devotion.

From a room somewhere further inside, she heard voices and she walked silently towards another door, which was half open. In the centre of the aquamarine room was a large hot tub with bubbling crystal water. A bottle of pink champagne was open and beside it, two glasses half filled.

Then with shock, she saw Zamforia and Tinky Bonk in the water, kissing passionately. His long legs were entwined around hers and both his hands were on her naked breasts. In horror she realised they were having sex and Tinky was moaning into his neck, her arms encircled around his naked waist. Zamforia was whispering passionately, "Darling, dearest heart … you are my life, how could I ever survive without you?"

Leticia blinked and then blinked again, rooted to the spot. Surely she was seeing things. Maybe someone had spiked her drinks! She watched in horror as they writhed and clung to each other as they reached their climax together.

With a frozen face, she turned on her heels and flew to the top of a tall tree. She sat there in total shock, the tears streaming silently down her face. It was obvious her spell on him had weakened or been broken somehow, she sobbed. All along he had still wanted Tinky Bonk. He must have asked her to the party. That's the only way she could have got here: by his permission. She sobbed and cried as never before. And then a terrible coldness engulfed her and she felt her heart turn to ice. She stood on the tallest limb of the tree, the wind whipping her hair into a black tangled mass. Reaching for her wand she pointed it in the direction of the pink pagoda and screamed like a banshee,

Witches of East and Witches of North,
Take this foul fairy and speed her forth,
Witches of South and Witches of West,
Take this foul elf with whom she's obsessed.
Banish his strumpet to rank smelling caves,
And make of his fate the wet sand and waves.

The sky became a deep swirling grey, which instantly blocked out the moon. A fork of lightning raced across the sky and Leticia knew that the spell had been cast.

She went back to the pagoda, empty now, and with a final wave of her wand, she magically sealed the door so nobody would ever find their way into it again. She turned back to the house, where her daughter and her friends were still sleeping, completely unaware of what had happened.

***

Leticia leant back onto the pillows and put her pen down. She closed her eyes wearily. The whole sad tale was down on paper at last, and she was exhausted. Her mind drifted to Spellbound. She had been inconsolable by her father's disappearance. Every day she had cried and ranted for his return until Leticia couldn't stand it anymore. In a fit of desperation, she had decided to perform a well-being spell on Spellbound to quieten her down. Gradually over the last three years it had decreased its potency to allow her child to re-adjust and become normal again.

Pushing a lock of her silky black hair away from her eyes, Leticia sighed bitterly and thought of Zamforia on his desert island in the middle of an ocean. At least there was food and water there, she grimaced. She had provided him with that, not that he'd deserved it. She hardly spared a thought for Tinky Bonk, who had been taken away to dwell in deep dark caves, where unseen and unheard of creatures lurked.

Shortly after Zamforia's banishment, the beautiful house they had built together had been made invisible and inaccessible. His money had gone with him, as well as all of the trappings he had provided for them as a family. Even her powerful spell casting could not have the Zamforian wealth, which had been handed down over the centuries as his birthright.

She and Spellbound returned to Broomsticks Cottage to live modestly. The only thing they were allowed to keep was the *Toofy Pegs* dinner set, and Spellbound could sell it, if she wanted, when she was twenty and one years. It would make her wealthy beyond belief; the richest young fairy in the realm, but Leticia would never take any of it. She wanted nothing of that bastard Zamforia's wealth - not a thing!

Afterwards, the gossip had been rife and Leticia had to think quickly in order to avoid a scandal. She announced to everyone that her husband was away in the Austrial Realm for a few years on business. Eyebrows were raised and no one had really believed her story, especially as she and Spellbound were living so modestly back at Broomsticks. They whispered that Zamforia had run off with someone else and that Leticia was too proud to admit it. They dared not ask her outright as she might become angry and use her fatal wand.

Leticia placed all of the manuscript papers in order and zapped them into a large brown envelope. She knew it would be a bestseller for *Spells and Swoon*, and if she could make some money from selling her story, then all the better for her and Spellbound. She had been careful to hide the true identity of all the characters in the story. No one would ever know.

She still loved Zamforia, and would always love him, she mused bitterly. Aunt Hester's genes had been well and truly inherited by her and she would never be able to find happiness with another partner. She bashed her pillow despondently and lay down into the bergamot scented sheets. She must sleep now, and she must try to put it all behind her.

Chapter 9

You're it!

The evening was warm and sunny and Spellbound was ensconced inside the wing hangar at Molars Inc. with Steffan Hogsbeer, awaiting her next tooth mission. Oh, how she would love to be sitting outside right now, hanging out with all her friends at the lake.

This job was fast becoming a pain and she still hadn't got over her fear of the dreaded widder spiders. They were very unpredictable and one of them had cornered her only yesterday. She had zapped it with her wand and it had shrunk down to the size of her little finger nail. The trouble was there were so many of them and they were always breeding. The baby widders had no manners and would bite just for the hell of it. You had to have eyes up yer bleedin' arse and that was for sure, she thought miserably.

All this danger and work for no pay, well not until she had completed a three month probation period. That was the law at Molars Inc. If the boss saw fit, he might reward a good day's work with a gift of gemstones, but no money could change hands until you had passed the final test. Mamma had said she must persevere and face her fears. Yeah, great! Why didn't she go and face them fookin' spiders? And then she remembered, Mamma had an affinity with spiders and kept a huge hairy one in the biscuit tin as a pet. This made blewdy sure she never got any biscuits.

Mamma had also said, "Look on the bright side, the gemstones are a real bonus, especially the emeralds," and that she should try and get as many as she could in the time span as they were extremely fine and sought after. For Spellbound though, a bit of extra pocket money would come in really handy right now, especially as she had her eye on a new top of the range set of Trendy Tress hair tongs.

If only Papa was here, she wouldn't have to worry about money. Her heart sank. If he were here, she knew everything would be okay again. She missed him so much, sometimes she thought her soul would burst. And lately the yearning feelings she had inside for him were getting worse and worse. Little did she know that the *Wellbeing Spell* Leticia had cast on her three years ago, after Zamforia's disappearance, was decreasing by the day!

"Cheer up, Spell," Steffan said with a cheesy grin. "It's okay, honest it is, sometimes you 'av to kiss a pond full of fwogs before you find yer pwince! Blinding ... hey, hey!"

"I don't want no frogs and no princes, thank you very much."

"Awwww, just thought wiv ya being all down and all, that some pixie had gone and bwoke yer heart!"

Spellbound shook herself out of the black mood that was about to engulf her. "I have no pixie about to break my heart. My Mamma is right, they are all bastards and cos of that I don't want anything to do with them."

"Oooh ... that is pwetty harsh, Spelly. Eddie likes you, why don't you give 'im a go?"

"Eddie is a twut," she said finally. "Just like all the rest of them and I have no intention of ever, ever having a relationship with anyone ... EVER!"

Just then, raised voices echoed throughout the hanger and Steffan and Spellbound turned to hear what the commotion was about.

"What do you mean you can't arrange the meeting with Incisors Limited?" a cultured voice bit out. "You know damn well I intend to take over the company in the autumn. Get me the MD on the phone right now or I shall demote you, girly!"

Spellbound looked through the open door and saw Drillian MacCavity taking large strides towards the hanger, followed by fifteen or so fairies and elves. His PA, a striking fairy with big boobies and platinum blonde hair, was running at his heels.

"What could I do, Drill?" she shrieked. "He said he doesn't want to see you. I can't make him see you if he doesn't want to!"

Drillian stopped dead in his tracks glaring down at her.

"My PAs in the past have always being capable of getting me exactly what I want, Miss Copper-Penny, so how it is that you never seem to be able to manage the simplest of tasks?" He paused for breath and then sniped cruelly, "It's a pity you are not as efficient at work as you are in my bedroom! I demand that you get him, on the phone, right now, and I don't want anymore of your pathetic excuses."

"HE'S NOT IN THE OFFICE, DRILL," she cried.

"WELL WHERE THE HELL IS HE, THEN?"

Between sobs, Miss Copper-Penny said, "He's on a train, *The Hornymental Express*, going somewhere on holiday!"

"Well buy the blewdy train, then!" he spat out furiously. "Just get me that meeting and get it NOW!"

"I tell you what, Mr. High and Mighty," she wailed, the tears streaming down her cheeks, "arrange your own meetings from now on. I am done with you and your impossible orders, not to mention your insatiable sex drive. Go and find some other shmuck to do your dirty work. And don't come banging on my door for anymore nookie, okay? Because that's off limits now, FOREVER!"

She threw down her planner and ripped off her name badge. She was so upset, her wings refused to work and they flapped limply behind her in total disorder. With a stifled cry, she turned on her heel and ran out of the hanger.

"Oh great!" Drillian sighed, pushing a hand through his thick black hair. "What now?" He glanced around at the other members of the group who were all looking at their feet in embarrassed silence. None of them could do the job, he thought irritably, they were all hopeless and pitiable. He cast his eyes around the reception and then in the direction of the hanger. Just then, he saw Spellbound, sitting open mouthed on the back of her bat.

"Hey you ... fairy girl!" he shouted, pointing at Spellbound. She looked behind her and then back at Drillian before finally pointing her tiny manicured finger to her chest and mouthing the words, "Who ... me?"

"Yes, yes, you," he replied impatiently. "Get down from that dratted bat and come here. Let me take a look at you."

Spellbound gulped and looked towards Steffan, who was wondering what Drilllian was going to do next.

"Better do as he says, Spell," he warned under his breath, "Don't wanna piss off the big boss man now, do you?"

Spellbound slithered clumsily down off the huge bat and walked nervously towards Drillian. He stood a good centimetre taller than her, making her feel quite intimidated. He eyed her from top to toe and then a cynical smile touched his lips. "You have the exact ingredients that I need," he said, walking around her in a circle, "but tell me, you look a little familiar, have we met before? I seem to remember you from somewhere, now where was it?" He scratched his chin thoughtfully and stopped to face her.

Spellbound glanced up haughtily into his grey eyes. "If I remember rightly," she said disdainfully, "you were cavorting with my friend Pumpkin. She was the one that introduced you to me only a few days ago; you obviously have a very small memory."

He ignored her comment. "Of course, I recall it now, how could I have forgotten? You deliberately sat on your hands, didn't you?" He raised his head to the heavens and laughed a deep throaty laugh. "You're not quite like all the others, are you?" he chided. "Well, well, never mind that now. I need a new PA ... pronto and ... *you're it*, so get out of those red jeans, make yourself look presentable and be back here in an hour."

He turned to leave but then stopped suddenly and glanced over his shoulder. "Oh, and what did you say your name was? I will need to have you badged up and cleared for security." She glared at him. Pompous git, he couldn't even remember her name. She gave him a withering look.

"My name is Spellbound Zamforia," she said in her snootiest voice.

Drillian whistled through his teeth, "What, *the* Zamforia daughter? And your Mother, of course, is the hi-tech, fairy sorceress that everyone talks about, isn't she? Don't make her angry and stay well out of her way, that's what the local gossips say. Great ... we like only the best employees for Molars Inc. and we like the finest pedigree families. You'll be a real feather in our fairy bonnets."

He held her gaze for a moment, and then winked a sexy wink before striding out of the hanger towards his offices, followed by his adoring entourage. Spellbound stood and watched his departing back. For once, she was speechless!

Steffan nudged her, "Better do as he says, gal. At least you'll get a fantastic wage stwaight away and your vewy own top of the wange *Damselfly*. They've just bwought out the latest designs for this year, so there won't be any mileage on their clocks. Blinding, hey, hey!"

She felt a little tingle of excitement in her tummy as she realized something else about this new job: no more spiders! It might not be so bad, she thought, to be earning some real cash for a change and Mamma would be over the moon to hear she had got the best job in the realm. She'd be on the blower to all of her fairy girlfriends, praising her and being proud of her. Plus, she wouldn't have to tell Mamma where she was all of the time. Yeah, she was really going to enjoy this. But just let the bastard try any funny business and she would zap that ever so famous todger of his into a gnat's knob as quick as a flash. Boss or no boss!

***

Spellbound whizzed into Broomsticks in a gust of wind. Leticia's eyebrows disappeared into her thick fringe.

"Spellbound! You frightened me to death, what's the hurry, girl?"

"Mamma ... you are going to be so proud of me, really you are. I have just got a new job as ... wait for it ... Drillian MacCavity's PA! And I have to be back at base in," she peered closely at her Tumex watch, "gawd, in thirty minutes!"

Leticia jumped to her feet. "What!" she screeched.

Spellbound was halfway up the stairs. "He says I must wear something more appropriate!"

Her mother raced up the stairs after her and before Spellbound could get through the bedroom door Leticia had flicked her wand and changed Spellbound's outfit. Leticia began fanning herself with the back of her hand.

"Now sit down just for a second and tell me what's been happening, child."

Quickly, Spellbound related the whole story and Leticia clasped her hand together delightedly. "Do you realize you have just got one of the most desirable jobs in this realm? You clever, clever girl! You're so like your Mamma. I can't wait to tell the girls at the Fairy Fraternity, they'll be so envious! Now, dear," she lowered her voice to a dramatic whisper as she leant forward, "I have heard on the grapevine of Drillian MacCavity's reputation, so be very careful. He's more dangerous than any of those widder spiders you've encountered. He screws anything that's not nailed down."

Spellbound was hunting around for her favourite silver hair clip. "Don't worry, Mamma, I ain't interested in him anyway. He's a big headed pulluck, with far too much dosh. If he were the last living elf in the whole of the realm, I wouldn't consider him."

Leticia breathed a sigh of relief. The last thing she wanted was her daughter being a notch on that elf man's bed post. There were too many others on it already!

***

Spellbound's top of the range gnome desk was rather superior in comparison with all the other desks in the company; but then when you were the PA to the boss's son, you wouldn't expect anything less. She had sped back to Molars Inc. and headed out to seek Drillian, but one of his entourage had said he was in a meeting and showed her to her new desk.

"He'll call you when he needs you," the fairy had said to her. As she sat there waiting, she wondered if she should file her nails or something, but *Drillian the Millions*, might not approve. No, she would just sit here and twiddle her thumbs and await his instruction. As if he had read her thoughts, his voice came out of the speaker phone, which was in front of her.

"Can you come in here, please?" he ordered. "Pronto!"

Darting towards his office door, she went straight in without knocking. She screeched to a halt as she saw the scene in front of her and blushed a furious crimson.

There, sprawled on the large mahogany desk, lay a half naked, red haired fairy, looking all flushed and dreamy eyed and Drillian, who had obviously been giving the fairy a good seeing to, was quickly adjusting his attire.

"Pop off and find Delilah a cigarette, would you girly, and make sure it's a Camel; that's the only brand she likes," he drawled lazily.

Delilah smiled sweetly at Spellbound and mouthed a snooty *thank you* as she adjusted the strap on her *Hairmarni* top.

Spellbound was gobsmacked. Find a fookin' cigarette? So this is what her job would entail. Mopping up after he had had his wicked way with all the fairies in the realm. What a creep, what a shit 'ed, what a bastard, she fumed.

"Oh and empty this bin would you, on the way out." He paused for a second, looking confused. "Sorry, what did you say your first name was again?" Spellbound walked over to retrieve the bin and as she bent down to pick it up, he trailed a finger down her back.

"Oi!" she shouted, "get yer grubby hands off me! I'm not one of your floozy fairies that'll drop at yer feet, MacCavity!"

"Drill," he spoke quietly. "Call me Drill." Spellbound tossed her head in the air and looked up at him disdainfully.

"I shall empty your bin and I will find a cigarette for your … *friend* here, but listen carefully, Mr. *Drillian* MacCavity, I will not be elf handled, do you hear? If you so much as lay another finger on me, I'll wear your mushrooms for earrings. Got it?"

Drillian looked thoughtfully at Spellbound. What a challenging little ladybird, and cute with it, he thought. A real little firefly if ever he saw one. He'd never met a fairy that wasn't interested in him before, let alone sex. Totally unique, completely brilliant, how very refreshing, he mused! Mmm, it would be nice to have a challenge for a change and very interesting indeed to see how long it would take him to bed her. Spellbound stomped out with the bin under her arm and handed it to one of the office juniors.

"Anyone smoke Camels here?" she asked irritably, as her eyes swept around the room. A trendy elf man who was in charge of admin took one out of his jacket pocket and handed it to her with a cheesy smile.

"Wanna light, gorgeous?" he asked, as he raised one eyebrow.

"No, it's not for me, it's for MacCavity's bit of crumpet."

He nodded his head knowingly and rolled his eyes upwards before laughing heartily, "You'll get used to him and his ways ... he's not a bad boss really."

She took the cigarette and held it well away from her, crinkling her nose in disgust.

Back in the office, she handed it over to Drillian, who now had the amorous fairy draped over his lap. He gave the cigarette to Delilah.

"Thank you ... umm ... what did you say your name was?"

She glared at him before she spoke. "Just call me Miss Zamforia, my first name needn't bother you. Now, what are my duties because I am ready to crack on?"

He lifted Delilah to her feet and gave her backside a little slap. "Off you go, butterfly, and I'll call you later." She gave him a gooey smile as she disappeared around the door taking her nauseous cigarette with her.

Spellbound stood silently in front of Drillian's desk, her wings as stiff and pert as her facial expression.

"What's with the look?" Drillian asked, with half a smile.

"Oh, I don't know. These silly fairies, they must be so stupid to fawn over an elf in such a way." She lifted her chin and proceeded to look down her nose at him.

"Well, all fairies enjoy a bit of slap and tickle. Don't tell me you haven't had your moments."

"Actually, no, I haven't, and I have no intention of doing so ... not till I'm married anyway."

Drillian leaned back in his chair and placed his hands behind his head.

"How very intriguing," he said with a glint in his eye. "I can't say I have ever met anyone who hasn't indulged in the carnal pleasures before wedlock."

Spellbound raised her nose a little further and looked at him disdainfully before turning away again. "I have my Aunt Hester's genes and so has Mamma," she said snootily. "The Zamforian fairies wait until true love comes before giving themselves freely. Now, could you please tell me my duties so that I can get on and do my job?"

He lifted a black eyebrow and smiled a dazzling smile, "So, tell me, I am curious ... who is this Hester?"

Spellbound paused for a moment and collected her thoughts. "She is my great aunt and she is very Victorian. 'No sex before marriage' is her motto, and her grandmother and great grandmother before her thought the same. We can't change our genetic makeup. Until we find love ... we're just not interested, it's as simple as that. Now please, is there someone around here that can tell me what it is I am supposed to do?"

"And have you ever been in love?" He gazed into her incredible green eyes.

Spellbound glanced back and then quickly shook her head. "Will someone train me or do I cobble it all together as I go along?"

Admitting defeat, he stood up and walked over to her, "You may have heard of my northern branch in Toncaster. We'll be going there for approximately six days. We are already booked in at The *Glitteritz*. I have a whole floor at my disposal at all times. You'll have your own suite of rooms and," he stopped suddenly; "I've just remembered your name ... Spellbound!" He smiled as if he was rather pleased with himself. "We're leaving tomorrow so ..."

"TOMORROW?" Spellbound's eyes shot up to meet his. "I must go tell Mamma and I need to get her to zap me some clothes as well," she babbled.

"By all means, ask your Mamma but don't worry about clothes. The hotel has an excellent shopping mall and I have your credit cards ready; just charge whatever you need to the company."

Spellbound gulped, "Fookin' hell! What a job!" Then she turned and rushed home.

Chapter 10

An Evening Visitor

Spellbound lay fast asleep in the darkness, tucked up safely under the mass of lavender-smelling covers on her bed. It had taken her some time to drift off as she just couldn't get her beloved Papa out of her thoughts. His absence in her life had seriously begun to affect her and the pangs of pain every time she thought of him were fast becoming too hard to bear. The only thing that distracted her from these awful feelings was the excitement of travelling to Toncaster the following morning.

She was dreaming restless dreams, when suddenly she felt the spirit within her tiny fairy body rise upwards toward the ceiling of Broomsticks Cottage. A little frightened, but not knowing whether she was actually asleep, awake or levitating, the feeling was so mind-blowing that she just went with it, allowing whatever it was to take her to greater heights.

Very quickly, she found herself whizzing through the trees of the forest, but instinctively she knew she was still tucked up in bed. "This must be what they call *astral travel*," she said to herself in her semi-sleep, and she knew this was not allowed in the fae realms until one was ten and eight years. Spellbound spiralled higher and higher, faster and faster, as if a higher power were controlling her movements, until her heart was beating quicker than a bee's wings could flap.

Without any warning, she was rocketed into space. She tried not to panic, but then all of a sudden she was plunged into a fairy pink paradise surrounded by huge pink candyfloss clouds and silver stars. She stopped abruptly and gazed down at her body. She had no body. All she could see was the transparent form of her fae self encircled in a golden light. "Oh blewdy hell!" she swore silently. "Where am I? Have I died and gone to heaven?"

As if someone was reading her mind, a gentle musical voice answered her.

"Ah, Spellbound, I can safely say that you are not dead."

Spellbound whipped around to see where the voice was coming from but there was no one there. "Who's there? Where are you?"

Before her eyes, a glorious vision began to unfold. Tiny sparkles of silver orbs appeared in a flurry of purple light and within the image were flashing beams of gold, that escalated upwards into a mystical whirlwind. After that, as if this was not spectacular enough, a stunning fairy appeared. Her hair was the colour of wheat, her eyes were sparkling blue and her sweet rose bud mouth smiled tenderly. Then her wings appeared, wings like nothing Spellbound had ever seen before, huge feathered wings that oscillated translucent light, changing colour every few seconds.

"Wowee!" said Spellbound, completely taken aback. "Who are you? And more to the point, why am I here?"

The fairy smiled again and turned to face her. "I am Moonflower, and in the fairy realms, I suppose I might be referred to as your fairy godmother. I have been assigned to you since the moment of your birth. If you like, I am your spirit guardian, always watching, always observing. You have never been alone child. I have been here for you always."

Mamma had told her that there were such things as fairy godmothers, but many folk thought that they were just a myth. These legendary beings were known to be above any fairy and their magic was so incredible that no fairy, witch, wizard or warlock could influence the power they had. She fidgeted nervously.

"I have summoned you here, Spellbound," the fairy godmother spoke, "for a very special reason. We are all concerned for your safety. You see, you are entering into a very negative place at the moment. We call it the '*yearning*' phase, dear. You are missing your father so much and it is getting worse by the day."

Spellbound gulped and nodded. "Yes I miss Papa terribly," she whispered forlornly.

"Three years ago when your father went away, your mother cast a powerful spell on you, dear, to stop your heart from hurting, but the spell can only last for so long and can never be repeated. If your yearning starts to get out of control, the Elders of this realm fear that your magic will vanish, and everyone knows what happens when a fairy's magic vanishes!"

Suddenly Spellbound began to realize the seriousness of what her godmother was saying. It was common knowledge that if a fairy lost her powers then her wings would disappear and her fae form would fast turn into a golden hare. She gulped again; she didn't want to end up eating grass all her life and being bonked senseless by them sex mad bunnies. And if that happened, she would have to learn to box when it was full moon and then she'd be called a fookin' mad March hare ... and have endless baby leverets. No, it would never do and Mamma, well ... what would Mamma tell all her friends when they came to visit?

Spellbound cleared her throat and asked in a very small voice, "Why is it, Moonflower, that my heart is yearning so much for my Papa? I know lots of folk back home whose Papas have all fooked off and they're ok with it."

Moonflower sighed, "Shush child, and try not to swear so much. We were hoping you would soon grow out of this unfortunate habit. You are so much like your mother," she added kindly. Moonflower smiled compassionately at her charge and changed her tone to one of kind authority. "We all belong to a circle of souls, Spellbound. Your parents are part of your soul group. That is why you miss him so much. If you don't get to meet the members of your group, you don't really miss them, but because you already know your father, your feelings are becoming just too intense."

Finally she was beginning to understand. And why had Mamma never told her about this, she frowned.

"Spellbound, it's imperative you find your father. It is so important that you should focus on nothing else. Once he comes back, your magic will return to normal and everything will be well. This is your mission."

"But how do I find him? I have no idea where to start looking and my magic isn't that great either, if you haven't already noticed! Last week I tried to cast a spell to find me flute and everything went terribly wrong. It ended up in a field full of fox shit! The ritual just didn't go right and just before I knew it, I had burnt out yet another wand and ...."

"Shush, sweet Spellbound, you're droning again. You must go to Clifford Eyesaurus. He knows exactly where to find your father. Ask him to help you. He is the key!"

Spellbound sat bolt upright in bed. Her heart was pounding and her head was really fuzzy. "I think I just had contact with my fairy godmother!"

Without another thought, she quietly slipped out of bed and went down the big oak stairs and into the kitchen, trying hard not to make a sound. There on the rustic table sat Clifford, covered in his piece of purple cloth. She sped over to him swiftly and removed the fabric.

"Clifford, wake up, wake up! I need to talk to you NOW," she whispered loudly.

Clifford's eye appeared suddenly after being jolted out of his sleep. He blinked several times and then glanced upwards when he saw Spellbound's nose pressed hard on to the glass.

"It's the middle of the night!" he said. "Go back to bed, child; can't you see I am trying to sleep?"

"Never mind that now," she replied impatiently. "You know where my Papa is and I am not going anywhere until you tell me EXACTLY what you did with him."

"What I did with him?" he spat out irritably. "Now listen here, Spellbound, I have done nothing with your father. His whereabouts are nothing to do with me whatsoever. Go to bed and leave me in peace before you wake up your mother."

"I was summoned to my fairy godmother tonight, Clifford, and she told me that you DO know where my Papa is. Now tell me before I throw you and your glass fookin' ball into the lily pond!"

Clifford went a pale shade of white. "Your fairy godmother, eh?" he said quietly. "Don't be silly, Spellbound, you were probably dreaming. There are no such things as fairy godmothers."

"Oh yes there are, as you well know. Moonflower is her name and she said I was in danger of going into something called the *yearning* and if I didn't find my Papa, my fairy magic would disappear and I c..c..could turn into a golden hare ... and if I do, Clifford, it will be YOUR fault entirely!"

Just as Clifford was going to respond, Leticia came storming down the stairs in a fit of rage, her white satin nightgown billowing around her.

"What is all this commotion about? And why the hell are you talking to Clifford at three in the morning, Spellbound? You know Clifford is out of bounds to you at all times. Get back to bed this instant and stop marauding around the house in the dead of night." In a flurry Leticia threw the purple velvet cloth back over Clifford. "Goodnight, Clifford dear, I am so sorry Spellbound has disturbed you."

"But Mamma ..."

"Now, Spellbound," Leticia spat back. "I have a heavy day of writing tomorrow and my deadline is Friday. If I don't get this blewdy book finished, we will all be done, done, done! And I will have to keep spelling for our food and as you know, spell food doesn't fill you up! Now get to bed and do as I say. RIGHT NOW!"

It was no good, thought Spellbound. There was no talking to her when she was in one of these moods. She would just have to try to talk to Clifford tomorrow before she left for Toncaster and in the meantime, maybe she could contact Moonflower again and see if she had any ideas on how to make the silly one-eyed Cyclops spill the beans.

Once her daughter was out of sight, Leticia looked around cautiously and removed the cloth from Clifford.

"What was all that about?" she whispered, "and why in heaven's name was she down here half screaming at you, Clifford?"

"You really don't want to know!" he replied in a deflated manner. "You had seriously better watch your back, Leticia. The Elders are onto you and I don't mean maybe, my dearest. Your precious daughter was summoned by her fairy godmother tonight on the Astral. Moonflower is her name and she has kindly informed your daughter that … I … yes, me, the idiot in the glass ball, knows exactly where her father is!"

"Oh fooking lordy lord, Clifford. Lordy fookin' lord!! Not the Elders! What are we to do? I can't believe she has met her godmother, but there again she's always dreamt about things from the future since she was tiny." Leticia was becoming frantic. "I have never ever in my life met my godmother and Spellbound is so young. How can one so young meet her godmother, Clifford … how? Maybe Spellbound is to be as powerful as me," she said, "maybe even more so! Well, you must not breath a word to her, do you hear, Clifford? Not a word. If she ever finds out, I shall know it was you who told her and …"

"But Leticia …"

"No, I mean it, Clifford. This will all blow over, you'll see." She bent over to retrieve the velvet cloth.

"There's one very important thing, Leticia."

"Not another word, do you hear, Clifford? No excuses!"

"But Leticia …!"

It was too late. She had covered him up and stomped back up the stairs. Somehow he had to tell her about the *yearning* danger Spellbound was in, but how? Because of Morgana's curse, he could only converse with the fairies if they needed to speak with him, not the other way around. Oh, what a mess Leticia had got them all into, he thought despairingly.

***

Spellbound was dreaming again. This time in her dream, she was sitting in her room staring at the computer screen. The pictures showed flowers and mountains, all living and moving in unison with nature. Suddenly, Moonflower appeared on the screen, dressed in pale blue and topaz. In her hands she held a glowing tiny white orb which she was holding out to her.

"Give Clifford what he wants," she spoke. "Use this magical orb to give him his heart's desire."

Moonflower's image disappeared and once again Spellbound sat bolt upright in bed.

"What a fookin' night!" she said out loud whilst rubbing her eyes. She moved her body sideways to lie back down and just as she did, she felt a small round bulge in the covers. Tossing them aside, she saw a perfect white orb, which fitted snugly in the palm of her hand. She gazed at it for a few minutes and as if by magic, it telepathically told her *exactly* what to do.

Chapter 11

Toncaster

Spellbound was so excited; she had never been in a *Swirlybird* before. She looked down at the tree tops and actually saw the roof of Broomsticks Cottage as the vehicle rose up and they started their journey towards Toncaster. Leticia, who was slightly concerned that her daughter would be staying away for a week with a sexy rogue like Drillian, had flown onto the chimney and was waving a piece of red chiffon.

"Oh I do hope she'll be all right," she said over and over to herself. "That elf man is so dangerous."

Drillian, who was lazily snoozing, had stayed in the *Swirlybird* outside Broomsticks Cottage while Spellbound had collected the last of her bits and pieces. He half-heartedly shouted to Leticia that they would be arriving in Toncaster within the hour. She flitted down gracefully from the roof with her wand in her hand and eyed him sternly.

"You will take care of my girl now, won't you?" she asked with an acid smile. "Make sure there are no shenanigans and remember she is a Zamforian fairy." She waved her wand in a slightly menacing way.

Drillian looked up through his half closed eyelids and nonchalantly nodded his head. He wondered if the rumours about Leticia Zamforia were true and if she could really banish fairies to the end of the earth. He decided it was all gossip.

Spellbound was gazing out of the window. With all the fuss Mamma had been making about the trip, she hadn't been able to get Clifford to one side and question him. It would just have to wait until she got back and hopefully this nagging pain in her heart would subside a little. Spellbound was still lost in her yearning when Drillian interrupted her thoughts.

"So who was your latest crush, Spellbound, and does he live locally?" He threw her a sexy smile and for a second, she thought she had never seen such perfect white teeth. But then, being the son of the owner of Molars Inc, didn't that come with the territory?

"Was he pixie, elf or fairy type?" He chuckled a little. "Or is it gnomes or trolls you are into?"

Spellbound sighed as her eyes drifted over him coldly. She really didn't want to be sharing any of her secrets with this sex maniac.

"I'd rather not talk about my love life," she said primly.

"Aww, come on, Miss Zamforia," he said in a low drawl, "spill the beans, I'm your boss now and I should really know a bit more about you."

"That's my private life and it has nothing at all to do with my work. You wouldn't want me asking about your love life now, would you?"

"Ask away, sweet fairy. Anything you like. I don't mind."

Spellbound. just wasn't interested and so decided to quickly change the subject.

"What do you want me to do when we get to Toncaster and what will my duties be?"

He sighed and shrugged his shoulders before replying.

"Make sure my life runs like clockwork. Handle the female fairies and whatever you do, don't get their times and dates mixed up. Be charming to my clients and see to their every need: the usual PA stuff. You'll soon pick it up."

Suddenly he stretched over and grabbed her hand and within a flash, pulled her swiftly onto his lap.

"Now, how about a nice little kiss? We've got nearly an hour to kill till we reach our destination."

Spellbound looked into his slate grey eyes which had suddenly become very dreamy. For a second she was drawn into the depths of them. Did this elf have some sort of magic charm? First she cops a look at his dazzling smile and now she's in danger of getting lost in those magnificent eyes. She mentally shook herself and without warning, she boxed him hard around his ears, making them ring like a chamber of church bells.

"Are you thick … I mean … are you really, really thick? I've made it very clear that I am not in the slightest bit interested in you and whether you believe it or not, you don't do a blewdy thing to turn me on. I'll tell you this, Mr. Snog Everyone's Face Off, when we get to Toncaster I will fly the fastest bee out of there and you can get yourself another silly fairy PA to mess around with!"

He gazed at her in amazement for a moment and then said in an exasperated tone, "Okay …okay, I give in. You win fairy; from here on in, I'll behave myself. I've got the message. It's a first for me but hey ho, I'll live."

She glared at him sullenly as she slid back into her seat.

"But don't go buzzing off on some bee, Spellbound," he said a little more humbly. "It's a good job at Molars, with fantastic wages and it's kinda nice having you around."

Spellbound glared at him again.

"Can't we at least be friends?" he asked. He held his hand out and she reluctantly placed her small hand in his. "Friends?"

She nodded warily and then deliberately looked out of the window, remaining silent for the rest of the journey.

***

The hotel was fantastic, just like an ice palace. The colours were themed in pale peach and lime green and there were major-domos on every floor. With a flick of a finger, they were known to give the best service around. Drillian and Spellbound sped to the top of the hotel in a crystal lift, illuminated with the newest *whizz wave* lighting. As they walked along the huge, softly lit corridor, Drillian stopped at his door.

"Well, this is me. You have to tap your door three times for it to open," he said, pointing to the door opposite his. He handed her a small laptop. "Give the girls a call for tonight, just four will do, and tell them to meet me in the sauna on the fifth floor. You'll find their names in the file marked *Totty*."

Spellbound explored her room, which was the most sumptuous thing she had ever seen. The bed was a four-poster with white satin coverlets and lace drapes, and through a door, she could see a sunken bath already drawn, with sweet smelling aromas wafting over her nose. There was a huge plasma screen TV above it and soft cream rugs beneath her feet. This job certainly had some wonderful perks, she sighed dreamily, and then she shed her clothes and sank down into the perfumed bubbles of her bath. Bliss, utter bliss!

All the commotion the night before, as well as the trip this morning, must have completely exhausted her because the hot, aromatic water made her fall asleep almost instantly. She was drifting in and out of peaceful slumber when a loud ringing object, which was dancing over her nose, rudely awakened her, saying, "Please answer your spell phone." She grabbed it quickly and saw Drillian's name on the screen.

"Spellbound, have you been in touch with the girls yet?"

"I am on the case right now," she lied convincingly.

"Tell them 8.30 p.m. and not a minute before. I'll be busy with the maid until then."

The phone went dead. She hopped out of the bath and, as naked as the day she was born, raced to the computer, wings limp and water dripping all over the place. She would try to spell the puddles away later with her new wand. She clicked on the file *Totty* and a hundred or more names were laid out in columns. She quickly rang four numbers at random and breathed a sigh of relief when they all eagerly agreed to come.

Some time later, she was just about to snuggle down to sleep when her spell-phone hovered in front of her face again.

"Spellbound, could you go into my room and get my robe and body rub? Bring them up to the sauna with the felento you'll find in the drinks cabinet," Drillian told her. "It's my own brand," he added arrogantly. "I can't stand anything but the best." Once again, the phone went dead.

Five minutes later, she was outside the sauna doors with everything he wanted. She was even quite prepared to close her eyes quickly if she had to. He was standing like a Greek god, up to his waist in the middle of the lavender bubbling waters, with three naked fairies draped all over him. Suddenly a head bobbed up from under the water. The fairy took a deep breath and ducked down again. Drillian groaned as he kissed another fairy passionately. Spellbound, having never witnessed passion at first hand, placed the robe, body rub and the felento on an ornate table and tried to slip out unnoticed.

"Filthy pullock!" she grated out under her breath.

"Thanks, Spellbound. You can have the rest of the night off."

As she turned to look at him, the fairy under the water pulled him down with her and the other three giggled.

"Pervy git," Spellbound snorted in disgust.

His head appeared above the water again. "I heard that, Spellbound!" he bit out and then all four fairies had their wicked way with him.

***

She had been given instructions to be ready at 9 a.m. promptly and to wait outside his room. At that exact time, the door flew open and the four fairies trailed out, with Drillian bringing up the rear. He slapped each one of them on their bottoms and promised to see them soon. Spellbound stood back with a bored expression on her face and sighed irritably.

"I'm starving; let's go and eat," he yawned.

Over breakfast he tried to engage her in conversation. "Did you like your room; is everything okay?" he asked.

She nodded and bit delicately into a banana bug burger. "Yeah, fantastic thanks. Talk about being spoilt; the room's a dream."

He placed his napkin on his lap and smiled, "Did you sleep okay?" he asked, this time looking directly at her. Not looking up, Spellbound nodded again and proceeded to spread a thin layer of celandine butter on her toasty.

"I bet *you* didn't get much sleep though," she sniffed disapprovingly. "I mean really, you are nothing but a male bleedin'slut …"

Drillian choked on his fairy flakes and without having time to finish her sentence, she had to slap him really hard between his shoulder blades. When he finally got his breath back, he was steaming with anger.

"Spellbound, do you have to keep cursing so much? And please remember you are my employee. Have some respect for goodness sake! How I conduct my life is none of your business. Do I make myself clear?"

Spellbound gave out a sarcastic laugh. "Conduct your life? I'd heard about you and your shenanigans," she laughed, "but I never thought for one minute to believe them." She stuffed the last of the banana bug burger into her mouth and wiped the corners of her lips daintily on her napkin. "You seriously need to go and get some sex therapy, elf man."

Suddenly he stood up and threw his napkin on the table.

"And you are the most inflexible and difficult female I have ever come across, you're just impossible. Maybe it was a big mistake hiring you!"

As he turned to walk away, she glanced up. "Whore bag!" she spat out sulkily, under her breath.

***

The rest of the week passed very quickly, with Spellbound hopping and jumping to Drillian's every command. Each night he had another succession of fairies in and out of his suite, and the more she saw, the more she realised that males, whichever form they appeared in, were definitely off the agenda.

On three occasions he had tried hard to win her around by taking her for a nice meal and then suggesting that she cancel his female entertainment for the night and join him instead. Spellbound had just given him a pitiful look and told him in no uncertain terms to go and fook himself.

Leticia had been on the spell phone every day, checking to see if she was okay and to be honest, by the fourth day Spellbound was beginning to miss her. The only consolation was that while Drillian was busy with his fairies and his meetings, she got to trawl around endless stores and buy some of the most fantastic clothes without ever having to look at the price. One dress appealed to her so much that she bought it in six different colours.

When she showed up for work that evening, Drillian's eyes nearly popped clear out of his head when he observed his sexy little PA in a cherry red, low cut mini dress, edged with gold thread and killer-heeled shoes. She seriously had to ditch the twinkly frocks, she thought to herself. When dressed to kill, she felt so empowered. This was the only way forward for her and deep down as much as she disliked the smarmy, sex crazed boss man, she was secretly pleased that she had got his attention.

The journey home proved to be long and laborious. Drillian spent the entire time on the phone to a fairy girl who had become clinging and wouldn't take no for an answer. He was fast becoming impatient and was trying very hard to tell her to get lost. When he finally did get off the phone, he was in a sour mood. "Why didn't you make it clear to her that it was just a one off?" he spat at her.

Spellbound glared at him from across the cream leather interior of the *Swirlybird*.

"You know damn well I hate that sort of pressure from females," he went on. "And being my PA, it is your job to see to it that I don't get hangers-on."

It was true. Spellbound's job was to make sure that no gals got hold of Drillian's personal number and stupidly, she had left his private business cards lying around while she went down to breakfast that morning. The loved-up fairy must have sneakily picked one up on the way out of his bedroom.

"Maybe you shouldn't be such a stud," Spellbound said yawning. She stretched her arms above her head, and then rubbed her nose a few times, something she always did when she was tired or bored.

"You are paid to make sure that ALL my needs are met," he said irritably.

"Ha! Not all, Drill, just remember that," she shot back.

Drillian eyed her curiously. Was she seriously trying her best to remind him again that she wasn't the least bit interested in him? It was only a matter of time, he thought, as he turned away and rested his head on the window, before falling asleep for the rest of the journey.

Chapter 12

Come Dine with Me

Eddie was seriously excited. It had been three long weeks since he had seen Spellbound at Broomsticks Cottage for supper and tonight he would be dining at Elf Hall with the very delectable fairy herself. There would be absolutely no way that she could dodge him now. His Mammy, Lady Elf, had returned the compliment and invited Spellbound and Leticia over for supper. Okay, so she had been busy with her toofy job at Molars but tonight he planned on setting the scene and having her all to himself!

As he stood in front of the full-length mirror in his luxury oak-beamed bedroom, he admired his appearance. Turning to the left, he stuck out his chest, and squirted some 'Minty Mouf' to the back of his throat, and then he carefully ran his fingers through the thick mass of golden curls that fell around his handsome face. Eddie grinned at his reflection and then blew a little kiss at the mirror. Taking great care, and pulling a seriously sexy 'come to bed' face, he proceeded to snog the back of his hand whilst still keeping one eye firmly fixed on his reflection.

"Mmm, you are definitely the biz, Eddie, a real Adonis!" he said out loud. "Spelly is gonna be blown away tonight, man, blown away!"

"Edward," Lady Elf shouted. "Edward, come down, dear. Our guests are expected in less than ten minutes and your Father would like a word with you before they arrive."

Eddie stopped snogging his hand and grimaced. "Choofing 'ell," he whispered. "Here I am trying to get myself prepared and me Papa wants an elf to elf talk. Talk about bad timing."

"Edward dear, get yourself down here NOW!"

"Coming, Mammy," he replied sweetly, leaping onto the swirling walnut banister, and sliding down to the bottom of the staircase in a flourish.

"Oh, I wish you wouldn't do that, Edward. The cleaners do complain so when you put your dirty feet all over the woodwork, dear, and it makes the seat of your trousers shiny."

"Sorry Mammy," Eddie said with a twinkle in his eye. "Just being an elf boy an' all!"

"Mmm, well, off you go into the parlour. Your Papa is waiting and I must say, dear," she said in a proud voice, "you look positively dashing tonight. Have you made an extra effort because the lovely Miss Spellbound is joining us?" She patted his shoulder in an affectionate manner. "Oh, and one more thing, please be polite tonight. We don't want a repeat performance of what we had at Broomsticks Cottage, now, do we? Spellbound is to inherit a huge fortune when she's older and already owns the *Toofy Pegs* dinner set. You won't find a finer nor richer fairy in all the realms. Her Mamma and I would really like you two to get together. So no leering, dear. It is common knowledge that she has her Aunt Hester's genes and will not be wooed with lewdness."

Eddie had the grace to look a little ashamed but then scooted off down the long corridor that led to the parlour, and threw a chuckle over his shoulder.

"I'll be good, Mammy," he laughed.

Inside the parlour, Lord Elf stood with his hands behind his back, rocking backwards and forwards on his heels, facing the huge gold and silver fireplace. His presence was astounding. He was one tall elf (if there was such a thing!) His neatly trimmed beard showed off his regal features and his mop of golden hair was still as thick as it was when he had been Eddie's age.

"Pops!" said Eddie, as he ran quickly into the parlour, slightly out of breath. "You wanna see me?"

Lord Elf turned around to face his son. His expression was serious and his eyes showed a little apprehension, not something Eddie was used to.

"Son, I think it might be time to have that elf to elf talk. Have you ever heard of the 'birds and the bees'?"

Eddie cast his mind back to the sweet-as-a-buttercup fairy he had happily bedded the night before. Mmm, she was a real little corker, he thought to himself, but seeing his father's anxious expression, he just couldn't miss this for the world.

"No Papa, can't say I have", he replied innocently.

***

"Hellooooo, hellooooo," trilled Leticia. "How nice to be invited. Come along, Spellbound, and wipe your little feet, dear, on the fairy expensive mat." She smiled nervously. This was her first visit to Elf Hall and she really wanted to make a good impression.

"Esmee, dear," she enthused, as Lady Elf greeted her with open arms. "I must say, Esmee, you look a picture of perfection."

"And you too, dear," came the reply. "Utterly sensational. I love your gown, Leticia, where did you get it? Or did you zap it up like the clever witch you are ... ha ha!" Lady Elf joked.

Leticia handed Esmee a hand-wrapped box of Blake Magic chocolates from *Elfredges*. They tittered like fairies do about the naughty treat!

Spellbound looked spectacular in a raspberry coloured lace mini-dress, with thin shoulder straps. Her shoes were cute ruby and diamante pumps with killer heels in crystal. Leticia had tried to insist that she wear a gown for the occasion, but Spellbound, who had started to choose her own fashion, was having none of it. In the end, and after an hour of quarrelling, Leticia had given in and was quite shocked when she saw her beautiful daughter descend the stairs at Broomsticks Cottage, looking very well groomed and all grown up.

Lady Elf escorted the two fairies into the drawing room and as Leticia looked around in wonderment at the sumptuous velvet drapes and hand-carved furniture, Eddie sidled up to Spellbound from behind.

"'Ello, Spelly," he whispered, so as not to let the adults hear. "Cor, you look the business tonight! I'm surprised yer Mamma let you dress like that ... jeeze and just look at the bling; must have cost her a small bleedin' fortune. Coo, Spell, I'm having all sorts of loving thoughts now."

Spellbound turned around and shot him a look. "What is it with you, Eddie?" she asked. "Can't you think of anything other than slushy stuff and romance? You really are starting to make me feel sick with all this mooning around. It's not cool, Eddie, really it's not!"

Eddie sported a cheesy grin then cast his eyes over to the corner of the room where his mother and Leticia were now seated.

"Oh, don't they make a sweet couple, Leticia dear?" asked Lady Elf as she smiled a sickly smile in the youngsters' direction.

"They certainly do, Esmee," Leticia replied. "I know they are young and getting used to one another but I have high hopes, Esmee, high hopes!"

"I agree, dear, give them time and I am sure Spellbound will come to see that they are a perfect match. There couldn't be a finer fairy for him, especially as her father is the great Zamforia ... and speaking of which, when is the notable Zamforia returning, dear? I'm dying to meet him."

Leticia coughed and changed the subject quickly. "Was Eddie a good baby elf, Esmee, did he cry much when he was in hankies?"

"Not a bit, dear, no, he was the perfect child. Look, I'll show you." Lady Elf pulled a large book from under the table and began to show her pictures of Eddie as a baby.

"Oh Spellbound, do come over and take a look at these wonderful pictures of Eddie," Leticia called. Spellbound raced over to her mother's side - anything to get away from the dratted elf and his mushy comments. As Lady Elf turned the pages, images of Eddie with his little pointy ears and naked elfin body lying on a rug made Spellbound choke with laughter.

"Ha ha," she gasped, "look at his lickle winkie pinkie!" The tears streamed down her face and she laughed even harder. Leticia and Lady Elf couldn't help but join in with Spellbound's infectious giggling. Eddie stormed across the room and glared at the trio.

"Aww, Mammy, you really are embarrassing me," he screeched. "Whatcha doing showing everyone pictures of me dinky?"

"I beg your pardon, but your other guests have arrived, Lady Elf," said the butler in a snooty voice, as he entered the drawing room.

"Oh, please excuse me, Leticia," Esmee said, as she got up from the chair and walked into the grand hall.

Leticia stopped laughing and looked at Spellbound, intrigued. "Other guests?" she mouthed silently. "I wonder who they can be?" She strained her neck to see if she could take a peek through the door but the butler was well and truly in the way and just smiled in her direction.

Eddie began pulling rather strange faces, obviously still put out that his juvenile elfhood had been the butt of their jokes.

"Would you like to follow me through to the dining hall?" the butler said to the two Zamforian fairies. "Dinner is about to be served."

The dining hall was a vision. A massive table, which could seat forty guests, sat elegantly in the centre of the huge baronial room. Six candelabras, all lit with flashing ice blue flames, were placed an exact distance apart along its length. Abalone handled knives and forks were positioned with perfect accuracy, and before each setting sat a silver goblet with an image of the Lord and Lady Elf embossed on them. The chairs were gold and upholstered in royal blue damask, with silver threads that were woven into a fine pinstripe.

"Please do come in and take a seat," Spellbound heard Lady Elf say. "And I must introduce you to the Zamforian fairies. This is Leticia Zamforia and her daughter, Spellbound Elspeth."

Spellbound and Leticia turned around in unison to face Philip and Drillian MacCavity. Spellbound's eyes met Drillian's in surprise, as he casually strolled over to her. Taking her hand, he planted a kiss onto the back of it.

Just out of earshot he whispered, "Nice to actually be allowed to kiss these hands for a change, Miss Spellbound."

Spellbound looked up to the ceiling and sighed, and Leticia began to giggle nervously. Fookin' Philip MacCavity! How was she going to get out of this little scenario, she wondered.

"It is quite all right, Lady Elf, you don't have to introduce us," said Drillian in a low husky voice. "Spellbound and I are already acquainted, aren't we, Spell?" He lifted his head from the kiss and smiled at her. "Spellbound kindly agreed to join the company as my new PA last week," he explained, turning his attention back to his hostess. "She is doing remarkably well, considering." Once again, he looked intensely at Spellbound. "We've just returned from a week-long business trip in Toncaster, haven't we?"

"Oh, that is wonderful, just wonderful," Lady Elf gushed, clasping her hands together, "and what a fine assistant I am sure she will make. You didn't tell me about that, Leticia," she remarked, turning to her friend. "You must be so delighted for Spellbound to have such an important job. We were all thrilled that she had become a tooth fairy but to be the PA to the boss's son is indeed a wonderful promotion!"

Eddie was standing in the doorway with his father. No one had told him Spellbound was personally working for Drillian MacCavity! And what a liberty he was taking with HIS Spelly, he grumbled to himself. Everyone knew he was a sex maniac and could 'do' any fairy chick he wanted! Now I have to stand in line behind a male millionaire, sex-mad elfman. What next, he asked himself.

Throughout dinner, Leticia observed Drillian closely. He was sitting opposite Spellbound at the dinner table, staring directly at her the whole time. Oh, lordy lord, this guy is a handful, she mused.

Philip was trying very hard to make polite conversation with her but her thoughts were firmly fixed elsewhere. How was she going to protect her daughter's innocence from such a rake? If Spellbound couldn't handle him she was going to have to do some serious spell casting on her behalf; but then again, she did have Aunt Hester's genes, she thought, and breathed deeply to calm herself. On the other hand, would Spellbound know how to handle such a grown up, sex-crazy Adonis as this? Oh boy, if only she were ten years younger! She fanned herself slightly with her hand. Spellbound was still so young and innocent. She might look all fully-grown and mature but she was just a baby! Leticia continued to watch Drillian as he expertly engaged Spellbound in conversation and to be fair, her daughter looked calm and even a little bored. Secretly she was pleased. Perhaps she could handle him; perhaps she was a chip off the old block after all!

Eddie was becoming red faced and furious. His plans had been thwarted. He coughed and interrupted the hum of conversation. "Hey, Spelly, why don't ya come to the fairy flicks with me tomorrow and we could go dancing afterwards?"

She looked up from her frogs legs. "Nah ... thanks but no thanks ... I've got better things to do," she said, tossing her glossy black hair over her shoulder. Eddie looked downwards in disappointment.

Leticia was trying to listen to the conversation but Philip MacCavity was demanding her attention. "Dearest Leticia, how lovely to see you, you look absolutely divine. It seems an age since we last met. Where is that quiet little dinner party you were going to host for just the two of us?"

Leticia was searching frantically for a reply, when Drillian clipped in.

"Father, please don't embarrass Madam Zamforia in such a way and don't forget you are a married elfman. Mother would be very hurt if you had supper with someone else, who is married too, in case you had forgotten. I am really surprised at you!"

Leticia let out a little sigh of relief as Philip hurriedly shovelled some food into his mouth, looking quite embarrassed. For the moment, she was off the hook.

Not to be thwarted, Eddie looked up from his plate, seeing a chance that he could score himself some brownie points with Leticia and bring himself closer to Spellbound at the same time. He directed his words to the older MacCavity.

"If you don't mind me mentioning it, sir," he said bravely, "I didn't see Mrs MacCavity at Spellbound's birthday ball, and she is not here tonight. May I ask where she is? I do hope everything is all right with her."

Drillian almost choked on his food, as Lady Elf went red in the face, and Lord Elf scrambled on the ground to retrieve the fork that he had dropped. Leticia gazed at Eddie in astonishment. They all turned to look at Philip who was calmly finishing another mouthful of food.

"Yes, of course you may, my dear boy," he replied smoothly. "Mrs MacCavity is in the best of health, thank you very much for asking. But she does have a rather pressing duty to fulfil regarding her own mother. Some years ago, her mother had an unfortunate meeting with a cat, which left her wings in very bad shape, not to mention her state of mind. My wife has regrettably had to be with her since that day to take care of her, as she is the only fairy her mother now recognizes and will let near her, which means that she cannot always be at my side at social functions such as these. Rest assured, I always arrange to take her some of the wonderful food that is served - like these frog's legs, absolutely delicious, Lady Elf," he said, expertly changing the subject, and raised his wine glass in her direction.

"Why, thank you, Mr. MacCavity, cook will be very proud to prepare a doggie bag for Mrs. MacCavity later. Please send her all our love and good wishes, and do forgive my son his blunt curiosity," she said, rather embarrassed.

Drillian could see what Eddie had tried to achieve by asking about his mother, so now his attention deliberately went to Leticia. Perhaps if *he* got her on his side he would stand a better chance to win over the lovely Spellbound.

"So, Madam Zamforia, I hear you make fantastic magic. Have you inherited this great gift from an ancestor perhaps?"

Leticia's violet eyes flicked coldly over his face as she gave him one of her polite little smiles. She should be courteous to him as he was Spellbound's employer after all.

"Yes, from my cousin Larissa. She was my guardian and mentor until I was ten and six. She taught me all I know and in turn, I shall pass that knowledge onto Spellbound." She looked towards her daughter and smiled.

"And does the great Zamforia have magic powers as well?"

Leticia swallowed very delicately and took a quick sip of her pink champagne. All eyes were turned in her direction. "He does indeed ... but he has a very different kind of magic to me."

Drillian gave her the full benefit of a dazzling smile, as he asked lazily, "When is he to return home? You must miss him."

"I miss him terribly," Spellbound piped up.

Leticia took a small breath and refused to be shown up. "Sometime in the autumn I think he said he would be returning. He has been very busy these last few years in the Austrial Realm, making sure his vast fortune stays intact."

Spellbound knew that Leticia had been backed into a corner and was lying through her teeth but she wasn't going to miss any opportunity to get as much information out of her as she could.

"If we are so rich, Mamma, why do we live in Broomsticks Cottage?"

Leticia threw her a black look as all eyes rested on the two fairies. Forming her words very carefully she explained evenly, "When your father leaves this realm, by the law of his ancestry, his fortune must go with him. That is his birthright and it cannot be changed. As you very well know, he did leave the *Toofy Pegs* set as your safety net, Spellbound, and when he returns, the beautiful house he built for us will be made visible again and we will dwell there once more."

Lady Elf nodded. At last some of the mystery surrounding Zamforia had been explained. "They say the house was magnificent, Leticia, and set in vast grounds ... is that so?"

Leticia nodded to Lady Elf and smiled dreamily, "Yes, a beautiful house; we even had a crystal stream running through the lounge. Zamforia spared no expense - he was always so generous."

Drillian was confused, "Pardon my curiosity, Madam, but why has he been away for so long?"

She sighed, her eyes turning to ice as they flicked over him irritably. He was as sharp as a knife and this was getting too uncomfortable for words. Spellbound's eyes were out on stalks as she cleared her throat delicately.

"Zamforia's absence has been a strain to say the least, but a part of his karma is to succeed in all things pertaining to wealth, business and privilege. So one must just shrug one's shoulders and accept it. After all," she lied convincingly, "he will be home soon enough and we can then get back to a full family life."

Lady Elf tittered and stretched her hand over to Leticia. "You are so courageous, my dear, and so brave to be on your own for so long; it must be an agony for you and of course Spellbound too. When

Zamforia returns, my husband and I will throw a huge ball in his honour, won't we, dearest?"

Lord Elf nodded, "It would be a great privilege to do that for you, Leticia, and I can't wait to meet Zamforia again. We used to play Bugbee together when we were at college. He is a fine upstanding elf with great dignity."

Leticia thought of Zamforia wrapped around Tinky Bonk in the sauna and tried her best to hide a scowl. "Yeah some fine upstanding bastard, my foot!" she thought.

***

Spellbound was in bed and Leticia was very disturbed. She was exhausted with having to pretend about Zamforia's disappearance to Lady Elf and their guests. Spellbound had been sullen on the way home and unusually quiet. Where would it all end, she thought, as she pulled herself wearily out of the chair and went over to Clifford.

As she removed the purple cloth, he spoke immediately. "At last, Leticia; I have wanted to speak to you for days about something very important."

She sighed; why was everyone so demanding? She raked her dainty fingers through her hair and irritably looked at the ball. "Fire away, Clifford, and make it quick. I'm shattered."

"Leticia, when Spellbound was summoned to the Astral by her godmother, she was told by Moonflower that you had cast a powerful spell on her three years ago to stop her from missing her father. The spell is wearing off very quickly and now she is in the *yearning phase* and you don't need me to tell you what happens when a fairy is in yearning!"

Leticia's eyes darted around the room in a blind panic. Slowly, her skin changed to a pale white and for a moment she felt she was going to faint. She clapped her hand to her mouth. "*Yearning phase*? Surely not! Not the yearning!"

Clifford blinked a couple of times and then continued. "If Zamforia doesn't return, Leticia, Spellbound will lose her wings and be transformed into a golden hare, and if that happens, there won't be a thing you can do about it, even with your powerful magic."

Leticia slumped into the chair opposite the ball and started to cry. This was just turning out to be the most awful day. What was she to do? How could she fix this mess? She lifted her head, revealing two very swollen and puffy eyes.

"How long has Spellbound got before the change?"

Clifford's eye rolled dramatically, "That I do not know; all I do know is that the Elders are not happy, Leticia ... something must be done soon to get Zamforia back or your daughter will be hopping off sooner than you think!"

She dropped her head into her hands. Everything was a crock of shit, Leticia thought despairingly.

"Clifford dear," she snivelled. "Look into the future. Tell me how long I've got to keep Spellbound from turning into a hare. To cast a spell to get him back could take months, and that's if I can even do it. You know and I know that I banished him for life. I would need a hundred wands and a thousand potions to sort this muddle out."

Clifford clucked like a mother hen, "Well dear, that's what you get for being so hot-headed and impetuous. Now try not to be too upset for a moment while I concentrate."

A full ten minutes passed and the crystal ball was a mass of magenta mist for most of it. Leticia paced up and down as she wrung her hands. Suddenly the ball cleared and Clifford's hazel eye became visible again.

"Well," she screeched impatiently, "what did you see?"

"You have three months and no more. Spellbound is fine for the present but you're going to have to get cracking and bring Zamforia back pronto!"

***

Later that night, Leticia was sitting in bed with four powerful spell books in front of her. She scanned the pages carefully. Each book told the same story: to reverse a spell such as this would take four months of constant spelling to return a banished soul - and that would be one month too late. My beautiful daughter is to become a golden hare and it's my entire fault, she thought sadly.

Downstairs, Clifford mulled over the events of the night. Seeing Leticia so upset had really unnerved him. How he would just love to embrace that perfect fairy and sweep her up into his warlock arms. Since the day she was born, he had watched over her, and from the time she was ten and four he had loved her. One thing was for sure, he thought to himself: if and when Zamforia did return, there would be no re-kindling of passion between the couple. The proud Zamforia would never forgive her for banishing him to some far off realm.

Chapter 13

The Inheritance

Spellbound was away in Toncaster with Drillian and his entourage again, giving Leticia some well-earned peace and quiet to get down to focussing on the magic she needed to perform. Leticia thought her daughter seemed to be handling the elf man and her job very well, all things considered.

The continuing spell to get Zamforia back was well under way and she had every confidence that it would be done in time. Larissa had spent an entire evening over at the cottage and given her some magical tips, along with a big confidence boost, and for now, all was well. However, if Zamforia was going to be conjured back to Bluebell Forest, she was going to have to look better than the bee's knees! There was little point in dieting; if her spell to bring him home worked, she simply had to change her outer appearance and quick. The last time that bastard had seen her she was as trim as a blade of grass and even though she hated him with a vengeance, she wasn't going to let him see her with these zippo hips!

Leticia had succeeded in recognising all of the ingredients from Larrisa's *get thin quick* potion and had finally finished concocting it, but had added an extra touch of her own magic so that the spell would never wear off. Oooh, if this works, she told herself, I could sell the potion to fairies far and wide and make my fortune!

Taking a tiny blue glass bottle, she submerged it into the copper cauldron that held the magical liquid. Filling the flume all the way to the top, she studied the contents with great interest. With a quick sniff and then holding her nose, she downed the fluid in one fell swoop. The familiar fizzy feeling engulfed her body and very slowly her shape began to change. Disappearing were the tiny lines around her mouth and eyes and her breasts automatically lifted into a perfect little bulge, spilling above her pale pink night shift. Her rounded hips were transformed into a slim yet voluptuous curve and as she turned to look behind her, she noticed that her backside was youthful and pert once more. With one last glance in the mirror, she grinned and then winked. "That'll do nicely!" she said. Little did she realize that Clifford had been watching through a gap in the velvet cloth and couldn't believe his eye!

Suddenly the musical door chimes rang out and she daintily flitted over to the large oak door to open it. A smartly dressed gnome in uniform grinned and saluted her respectfully.

"Recorded delivery, Milady, please sign here."

She took the long cream vellum envelope from him and stared hard at the red seal on the back. With a flick of her wand her signature was done. She closed the door and opened the letter; it looked very formal and more important than the pixie post she usually got. Seating herself comfortably, she unfolded the two embossed sheets.

> *Dear Madam Zamforia,*
> *We wish to inform you that you have been left a legacy.*
> *Please come to our offices at your earliest convenience*
> *for further instruction.*
> *Yours Sincerely,*
> *Peri and Manson*
> *(Solicitors)*

Her eyes scanned the pages excitedly. "A legacy, but from whom?" she said aloud. She just couldn't think, her head was spinning. She had not done any money spells lately so this must be for real. She couldn't possibly wait another minute without finding out exactly who had been so kind as to leave her money and how much!

***

As she was being ushered into the offices of *Peri and Manson*, her heart skipped a beat. A plump bearded gnome led her to an overstuffed chair and looked at her over his tiny silver spectacles. When they were both seated, he cleared his throat and proceeded to read the document in front of him.

"Madam Zamforia, some years ago you did a Tarot reading for a gentleman elf called Wilfred Pickel-Nickle. You advised him to start a new business and to move to the Zeeland Realm to make his fortune. Well, he followed your instructions to the letter and became a multibillionaire thanks to your advice. Sadly, he passed away a month ago but he has left you a sizable sum."

He wrote down a figure with rather a lot of noughts on the end and passed it to her. She gasped with utter astonishment.

"As it is such a huge amount, Madam Zamforia, we will of course help and advise you how best to invest ... so to speak!"

Leticia sat in a daze. She was rich beyond belief. Once Zamforia came back, he was sure to divorce her for banishing him for the past three years, but at least this way she would be made for life and not have to give readings to the fae folk anymore. Now she could write to her heart's content and be independent and comfortable and not have to hold her hand out for a penny of that bastard's money, she thought with delight.

***

Spellbound's fairy spell phone danced in front of her nose to let her know she had a call. As she held it to her pointy little ear, she heard her mother's excited voice on the other end.

"Darling, sweet, sweet fae child! You must come home this instant dear ... take a break! We have struck it rich; we will never have to worry about money again. Oh, and Spellbound dearest, you and Mamma are going to buy a new house, so hop on the swirlybird contraption and get yourself back to the cottage immediately: we are going shopping!"

Spellbound was sitting opposite Drillian at the luncheon table, pushing a snail around her plate. "What are you talking about, Mamma? Have you gone mad? I can't just hop on the swirlybird and ..."

"Hop on it RIGHT NOW," Leticia demanded excitedly, "I'm clearly not mad, dear, the most astonishing thing has happened. I've been left a huge legacy. Come and help Mamma spend it!"

Spellbound screamed in delight as Leticia flapped around on the spot with the phone in her hand.

"Oh, and Spellbound dear, Mamma may look a little different when you see her next, so don't be shocked."

Spellbound turned to Drillian excitedly. "I gotta take some time off to go to my Mamma. You won't mind, will you, Drill?" Flashing him an enchanting smile, she jumped down from the high stool. Her turquoise wings had stiffened in excitement and turned bright shades of orange.

She looked a vision when she smiled, thought Drillian, with her long dark hair tumbling around her face and her eyes flashing and dancing like a sprite on a lily pond. He couldn't ever recall seeing that sweet rose-bud mouth laugh or smile before. She really was something only an elf could dream about. He gathered his thoughts quickly and for a second froze. His jaw tightened and a knot began to form in his stomach. Spellbound waited for him to say something. Finally, he ran his fingers through his dark mass of hair and lifted his slate grey eyes to meet hers.

"What's so exciting; won't you tell me?" he asked.

Spellbound began hovering two inches from the ground, something she always did when she couldn't contain herself.

"Mamma has just received a whopping inheritance from an old client and we are going to buy a new home as soon as possible, can you believe it? Oh, this is so exciting, Drill! I always hated that cottage, all dark and drab. Now we can live in the lap of luxury, just like when my Papa was here."

Her face changed a little at the mention of her father and the dancing in her eyes suddenly clouded over. Drillian had come to the firm conclusion that Spellbound was indeed showing signs of the yearning. The vacant expression on her face didn't last long though, and before he could say another word, she hurriedly began to collect all her personal things together.

Drillian inspected his fingernails, feeling suddenly annoyed. "How long were you thinking of being away, Spellbound?"

She thought of the first thing that came into her head.

"A month? I dunno, haven't had time to think. Guess I'll be as long as it takes," she chirruped.

"A month, that's a little steep, isn't it? Hmm ... I'm not sure about that." He continued to look down at his nails, frustration engulfing him. Spellbound stopped dead in her tracks and turned her sweet little figure to face him.

"Take it or leave it, Drill, I couldn't care a gnat's fart. In fact I don't really need to work at all now, do I?"

Drillian felt his heart sinking at Spellbound's obvious change of attitude, and knew he had to think fast or he might lose her for good. "Okay, two weeks. That's all you're getting and then I want you back here with me, doing the job I pay you very well for doing. Enjoy your spending spree and ..."

Spellbound didn't wait for him to finish. She was heading out of the restaurant and towards the door.

"I'll miss you ..." he whispered under his breath, but she was already gone.

***

Drillian sank down onto the richly upholstered chair in his office. Why did he feel so dejected? Maybe he would get the laptop out and look at his *Totty* list, he thought. That should distract him. His eyes scanned down the fairy list but he couldn't summon the enthusiasm he usually had.

He could call Passionflower. She was very good at underwater activities, especially in the hot tub, and she could hold her breath forever and ... his thoughts drifted. Then there was Maybelle, she really knew how to mushroom bounce. He sighed. Just lately he had lost interest in them all. Why was that, he wondered despondently. Why, all of a sudden, had his desire in the fairer sex diminished like this? It was just so out of character. Then like a bolt of lightning, it hit him full in the face. That was it! For the first time in his twenty years, he was feeling an emotion he had never felt before. He had a crush ... he had a crush on a stroppy little cute-assed fairy called Spellbound!

***

Leticia and Spellbound had found the perfect house. It was situated in the very centre of Bluebell Forest in a large clearing. Nearby was a huge lake with over fifty pale blue swannikins gliding on its surface. The trees surrounding it were in an unusual shade of turquoise and pink. Little furry dodibells, in every colour, swung from branch to branch singing in tinkle-tones. One landed on Spellbound's arm and cuddled into her, sucking its furry thumb cutely. Spellbound stroked its little pointed ears and it trilled.

"Ahh ... Mamma, isn't she cute?"

"Divine, absolutely divine. I always wanted one as a child but was never allowed one and now we are overrun by them. Don't bring them into the house, dear, they disappear into all of the cracks and crevices and breed like mad, especially the yellow ones; plus they sing all night long and keep you awake. They also have a nasty habit of getting into the bedclothes. If you're sensitive, believe me, dear, you'll get the itch bug. Soon we will have to get the little wooden wheelbarrows out to collect them all and put them further afield."

They strolled back towards the house, which looked like a pale pink palace. There were two swimming pools and a fly zone. Spellbound had her own wing and could entertain as many friends as she wanted. She even had her own top-of-the-range bright red and white spotted *Ladybuggy*, a maid, and her own personal butler called Biff Wellington, who was rather snooty.

Life was just utter bliss and truly fantastic, she thought to herself. Leticia had also been very kind and affectionate and allowed her to choose all of her own furniture and drapes. Spellbound wondered about her mother's change of character, as she had suddenly stopped dominating her. It was all so perfect. She had her freedom, a fantastic job, her own house and a kinder, thinner more glamorous Mamma. The only thing missing was her Papa and as soon as she could get that bastard Clifford on his own, she would get him to spill the beans

Chapter 14

A Broken Ball

Drillian was riding around the forest on the most magnificent male dragonfly and was thoroughly miserable. It had been a whole week since Spellbound had sped off at the speed of light to spend her Mamma's inheritance and he was worried that he was in danger of going in to the *yearning* himself. This silly cock-assed fairy had filled his thoughts every single goddamn minute of every day and he just couldn't get a thing done. Luckily, he still had enough elf power to keep his business ticking over nicely, but the second he tried to make a conscious decision or put a deal together, the delightful little winged creature would invade his mind yet again. He was starting to get worried. This was seriously not like him. Sure, he was renowned for having a string of fairy gals at his beck and call but never, not *ever* had he had any kind of feelings for them. These days, his mushroom only twitched when he thought of Spellbound and he was fast becoming concerned that unless he got to savour the sweet flavours of her, it would never twitch again!

If he could bed her, that would do it, he mused. He needed to get her well and truly out of his system. If he had sex, just once, then his interest would wane like it usually did, he reasoned to himself. It was only because he couldn't have her he was feeling like this and the only explanation why he was so preoccupied with her was because she wasn't interested in him! If she fell into his arms or draped herself over his desk, he would be fine. He was sure of it.

"Well Drill," he said to himself, "You are just gonna have to try a bit harder, mate. Turn on the charm like never before and make her yours for the night." Not one to believe in the power of Aunt Hester's genes and certainly not one to be defeated, he steered the dragonfly towards Spellbound's home.

When he saw Leticia's new residence, he was totally taken aback at the awe-inspiring sight. He brought the dragonfly to a hover and there in the distance he saw Spellbound sitting by the edge of the lake, dipping her toes into the cool translucent water.

She was dressed in the cutest sexy denim cut-off jeans and silver diamante-encrusted top. She looked her usual delightful endearing self but today, her wings, which had transformed into an icy pale blue, weren't stiff and perky like before, they were hanging down, just like the sad and sorry state of her head.

He pulled in the reins and silently steered the insect a little nearer. As he got closer, he could see that she was crying bitterly, her tears falling like a river down her face. "Shit," he thought. This wasn't what he had expected at all. Nevertheless, he couldn't turn around now; if he did she would be in danger of seeing him. He swiftly steered the dragonfly onto the nearest reed and skilfully leapt off to face her.

Spellbound was shocked to see him, her green eyes swimming with tears. She shot him a 'how dare you disturb me' look before quickly wiping her eyes with the palm of her hands. The last thing she wanted was for him to see her crying. He observed the tears and her downcast expression and it just made him more compelled to throw his big arms around her and make all the pain go away.

"What d'ya want, Drill? I'm not coming back to work yet, so please just bogger off and leave me alone," she snivelled. "Just leave me alone."

"Hey you, what's wrong, why the tears?" The sympathy in his voice made Spellbound feel uncomfortable; thrusting her face into her hands, she tried to compose herself as she hiccupped softly.

"None of your business, Drill. Just leave me be … please."

"I shall not leave you be until you tell me what on earth is wrong with you!"

He strode over and squatted down in front of her, gently taking his finger and curling a lock of her dark hair behind her pointed shell-like ear.

"Go, this is really not a good time for me," she choked.

Drillian could feel hot tears pricking his own eyes. This fairy's pain was contagious, he thought. Why the hell do I want to cry like a baby when she does? She was damn right about one thing, he did need some therapy but it wasn't for his sex life, that was for sure.

"Listen, Spell," he said gently, "I haven't got a magic bone in my elfin body but if I could wave a wand of any sort and take all this shit away from you I would. Just tell me what it is that is making you like this, and I'll see to it. I promise I will."

"Well, Mr. fix-it," she sobbed, "I doubt you are gonna be this nice to me when I turn into a fookin' mad March hare!"

"A what?"

"A hare!"

"Did you say a hare?"

"Yes!"

"Damn, you ARE in the *yearning phase,* then," he said, looking horrified. "I kinda half guessed you might be. Some pixie boy really did get to you, huh?" He looked down at the grass feeling completely beaten.

"It's not a pixie or an elf, silly!" her voice quivered.

"Wait." Drillian lifted her face up with his forefinger. "If it's not a guy, then who?" he asked with concern.

She tugged hard on a blade of grass and sighed unhappily. "It's my Papa," she said. "He's gone and I need to get him back. If I don't get him back soon, I'm gonna yearn to death and turn into a hare. I know this because my fairy godmother came and told me."

Drillian raised both eyebrows. "Wow, you got to meet your fairy godmother? That's jammy, what did she say to you?"

"She told me off for swearing so much and said that I had to go and see Clifford. He's our warlock trapped inside a glass ball and she said he'd tell me where my Papa was."

"So, did you go and see him? Did you ask him?"

"I can't get near him," she said in an exasperated tone. "Mamma is watching my every move. He is her warlock, he serves only her. I don't get to consult him until I inherit him. Something fishy is going on, Drill, and I need to figure it out."

Spellbound continued to wipe her eyes. Looking over at the grand house, Drillian began chuckling.

"Erm … no time like the present, hun. Your Mamma has just left the building, basket on arm and ready to shop till she drops, by the looks of it!"

Spellbound shot a look in the direction of the house and swiftly stood up, wiping her nose quickly with the back of her hand. What she saw was Leticia walking towards the wood all dressed up in her shimmering peach gown, with her tiny wicker basket tucked neatly under her now, very fairy slim arm.

Spellbound and Drillian waited until Leticia was out of sight and sped into the house. Drillian looked around quickly. It was a very different picture from that of Broomsticks Cottage. Inside the grand hallway, they turned left and entered the beautiful library, full to the brim with many wonderful fairytales from centuries past, along with a selection of Mamma's raunchy *Spells and Swoon* books. There in the corner of the room was Clifford's ball, this time covered with a piece of the finest silver muslin. Spellbound stopped and ordered Drillian to wait while she raced upstairs to collect the magical orb from under her mattress. Once back in the library, she uncovered Clifford, who was waiting, wide awake.

"Spellbound," he said a little shaken. "Ah, I see you have brought a guest!"

"Never mind the small talk, Cyclops; it's time to rock and roll. Now spill the beans: what have you done with my Papa?"

Drillian stood back and watched speechlessly. The atmosphere in the room was electric.

"I really don't know what you mean," Clifford lied, "and I would like it if you showed some respect, young lady, and stopped calling me names. It is quite hurtful, you know!"

"Just tell her how to get her Papa back, mate, or I'll see to it that you never look out of that glass again!" said Drillian.

Spellbound turned in astonishment and looked at Drillian. "I can handle this, Drill," she spat. "If you must be here, at least be quiet. I am quite capable of fighting me own fookin' battles, thank you!"

Drillian didn't take a blind bit of notice and walked over to Clifford.

"Listen you," he said, looking directly at Clifford's eye. "You tell her NOW where he is, do you hear? We are running out of time and I am losing patience!"

"I am not breathing a word," said Clifford. "It is not my place to divulge the details of her father's whereabouts. Ask your mother if you really want to know, Spellbound. This family has got to be the most complicated and dysfunctional I have ever served. I am sick of all this, I tell you, sick, sick, sick of it all!"

Spellbound took the orb from behind her back and held it in front of Clifford.

"I know what you want, Clifford," she said quietly. "I know your heart's desire. I can feel it through the power of this orb. You want your freedom, don't you, Cliffy?"

Clifford gulped as he looked at the small round shining ball of light, sitting in the centre of the fairy's hand.

"You have a magical moon orb, Spellbound. Pray tell me, where did you get it? How did you come by such a thing? There are only two in the entire universe."

"Moonflower, my fairy godmother, gave it to me and she said you would know exactly what to do with it. But I think I know how it works, Clifford," she said cockily, "because it's MY magical orb after all and I am magic too, you see."

Spellbound was enjoying her power happy moment, tossing the orb from one hand to the other. "I can use this orb in any way I please," she taunted.

Clifford's voice began to shake. "Spellbound, I'll say it again. You have the one and only thing in the entire universe that can release me from this god-forsaken ball! You have to do it for me please. You have to use that orb to free me!"

Spellbound stood, looking thoughtful. "Nah ... I think I'll keep the wish just for myself," she replied, making Clifford even more frustrated.

"You have no idea what you have there, do you, child?" he said in a pained manner. "That orb will reverse any curse or negative spell instantly. It's not a wish ball, you stupid fairy, it's the most powerful magical thing that has ever existed in the land of the fae, now ..."

"Don't you call her a stupid fairy, you one eyed wozzack!" Drillian heard himself say, to his surprise. Anger had risen in his gut and all of a sudden, he had become completely protective of her.

"Drill, will you just shut it for a sec please, hun," Spellbound whispered behind her hand. "I am trying to blackmail the snoop! If I'd known you were gonna play big brother I'd have left you outside on yer winged thing!"

"Spellbound, sweet, sweet child. Now be a good girl and release me from the ball. There's a good fairy."

"What's it worth?" she asked with a twinkle in her eye. There, she had said it: the bartering had begun.

Clifford looked at her, his one eye disbelieving that she could hold his entire future in her hands and with such contempt. What could he do? His loyalty and love for Leticia went without saying, but to be free, free from this piece of glass, free to walk again and free to eat, free to practice his magic and one day open his school of sorcery like he had always planned and perhaps have Leticia at his side ...

There was no contest. For hundreds of years he had been entrapped following Morgana's curse and now, today, this very day, he could be free to live out his life. He sighed and spoke very quietly. "Okay, Spellbound ... you win. Release me from this ball and I will show you where your father is."

"Oh no, Cliffy! I wanna know everything first. You don't think I am THAT stupid that I would set you free before you give me the answers I want. You are going nowhere until I have all the facts." Spellbound stood her ground, and Clifford knew he had been beaten.

"Okay," he sighed. "Look closely into the mist."

Spellbound and Drillian both took a step closer and peered into the swirling fog. At first, they could see nothing at all, but then slowly the visions began to emerge. There before their eyes was the fateful scene. A beautiful golden haired naked fairy was wrapped like a silken ribbon around her beloved Papa in a hot tub. They were kissing passionately, completely absorbed in each other.

"Ouch!" said Drill. "Not good that ... nope, doesn't look good, nope not at all!"

"Who the blewdy hell is that fairy gal, Clifford?" Spellbound screeched.

"That, my dear, is Tinky Bonk, your father's ex-fiancée, and the reason your mother banished him away on a desert island three years past. Your father was engaged to Tinky before he met your mother. Leticia walked in on them having sexual relations in their new home and was heart broken. She then became very angry and sent them both away in opposite directions for the rest of their lives."

"I can't believe it," Spellbound cried. "My lovely Papa cheated on my Mamma? No ... not my Papa! He would never do such a thing, no, no, no ...it can't be true, the ball is lying, Clifford."

Spellbound's breath started to shudder and she could feel the tears begin to well up in her eyes again. Drillian was there like a shot and enclosed the sad little fairy in his arms.

"The ball never lies," said Clifford matter of factly. "What you see is what happened. Your mother was inconsolable; she loved him so much, you see. Zamforia was her one and only romance. She wanted your father so much that she spent an entire month casting a powerful love spell to make him leave Tinky and come to her."

Spellbound couldn't believe what she was hearing and glanced up at Drillian with disbelief. He looked at his feet for a second, feeling he was intruding on something rather personal.

"Zamforia was betrothed to Tinky for quite some time, but your mother, having Aunt Hester's genes and all, knew that she could never love another and took him away from her. She used all the magic she could muster and programmed him to love her for life. For some time after she had caught the two of them together in the Cherub Pagoda, she did feel pangs of guilt for using her magic in this way, and she quickly reversed the spell, so at least he is free of that now. What your mother did was wrong, Spellbound, but in all fairness, she has put things right, to a fashion."

"So what are you telling me, Clifford, is that Papa never really loved Mamma anyway; that she used enchantment to get him and Tinky Bonk was his true love?"

"It would seem so, child," Clifford replied in a soft voice. "It would seem so."

Spellbound started to sob uncontrollably. All of her young dreams and aspirations had just crumbled in front of her. As much as Clifford had his issues with this young wild fairy, he hated to see her so disturbed.

"Your father truly loves you though, Spellbound, as does your mother," he added kindly. This made her cry even harder.

"It's okay, Spell," Drillian said quietly. "Don't cry." He lifted her chin and gazed sadly into her tear-drenched face. Just how much could one fairy take, he wondered. Why did life have to be so rotten for such a lovely little thing as this? There I go again, he mused. Every time I'm around this chick, I go all GOOEY! I seriously must get a grip, he told himself firmly. Then, without even knowing what he was doing, he lowered his head, kissed her cheek and waited for the slap!

***

Leticia placed her basket on the table and smiled smugly. She had bargained ruthlessly with the jeweller for the triple stranded emerald necklace and earrings and had got the best price ever. Of course, she could have afforded to have paid the full price on the gemstones. But once a thrifty fairy always a thrifty fairy, she told herself.

The much-needed shopping spree had temporarily taken her mind off the need to get Spellbound free of the *yearning*. She was spelling like mad to get Zamforia back in time. Larissa had said it would be a close shave and nearly impossible, but Leticia had always achieved success with every spell she had undertaken in the past and so she felt confident that this would be successful too. It had to be. After all, she couldn't have her only child turning into a mad March hare!

She made her way over to the ball to see if Clifford could predict whether she was on target or not. She removed the muslin cover with a flourish and stepped back in amazement to see the familiar ball smashed clean in half.

"OOOOOOOHH! Fooking lordy lord. Ohhh!!!!! Lordy lordy fooking LORD!"

Leticia began wringing her hands frantically, her eyes darting around the table in a frenzied fashion. "What's happened ... what's happened to the ball?" she asked breathlessly, "Clifford, oh my word, Clifford, Clifford, where are you?"

"Right behind you," said a sexy deep baritone. She spun around in a flurry of fairy dust and found herself face to face with a stunningly handsome stranger.

"Who the fook are you?" she screeched like a harridan.

He smiled a dazzling white smile, his hazel eyes crinkling at the edges mischievously. His eyelashes were longer than she'd ever seen on anyone and his hair was a thick glossy shade of deep chestnut.

"Clifford Eyesaurus, Milady, at your disposal." He bowed ever so slightly and his purple velvet cloak billowed to show a long lean athletic body and broad chest.

Leticia gulped. "Clifford? But it can't be," she said in a small whisper. For a moment she stood in complete silence, her mouth slightly open. She glanced quickly again at the broken ball and then back at him. He approached her and knelt at her feet, kissing the hem of her gown.

Not taking any notice of his romantic gesture, Leticia gawped at him with total disbelief. "I...I...I don't understand," she stuttered, still suffering from the shock. "How did you get out of the ball?"

He led her to her favourite chair, sat her down, and knelt at her feet again, his hands cupping hers as he drank in her beauty. To finally touch the object of his affections was better than he could have possibly imagined. He gazed up into her eyes and took in the vision of her creamy white skin and delicate frame, as her perfume drifted into his nostrils.

Pulling himself back to the present with a jolt he replied earnestly, "My sweet Leticia, when Spellbound met her fairy godmother Moonflower, she gave her a moon orb." He smiled excitedly.

"A moon orb? I've only heard of them, never seen one," she breathed erratically.

"Moonflower told her to bring it unto me and give me my heart's desire, but alas, my sweet," he said more seriously, "in return I had to tell Spellbound everything about her father and how you had spelled for his love, only to banish him once you found out about his deceit."

Leticia looked dazed and bewildered; for a moment, she thought she might faint.

"You have to understand, Leticia, I couldn't refuse. It was a direct order from the Elders and it has brought me my freedom."

"So what exactly does my daughter know and what did she see?" Leticia asked in a faint whisper.

"She knows the truth, my princess. And she has seen all that she had to see. There are no secrets between you now."

Leticia dropped her head into her hands.

"No ... no ... this can't be so. I am so shamed."

Clifford grabbed Leticia's hand and pulled her to her feet. He put his arms around her and stared straight into her beautiful violet eyes. "Let us not talk of shame, Leticia, not now," he said, as he cradled her head against his shoulder. "I have looked after and cared for you since you were a little child. I have watched you grow and blossom into the magnificent fairy that you are today. We have shared so much together and no one knows you as well as I do, would you not agree?"

He held her face tenderly in his hands and she nodded as the tears ran down her cheeks. In a flash, he magicked up a snow-white hanky and dried them. "I have to tell you this," he said, looking deeply into her eyes. "I love you, Leticia, more than you will ever know. I have always loved you and for ever more my heart will be eternally yours!"

Suddenly he kissed her full on the mouth, taking her by surprise. Only Zamforia had ever kissed her before, and with only a little hesitation, she pulled away.

"I have dreamt of this moment, of being with you, putting my arms around you, having you for my wife."

"But ... but ..."

"Shush, my sweetest," Clifford spoke. "When Zamforia returns he will certainly want a divorce, especially since you took the love spell from him. He belongs to Tinky Bonk now, you must realize that."

Leticia gazed back into his eyes sadly and nodded again. A little hiccup softly left her mouth and she started to cry again.

"He was never mine, was he, Clifford? I should have been wiser and not so free with my wand and spells and potions."

"You were but a hot headed child, dearest, and all is not lost, you do have Spellbound from the marriage and she is a joy among joys."

Clifford pulled her close again and Leticia frowned slightly at the thought of the little fairy. "Where is Spellbound now?" she asked him.

"She is with Drillian, and before you say anything else, I think he is falling in love with her. You must promise me you won't meddle or interfere with her karma, like you did Zamforia's. I know you want her with Edward, but let fate decide. Promise me?"

Leticia sighed wearily, pulled away and went back to her chair.

"My life is shattered, Clifford. I have all of this money, all of these things and no happiness. Spellbound could turn into a hare if I don't get that spell right. And to top it all off, I have to bring back the very person who lights up my soul and breaks my heart all in an instant." She smiled sadly, her nose a little red from all the crying. "Your magic is as powerful as mine, Clifford, can you help here? Do you think that you could help bring back Zamforia so I can put all this sorry mess behind us?"

Clifford stood before her, feeling empty because she was no longer in his arms.

"Spellbound has the key, my sweet. She has the magical moon orb, which can reverse spells and curses. We must speak with her soon and show her how to use it, so that she herself can bring back her Papa."

Suddenly a weight lifted from Leticia's shoulders; of course, the orb would solve all of the problems and Spellbound would be released from the curse of *the yearning*.

"Leticia … I know a lot is happening to you at the present time and your head is all over the place … but … I … I … will you … marry me after the divorce?"

"Marry you, Clifford?" She turned her attention to him and spoke gently. "My dear, I am flattered beyond belief but I am already married and …"

"You will get over Zamforia and he will be happy with Tinky and pick up his life again. You have stolen three years of his life. Don't make him any more miserable than he already is, Leticia. You're not a child now."

"It isn't as easy as all that, Clifford," she objected. "I cannot just turn my feelings on and off at the drop of a wand. I have loved Zamforia for so long. It would not be fair to marry you and still be in love with another. If circumstances had been different then I would consider but …"

Clifford quickly interrupted. "If you would desire it, I can conduct a special ritual that will make you feel nothing for him ever again; your heart will be free to move on and begin anew."

Leticia was shocked. This type of magic could only ever be cast by a warlock and it went against the rules big time. To interfere or influence a person's mind carried great consequences, especially if the Elders ever found out.

"No, Clifford. I would never ask such a thing of you. This is my muddle; I caused it, I created it and therefore I have to live with the consequences. After casting such a powerful love spell on Zamforia, I have to take my punishment and if that means having a heart that hurts for eternity, then so be it. I deserve much worse."

Clifford brushed his hand over Leticia's cheek. A pained expression filled his face. "There would be no price to pay, Leticia. If it means that I may have the chance to live out my years with you by my side then I would project my power to a thousand realms and face any consequence."

"No, but thank you dear," Leticia said with a quivering voice. "Your offer is kind but I have made up my mind. I will do the right thing this time."

"Then think about my proposal of marriage; we would be a good partnership. You could teach me your gifts and I could teach you mine."

She was quiet for a long time and gazed at the tall stunningly handsome warlock. In all of her years she had never had feelings for Clifford, but looking at him now, he was amazingly attractive and he oozed power. Maybe someday this could be a good partnership, she thought silently. She did have a strong fondness for him, and it was clear he loved her more than life itself, which she had always secretly known, even when he was entrapped within the glass ball, and that was more than could be said for Zamforia!

Pulling her up again, Clifford wrapped his arms around her and held her against his young strong body. "I love you, Leticia; let me look after you as I have always done; let us raise a new generation of Eyesaurian fairies. You are young and healthy; we could be happy and have our own family. But don't ban me from your life, Leticia," he said in desperation, "for that I could not bear!"

***

Spellbound entered the hall of their house and dragged herself upstairs. Seeing her father having sex with Tinky Bonk had shocked her so much that she felt she would never recover. It had also been a shock to see Clifford crash out of the glass ball in a flurry of electricity, which nearly knocked both her and Drillian clean off their feet.

Throwing herself on the bed, she continued to cry her heart out. She could not stop this infernal weeping. It was draining the life out of her and her eyes were swollen beyond recognition.

"I'll have a long soak and try to do some meditating. Maybe Moonflower will come to me," she said to herself dejectedly.

Sinking into the golden bath tub, she closed her eyes, but the pictures she had seen in the ball kept coming back to haunt her. "No … Papa would never do such a thing no … no …" she told herself.

She started to cream her little body with expensive fairy gel and then suddenly let out a huge scream.

"Ahhhhhhhhhh!!!!!! Ahhhhhhhhhh! Ahhhhhhh!! No!!!!!!!!! No!!!! No!!!!!!!!!!!"

Leticia and Clifford heard the screams from the east wing of the house and tore up the stairs in a whirlwind, throwing open the door of Spellbound's bathroom. She was stood in the middle of a puddle examining her bottom in the full-length mirror. She continued to scream and wail at forty decibels when she noticed a long golden ear pop out of her head.

"Mamma, I've grown a hare's tail and look, I've got another ear! Mamma, make it go away … make it go away now, I can't bear it!" she screeched hysterically. As she spoke, golden hairs started to appear on her arms and legs and her nose was already beginning to change shape.

Leticia swooned and fell into Clifford's arms. As he patted her cheek repeatedly, he could see that the blood had drained from her face.

"Oh, lordy lord, Clifford, it's started, do something, please!" she gasped weakly.

"Now everyone calm down," he said steadily. "Spellbound, stop this wailing, and Leticia, sit down before you fall down. Let me think."

Leticia was wringing her hands in consternation and Spellbound continued to scream at the top of her voice as another ear appeared. Clifford wrapped a sheet around Spellbound to conserve her modesty and went back to Leticia.

"Right, we have to work quickly, we need the orb right now. Where is it, Spellbound?"

Leticia pulled herself together somewhat, running over to her child and staring into her hysterical face, "The orb, where is it, sweet child?"

Shaking uncontrollably, Spellbound pointed to the top drawer of the cupboard in the corner of the bathroom and Leticia quickly retrieved the orb and passed it to Clifford.

"We must all do this together," he said. "Spellbound, come here and put your forefinger on the globe. You too, Leticia; your magic will enhance the spell, we have but a few seconds."

All three stood in a circle as Clifford held out the orb, which oscillated and throbbed, changing colour constantly.

"When the orb is pink and *only* pink, say this in unison," he spoke tersely.

Three forces together,
Three forces we be,
Magical orb of strength and power,
Set the enchanted ones free.

The orb left their fingers and flew around the bathroom, growing larger and larger and then it exploded with a resounding crash and disappeared into the ether and back to Moonflower. Spellbound fainted and Clifford caught her before she dropped to the floor. Leticia swayed with not an ounce of colour in her face. Dragging her breath into her lungs, she went to her daughter's side. The tail and ears had disappeared and her skin was free of hairs. She was in a very deep sleep.

Gently Clifford carried Spellbound to the adjacent bedchamber and laid her in her bed, pulling the covers up to her chin.

"She will sleep in enchantment for two full days, Leticia, and she must NOT be disturbed; don't even look into her room. She will wake up renewed, happy and free of the yearning, so fret no more, my darling."

Leticia clung to him as he wrapped his arms around her quivering body.

"You must sleep too, Leticia. The spell was powerful and I can see it has drained your strength. We won't know when Zamforia and Tinky and will come back, probably after Spellbound's recovery, but for now … rest. The ordeal is over."

He gazed into her beautiful violet eyes and snapped his fingers once. Her eyes closed and he lifted her into his arms and carried her to her own room.

Clifford dared not rest and sat by Leticia's bedside watching her sleeping. He would guard her until she had her full faculties again. The last thing he wanted was for some dark force to enter her when she was so unconscious and vulnerable. He knew Spellbound would be protected by Moonflower and breathed a huge sigh of relief that this whole sorry episode was nearly at an end.

He gazed down at the sleeping sorceress. Her hair tumbled all around her heart shaped face. Her skin was as creamy as alabaster and his heart yearned for her to be his. Zamforia was now free to wed Tinky, and he would make sure Leticia would stay safely by his side forever.

Chapter 15

Fenella Phlegm

About eight miles south of Bluebell Forest, there was a dank, dark wooded area hidden away, surrounded by a filthy, dirty swamp. Very few would go anywhere near it because it was renowned throughout all the realms for its sinister energy. The ghosts of evil and depraved witches, corrupt and banished wizards, as well as the souls of malevolent warlocks who had fallen in battle, were said to haunt the deep hollows, and those that practiced the dark arts would gather to cast their evil deeds. No birds or animals went there, as the air was fetid and stank of rotting flesh and vegetation.

The only reason that any fairy or elf would venture into this part of the realm was for the most fantastic *sillypscilly* mushrooms, that when eaten, gave the hallucinogenic effect of astral travel. Trolls and ogres frequented the outer perimeters and, if bribed with enough poppy punch, could be persuaded to collect them.

Drillian was getting desperate. He simply couldn't function anymore. For the last three days Spellbound had continued to invade his thoughts. He had not seen her since the crystal ball had exploded and Clifford had leapt out into the room. Leticia had been polite when he had called at the house and asked to speak with Spellbound, but was resolute that she could not be disturbed. Clifford explained that Spellbound was recovering from the yearning spell and would not be around for a week or so. Every time Drillian so much as tried to focus on his business empire, she would pop into his head, and before he knew it, he was fantasising about laying her down on his king-sized passion pouffe and having the hottest sex of his life.

His appetite was more than quite elfy, but of late, nothing tempted his taste buds. He was walking around with a knot in his guts and had no interest in food or fairy gals. This must stop, he berated himself, and he had to get back to normal. Things had become so bad that he took Spellbound's advice and went to see Carmella

Cacklejuice, the local fairy shrink. She was well known for her wisdom and sound advice in such matters. Her sex therapy sessions were said to be phenomenal and she specialised in impotency and fairy *Frantric* sex, a skill she had learned during her numerous visits to the Asiatic Realm in her youth. It was rumoured that she could make an orgasm last half an hour!

After three sessions with Drillian, she told him that he was seriously obsessed, probably just 'in lust' and needed to get a grip. She also suggested that if he could take *her* to his bed chamber and have a steamy, mad, hot, rumpy pumpy session, his obvious obsession with Spellbound would probably be cured in an instant. A few months ago, he would have jumped at the opportunity of bedding Carmella, but for once in his life, he had declined. This was totally unheard of!

Being a MacCavity, Drillian had always got everything he had ever wanted in his life. As an only son, his parents had indulged him and tended to his every need. Not to have the very thing he desired sent him into a frenzy, so he needed to take drastic action and fast. He was behaving like a lovesick teenager. What he needed was some kind of spell that would make Miss Zamforia his for just one night, he had told Carmella.

The only problem was that with most spell casting, witches and warlocks had certain moral ethics about influencing another's mind. It wasn't going to be easy finding a spell that would circumvent Aunt Hester's Victorian genes for any period of time. No, this would call for one hell of a ritual. Carmella scratched her chin in deep thought.

"There is always Fenella Phlegm," she said, with a slightly worried look. "She's one of the more powerful fairy witches who dwell in the darker regions of this realm. Rumour has it that if you pay her enough, she can magic anything up; she was banished there for having sexual relations with a grasshopper some ten years ago."

"How do you know of such a witch?" Drillian asked with curiosity.

Carmella turned to him and slanted him a mysterious smile. "There have been times when things just don't happen naturally, so in my job I have to have a finger on the pulse and I have used her and her spell crafting a few times for myself and the more difficult clients. But perhaps you need to be extra careful, Drillian. After all, Spellbound's mother is the most powerful fairy in the forest and her father is Zamforia; if Leticia found out ... then woe betide you! You might find yourself banished to that godforsaken place yourself ..." she trailed off with a frown.

Drillian knew he was on dangerous ground but he spoke his thoughts out loud and shrugged his shoulders. "Sod it! I won't be denied her a moment longer." When he wanted something he got it. "To Fenella Phlegm I shall go!"

***

The verdant beauty of the forest had long since disappeared in this place. The trees were bare and putrid smelling mists hung around the rotting foliage. Drillian carefully picked his way along the overgrown path towards a gnarled stump that resembled the face of a demon. He glanced down at the map Carmella had given him. It had cost him a week's wages to get it but he was determined in his quest for the fairy Spellbound. Today he had decided not to bring his *Swirlybird* or dragonfly for fear of being heard and spotted by the locals. His reputation was too important and if he was seen, tongues would definitely wag.

A clearing came into sight and up ahead was an old rickety cottage with peeling plaster and a wonky chimney. The windows were filthy and covered in sinister insects and strange noises could be heard here and there in the undergrowth. It had a threatening, disturbing look about it, a place where one wouldn't enter unless they were desperate, which of course he was!

As he stood in front of the old wooden door, the ivy that clung to the walls of the building began winding itself slowly around his ankles. He pulled his dirk from his belt and slashed at the vine. A piercing screech came from behind the door and it was obvious that someone was pulling across a rusting bolt. With a deafening creak, the door slowly opened to reveal a wizened creature. Her matted salt and pepper hair was long and disorderly. Disturbingly, there was a nest of the dreaded widder spiders crawling on her greasy fringe and when she eyed him cautiously, he could see the signs of blindness in one of her opalescent eye balls.

"What do ya want, pretty boy?" she wheezed, showing her stumpy discoloured teeth. Her breath stank and he stepped back a few paces in alarm. The ragged black and magenta wings twitched from side to side in a sinister fashion. She stepped nearer to him, and the tip of one of them stroked his face, as she cackled. "So ... you are the sex pot of Bluebell Forest. I've watched you a few times in my ball when I needed a little *stimulation*," she grinned lecherously. "You're better than any porno movie. Can't say as I remember your name though ..."

"My name is Drillian MacCavity and I have come to ask your assistance in a matter," he said, speaking with more courage than he felt. This female was gross.

Fenella cackled again, the lines on her face becoming more obvious. She took another step forward to get a better look at the handsome elf that stood in her doorway.

He was dressed in light stonewash denim jeans, a crisp white t-shirt, which proudly revealed his tribal tattoo, and a pair of Fleabok trainers. He ran his fingers nervously through the sides of his hair to reveal his two perfectly formed, pointy ears. He wasn't so sure that he liked being scrutinised in such a way but felt it best not to comment, under the circumstances.

"Aye, you're a fine looking specimen, that you are, and I can see why you have the fairy fan club," she leered, stroking a gnarled stinking finger over his lips. Drillian pushed her hand away and stifled a wretch.

"What is it that you want from a poor old witch such as me … perhaps some scintillating sex?" She screeched with laughter, her bony frame shuddering in mirth and turned back into the cottage, leaving the way clear for him to enter. "Let me see. I remember your name now, the great Drillian MacCavity, son of Philip and heir to Molars Incorporated. In trouble, are we?"

"It is not that," he replied. "The business is doing very well, thank you. No, it is about another matter that I wish to see you." He hesitated for a moment. "A more personal matter."

Fenella prodded the open fire with a large log as Drillian observed the bedraggled fairy. He could tell that in her youth she had probably been quite a beauty but now all that remained was a skeletal caricature of a century-old witch.

"You had better tell me whatever it is you have come to say," she said, still stoking the flames.

A large bobbly toad suddenly leapt out from nowhere and landed on his trouser leg. He pushed it to one side but it immediately jumped back on his trainer.

"Don't mind Tiptoe, sir… she means you no harm."

"I need a spell to enchant a fairy and make her mine for the night," he said quickly and felt rather embarrassed about having to divulge such intimate information to this old crone.

Fenella spat a huge shot of mustard phlegm into the fire and it sizzled on a lump of wood. Drillian winced and tried again to remove the toad, which was stuck like glue to his other foot. He doubted whether he would ever wear that pair of trainers again.

"A handsome elf like you needs a spell to enchant a fairy? Surely not ... you surprise me, sir!"

"This is no ordinary fairy, Madam. She has Victorian genes, inherited from some obscure aunt. She will only succumb to a male if she is in love, and as she is not in love with me I can't have her, therefore I want her all the more," he sighed in exasperation.

Fenella turned and stared at him. Then she spat again into the fire and wiped her filthy hand over her mouth.

"So ... you need a love spell for the elusive Miss Zamforia! Yes, I know of whom you speak," she said, with a worried frown on her face.

"But only for one night. I don't want her permanently, you see. I just need to bed her so that I can get this obsession out of my head," Drillian said earnestly.

"Umm ... I don't know, elf man. Her mother is, after all, Leticia Zamforia; even I am frightened to death of her. If she were to find out it was I that cast the spell I would be dead meat and that is for sure. Perhaps this time I will have to say no to you. It's really not worth my while, you see. Spellbound is a Zamforian fairy; her father is very revered and Leticia also has the powerful warlock Clifford Eyesaurus as her devoted guardian. If I angered any of them, I would be finished!" Fenella frowned and shook her head. A widder spider ran over her weather beaten cheek. She gently lifted it into her hair.

Drillian shrugged arrogantly. "Surely this gossip about Madam Zamforia is just stupid supposition?"

"No ... you are mistaken. You must take care, too, if you cross her. She has great powers of banishment, and guards her only child with a vengeance. It is far too risky, you must leave. Go now!" She moved past him towards the door.

"Fenella," he said desperately, "I will be more than generous. I will give you five hundred fettials."

Fenella paused and brushed one of the larger spiders from her eyes. "For two thousand ginnagonds I might consider it," she growled, her eyes flickering greedily. "Just the one night you said?"

Drillian sucked in his breath and tried not to look shocked at the amount. Yes, he was rich but this was a six month's wages! "A thousand and no more, old crone," he bit out aggressively.

She hobbled back to the fire, spitting once more into the flames.

"I'll bid you good day then, sir."

He reached into his breeches and took out a black cloth purse bulging with coins, tossing it onto the table. "Here, you win," he snarled. "My only concern is that I don't want this spell to last. Just one day and one night, that's all I want of the fairy's favours."

Fenella's eyes lit up. She was money mad and always had been. She clawed the purse towards her and shoved it into the bodice of her filthy dress.

"The deal is done then, Mr. MacCavity," she cackled softly, pushing him out of the cottage. "Be back here for your potion after the cock crows twice!" she cried.

"What cock?" he asked, a little confused.

"In two days' time, you stupid fool!" she shouted, and slammed the door behind her.

Chapter 16

Spellbound's Seduction

"Spellbound dearest, please get down from the sweep fan. You'll bring the whole ceiling down in a minute and that will never do. You have been spinning around and around for over an hour now and frankly, dear, you are doing your Mamma's head in!"

Ever since Spellbound had awoken from her three-day rest and the yearning had finally dissipated, no one could contain her. She was stupidly happy and zapping dodibells at the drop of a cap. Every time someone spoke, she laughed loudly and Clifford and Leticia had had to cast a *reduce the volume* spell on her, for half an hour a day, just to get some peace.

"I'm so happy, Mamma," she shouted from the top of the ceiling. "All my sadness has left me and I have so much energy. I am on top of the mountains, on top of the ..."

The spell phone began to jingle in front of her nose and with a swift twirl in the air, she let go of the sweep fan and fluttered down on to the ground.

"Heeeellllllllllloooooooooooooooooo," she sang happily, "this is the one and only Miss Spellbound Zamforia at your service, may I ask who the devil is calling?" Spellbound was giggling uncontrollably as Leticia raised her eyebrows and gave Clifford a withering look.

"Spell, it's Drill here," a deep sexy voice spoke back. "Have you been on the poppyade?"

"HA HA HA ... no, I'm not drunk, silly Billy, I am just remarkably happy, that's all. I have good news, Drill, in fact, I have the bestest news ever," she said, pausing for a second and awaiting his response.

"And what would that be?" he asked, not really wanting to know, but rather more interested in summoning her cute fairy ass over to his place instead.

"I am completely free of the yearning," she said excitedly, "and somehow, all that depression has been replaced with sheer and utter happiness. I am so so so so so so so HAPPY ... heheheheheheheheHAHAHA!"

"Mmmmm," he responded. "Well, I am so relieved for you but I need your fairy happy backside over here, Spellbound, at my place, pronto. We have some serious invoicing to catch up with and as you have had quite a lot of time off lately, I suggest you tell your folks that you're not going to be back until tomorrow morning. I had the maid make up the west wing for you, so bring an overnight bag. My guess is that we are going to be at it well into the night." Drill slapped a hand to his mouth. Blewdy hell, did I really say that? "At the invoicing, that is," he amended quickly.

"HA HA! Glad you went and put that last sentence right, Drilly baby, 'cause you know I would never be at it with you, lover boy, not in a zillion years." She continued to laugh hysterically.

"MAMMA, MAMMA," she bellowed, causing Drillian to hold the spell phone away from his ear, "THE ALMIGHTY FOOKING TOOFY PEG MAN NEEDS ME TO WORK ... UGH ... WORST LUCK, EH? MAMMA, CAN YOU HEAR ME, I HAVE TO GO ... I'VE BEEN SUMMONED ... MAMMA?"

"Spellbound dear! Do stop shouting like a fog horn, I am right behind you! Yes, I heard you, who wouldn't?"

"Oh good, Mamma. Hey, I'll be gone until tomorrow morning. Is that okay, Mamma? Do you need me for anything? Will you miss me? HEHEHEHEHE!"

"No, not at all. Get yourself off, now," Leticia said exasperatedly. "And thank the lordy lord for that," she muttered under her breath. "A whole twenty four hours of peace and quiet ... I can't friggin wait!"

**

Drillian sent his Sparrow Hawk, *Jock Strap,* to collect Spellbound. She had decided to make herself look ever so sweet today and was wearing a lavender pair of cut of trousers and strapless silver top to reflect her mood. Her wings were changing colour by the minute. Each time she got a rush of happiness, they went a pearly pink colour and when her mood settled down a bit they changed back to lilac and bright orange.

The Sparrow Hawk sped in and out of the trees as Spellbound gaily waved down to everyone she saw. With her wand now fixed firmly in her right hand she was zapping and pinging magic all around her, sending a cascading array of silver fairy dust about the wood. She changed the Sparrow Hawk's plumage to bright pink with a luminous plume of green on its head and gave him a little golden crown just for good measure and a bright red saddle.

Spellbound's magic was now working better than ever. Her Mamma had figured that because she had been so depressed, none of her spells had given the desired results but as she was now free of being so utterly miserable, she had channelled something within her, which was making her more powerful by the second.

Drillian was pacing up and down outside Cummalot Castle waiting for the crazy fairy to arrive. He knew that she was getting nearer when he heard the distant sound of whooshing and whirring, followed by loud bellows of laughter. Jock, the Sparrow Hawk, looked positively petrified when he pulled up outside the grand entrance. Spellbound showered his face with a million kisses, tickling him under his wings. If this was to be the norm, he would bogger back off to Swopland, he fumed. "WOWEEEE ... Drill," she shouted as she leapt off the back of the bird, changing him back to his former plumage.

"I didn't know you lived in a castle!" she said excitedly. "What a place, what a wonderful place!" she exclaimed. "Not as big as Papa's castle or Mamma's palatial pad but, hey ho, I'm no snob. I don't mind slumming for one night." She laughed uncontrollably and slapped him on the back.

Drillian lurched forward, nearly losing his balance. He'd never been with a fairy richer than himself and he felt like kicking her ass right now for being so incredibly bolshie. Spellbound glided towards the large golden doors that were framed by two footmen, one at each side. In true fairy fashion, she did a sweeping curtsey and held her hand to her breast before speaking in her most lady-like voice. "Why thank you, kind sirrahs!" she said, as one of the footmen stood aside and ushered her in. In ten seconds flat both footmen were turned into giant green bunny rabbits chewing over-sized carrots.

Drillian looked up to the heavens and tutted as he followed her inside. "I do hope you will change my footmen back to their original form."

"Later, Drill, later, now have you got any cake? Do they call you Drill because you're always screwing? HA HA!" she said, skipping and darting through the great hall. "I'M SO FUNNY …"

He had a hard time keeping up with her. "I really fancy something sweet like cake or …" she paused, "Chocolate! I love human chocolate, bet you ain't got any of that!"

Drillian shouted for a maid to go and fetch the fairy some chocolate.

"It won't do your teeth one bit of good," he remonstrated with her sternly, as she sat with the chocolate bar wedged between her legs, greedily chomping big chunks off it.

"Never mind the teeth, Drill, this is heaven, I tell you, spaddy whacking heaven. You are so lucky to be able to get this stuff. I hear it takes some serious courage to rob a human child of its chocolate. Poor little spoilt bleeders!"

"You'll want a drink or something to wash that down, won't you?" he said, getting up from the couch and walking over to the drinks cabinet, as casually as he could.

The room was bedecked in rich fabrics, the tall arched windows were adorned with luxury cream drapes and on the floor were faux *hugga-hugga* bear rugs. The maid was hovering over Spellbound, collecting the stray pieces of chocolate that had fallen onto the carpet; she secretly pushed them into her pinafore pocket for later. Drillian poured Spellbound a glass of bluebellade and then, with only a moment's hesitation, he discreetly emptied the whole contents of Fenella's glass bottle into the fluid and watched it bubble and ferment. Finally, when the potion had died down to leave a clear, delicious tasting liquid, he walked over and held the glass out to Spellbound, who by this time had eaten her way through half the bar.

"Oh Drill, I couldn't possibly drink that!" she groaned, holding her stomach, her face going a little green. "I think I've eaten too much of the chocolate hun … oooh, my belly is growling like nothing I've ever known. Y'know, I think I'm gonna be …" She retched twice. "Mmmm … sick!" She careered across the room, knocking an antique standard lamp over and smashed the priceless Miffiny shade to a million smithereens. She shot out of an open window, yicking up all over the grass.

Drillian was motionless, holding the potion and wondering if he should forget the whole damn seduction scene! This was not working out at all as he had expected. He turned to the maid. "Put Miss

Zamforia to bed. She has clearly over-indulged herself with too much chocolate. See to it now," he snapped impatiently.

***

Spellbound lay flat on her stomach in the four-poster bed groaning, her wings pointing northwards and her legs spread wide, when Drillian came into her chamber.

"Feeling better?" he asked, as he placed the potion on the table beside the bed.

"A little," she whimpered. "I guess I was a little bit greedy, I ain't NEVER seen THAT much chocolate before," she said with a half hearted smile.

All Drillian could think about was just how much precious time she was wasting. Seeing her spread-eagled on the bed like that, looking all sorry for herself, just made him want to swallow her up in his big arms and kiss her to death. With a tender gesture, he sat beside her and stroked her dark silken hair away from her eyes.

"How's my poor little fairy? Would you like Drilly to kiss you better?"

"Just fookin' try it, git features … gerroff you, I know what your game is, trying to sweet talk me. Mamma has given me many lessons in chat up lines, so bogger off, Romeo," she said, swiping a hand out and luckily missing his nose by a cat's whisker.

"You really don't like me, do you, Spell?" he asked, standing up and looking hurt. "I've left your drink there for you; I'll be downstairs in the library when you feel ready for work."

His last-ditch attempt at trying to get close to her had failed miserably. She still hated the thought of him touching her, he thought. Ah well, as soon as she drinks Fenella's potion, I'll have her all to myself and hopefully, this time, she'll be willing and able and then I'll be able to get her out of my system. Just thinking about it put a smile back on his handsome face. Then she could go and fook herself!

When he had gone, Spellbound sat up in bed and admired the room. The walls were embellished with rich tapestries and the ceiling was ornately painted with cherubs and fairies from years gone by. In the middle of the ceiling was a huge mirror. Typical of him to want to look up everybody's arses, she thought. There was a series of buttons on the headboard and she pushed one curiously. Out sprang a pair of pink fluffy handcuffs. She tried another and a little white vibrator with bunny's ears plopped into her lap, making whirring noises. She threw it across the room in disgust and shouted, "Pervy git!" In the corner was a bath tub full of pink, warm bubbling water, surrounded by a beautiful shimmering net curtain. She noticed the tub and decided that as soon as she got home, she would beg Mamma for one.

Suddenly feeling thirsty, she spotted the inviting drink and reached out her hand. The first sip tasted like blueberries, the second like fresh oranges, the third was like an exotic passion juice. It was sensational, she thought. Without thinking, she threw the entire contents of the glass down her throat and all the sickness and bloaty feelings she had previously felt left her in an instant.

"Wow, that's luminous stuff!" she said aloud. "I must get Drill to give me some more of that." She leapt off the bed to go in search of him when all of a sudden, the sheer mention of his name made her feel all funny and gooey inside. "Oh … Drillian," she said out loud again, "Where are you, hun?"

Drillian was sat in the library, a very long oblong room filled with books from ceiling to floor. As he was flicking his way through the Carma Sultry, he heard a commotion from the adjoining hall. Suddenly Spellbound appeared at one end of the library, hovering just above the floor. Her wings were perky and bright silver and in the distance, he could see a cheeky intense look on her face. Without further ado, she flew as fast as her wings could carry her towards him, and wrapped her long fairy legs around his waist, holding onto him tightly. Drillian was so taken aback that he nearly fell into the fireplace, as she planted a thousand kisses all over his eyes and nose.

"Oh Drilly Willy," she gushed excitedly. "Wow, you are *such* a hottie. I have this funny feeling rushing all through my fairy veins … muah … muah … muah!" She continued to kiss his face, covering every inch with tiny kisses.

Drillian held the fairy in his arms and even though he had planned this whole event, he was still knocked for six at her immediate lust. Fenella had obviously decided that he was going to get his money's worth!

"I think I lurve you, Drilly baby," she cooed. "I do, I do, I luuuurrrrrrve you."

"You do?" he asked, looking shocked as she planted her lips onto his again.

"Oh yes, I do, I do, I do, I do. Come on, you little love god," she said, throwing her head back and bouncing on his hips, "Show me what all the fuss is about and get rid of my virginity, whatever that is! And show us your todger … I ain't never seen one up close before … is your mushroom twitching, Drilly boy? Is it … is it? Show me your pork chop, you gorgeous dazzling thing. Daffy said it's HUGE. I just have to see it … come on, whip it out and let's have a peek … don't be shy, baby!"

"Spellbound … er … Spell," he said, overwhelmed by her over demonstrative behaviour. "There's … er … plenty of time for that, now settle down, hun, just try and er …"

In a flash she leapt out of his arms, whipped out her wand, and zapped his clothes clean off his body. Drillian stood there butt naked, quickly covering his elfhood with both hands.

"Spell, hun … what have you done?" he cried, feeling suddenly abashed. She circled him, taking in every part of his lean, tanned, athletic body.

"Wowwee!" she breathed heavily. "You are cute, Drilly, and modest too. Cor, I never thought you would be the shy type." She took her wand and tickled his bottom with it, making him automatically remove one of his hands to push the staff out of the way. She eyed his manhood with wide eyes. "No wonder all the fairy gals want to have their wicked way with you. Pumpkin said you made her eyes water and I can see why!" She peered more closely at his elfhood, inspecting it with an eagle eye. "How does that thing work?" she asked, lifting the end with the tip of her wand. "I've never seen a real life todger before. Where exactly do you put it, Drilly? Which pee pee hole does it live in?"

This wasn't at all what Drillian had expected and he was getting more embarrassed by the minute. "Spell, listen …" he tried to say, but another zap of magic from her power happy wand saw her stripped off to just a tiny twinkling turquoise thong. Drillian gulped at the sight of the naked fairy and then a second later, Spellbound had zapped him again and they were both lying on the four-poster bed, covered in shooting fairy dust and romantic pink stars. She zapped her wand on the switches in the headboard and out dropped the hand cuffs, three vibrators and a porno magazine.

He was utterly astounded at the change in her, but still had the presence of mind to press another small button on the headboard. At once, an array of orange, green and blue fairy sparks whizzed around their heads and all around them, sending them into a giddy delight and obscuring them from view.

***

"Drilly … oh Drilly," Spellbound sang lightly in his sleepy ear. There was no response. After a few more minutes of tickling him, nibbling his neck and yanking on his todger, she decided to bounce frantically up and down on his stomach.

"UGH … HUH …WHUUUU."

"Wakey wakey, lover boy," she yelled, "I wanna go again … hehehe, do it again!" she bellowed, as she continued to jump up and down on his chest. Drillian, true to form, and with a hearty laugh, gathered her up in his arms again.

**

"I need to eat Drill," Spellbound said, after their sixth marathon session. "Rumpy pumpy don't half make you hungry. I never knew I would like it as much as this. Can we do it every day, Drill? And you'd better not be having none of them other fairies either, not now that I lurvvve you. Zamforian fairies are very jealous and as you know, we can do nasty banishment spells at the flick of a wand," she half joked. He gulped nervously. "Now that I lurve you so much, any funny business and I'll be banishing you, just like Mamma did with Papa."

Drillian lay completed naked and lifeless on the bed. This was one fooking energetic fairy. Sure, he had stamina, he was renowned for it, but twice on the bed, once in the bath tub, and three times on top of the wardrobe really had knackered him out!

"Banishing sounds like a very good idea right now," he said with a chuckle, rolling her over again.

**

"Something just doesn't feel right, Clifford," Leticia said as she paced the room. "Something is definitely amiss. I have this very strange feeling in my guts and …" she paused, scratching her head for a moment.

"I know what it is! It's Spellbound, she's … she's …" Swirling her wand three times around her head and chanting something in elfish, she cast a quick spell.

Back at Cumalot Castle, Drillian was seriously enjoying himself yet again. "Spelly … Spelly, darling sexy fairy," he murmured to her, looking down at her on the bed. In a flash, she disappeared into thin air.

Spellbound tumbled into the centre of Leticia's parlour as naked as the day she was born. Her lipstick was smudged across her face and her hair was sticking up like haystacks.

"MAMMA! What the fook do you think you're doing, spoiling all my fun?" Spellbound screeched, wrapping her wings around her body to cover her modesty.

"More like what the fook have YOU been doing?" Leticia asked frantically. "You've been having sex! I can't believe it, Spellbound, you've gone and had sex!"

"Leticia, now stop interfering with her karma," interrupted Clifford. "She has Aunt Hester's genes; if she's laid with an elf, I'm sure that it is all proper and she's in love."

Leticia ignored him. "Who have you been having sex with?" she yelled at her daughter.

Spellbound looked down at the floor and giggled. "I'm in lurrrvvve Mamma, I really am."

"WHO, SPELLBOUND?"

"Drilly, of course," she replied. "Ohh! He's a wonderful lover, Mamma," she sang, winding her finger around her hair.

"That sex-crazed elf guy?" screamed Leticia. "Oh lordy lord, what have you done, you stupid, stupid girl?"

Clifford could see things were getting out of hand and tried to calm the furious fairy. "Now, Leticia, just let her be. If she says she is in love with Drillian, then she surely must be. And he's a good catch, the second richest elf in the realm. Only Zamforia is richer. One can't complain about her choice for a husband."

"He's a grunt-futtock!" Leticia wailed as she wrung her hands.

"Well, that's a bit steep; more of a young rake, I would say," Clifford smiled. "But I'm sure he'll settle. I did say that I felt he was sweet on her, so maybe it's not such a bad thing."

"Yes, but he's still the worst sort of spaddy-whacker!" she groaned.

"Can I go now?" Spellbound asked impatiently. "It's just that, we were ... y'know in the middle of ..."

Clifford waved his hand over Spellbound's face and she vanished as quickly as she had arrived.

Drillian was lying in the ornate four-poster bed. Spellbound's sudden disappearance had left him feeling rather lonely. A puff of purple smoke engulfed the room and she appeared again. She crawled up the bed on her hands and knees and roared like a tiger. His frown suddenly changed into a smile as he reached for her.

"Welcome back, little pussycat!"

***

As the sun peeked through the gap in the curtain, Spellbound felt a tiny tickling on each of her toes. Little sensations of pleasure shot through every toe as she wriggled and giggled. She opened her bleary eyes and stretched her arms above her head. In true-to-form sleepy style, she lifted one leg high in the air and pointed her foot to the sky. This was a good way of getting her bones moving and ready for the day ahead. Suddenly she remembered the events of the evening before and she sat up bolt right in the bed covering her face with her hands.

A low throaty chuckle disturbed her thoughts and there at the bottom of the bed was Drillian MacCavity planting kisses on the instep of her left foot. With a kick like a mule, she caught him straight on the jaw and he back-flipped off the bed into an untidy heap.

"I can't believe I let you do those things to me last night, you sex mad grunt-futtock!" she shouted. And with a flick of her wand she disappeared.

Chapter 17

Zamforia's Return

Leticia looked at her reflection in the cheval mirror. She was an absolute vision; not one detail could be criticised. Her make up was perfect and had been done professionally for the cameras. Her ball gown was very tight and the bodice showed her curves off to perfection. The whole ensemble had cost her a small fortune and then she had used spell craft for the final exquisite details. Her hair was in a Grecian style and she had a tanzanite and emerald tortoiseshell comb holding back the raven black tresses. She had to look her best, for tonight she was going to be interviewed on live TV about the publication of her new *Spells and Swoon* bestseller.

"Wow Mamma, you look like a goddess!" exclaimed Spellbound, from the other side of the room.

Leticia smiled and went over to her daughter, who was dressed in divine emerald silk, trimmed with a little hood of fake wolverine fur. "You look very beautiful too, Spellbound, and your face is radiant. It's so good to see you happy and vibrant. Have you forgiven naughty silly Mamma for all that's gone by?" she asked in a strained voice.

Spellbound nodded and laughed as she rose two feet in the air and spun around, showering sparks everywhere. Since the yearning had passed, her magic had improved thrice fold and she knew she would see her Papa soon. She was so excited.

Clifford stood in the doorway, resplendent in jet-black silk with a white lace jabot at his throat. Spellbound darted past him, whizzing fairy dust everywhere with her wand.

"See you all later!" she laughed, and in a flash, she was gone.

Clifford smiled. "She is so happy, Leticia, and you … well…" He came towards her and held both her hands. "I have never seen you look so lovely."

She looked up into his hazel eyes, touching his cheek fondly. "I don't know what I would have done without you, Clifford, these last few weeks."

He lowered his mouth, savouring her sweet lips for a second. He knew she was far from being his but at least she hadn't pulled away. "Ready?" he asked, holding out his hand.

***

The house was alive with cameras and Jeri Swinger was swotting up on his notes before the interview. The make up girls were following him around like lapdogs with brushes and powder puffs at the ready.

Leticia lifted her skirts and stepped over a huge electrical cable, manoeuvring around the throng of technicians. Clifford's hand was under her elbow reassuringly, as he knew how nervous she was. There was less than twenty minutes to go before the broadcast. She welcomed her guests and thanked them all for coming. Philip and Drillian MacCavity bowed formally to her as she approached them. Spellbound left her group of friends and made her way over to Clifford and Leticia. "Hi Mamma, are you okay? Not long to go now, aint it exciting?" she bubbled as she deliberately ignored Drillian and his father.

Philip's eyes were out on stalks as they drifted over the gentle swell of Leticia's bodice. "Leticia, you look divine, my dear, truly divine."

She glanced up and nodded.

"And this must be Clifford, your warlock, is it? I bet you are relieved to be out of that dratted ball!"

Clifford pulled Leticia protectively in a little closer to him and stared back at him haughtily.

"Madam Zamforia, you are wanted in the library ready for the broadcast," informed the producer's PA, thankfully interrupting the awkward silence that had fallen.

Leticia followed the PA, saying small hellos to everyone as she went by. She mouthed "See you later" to Lady and Lord Elf and Caitlyn as she waved to them gaily. She hadn't realised how many people she had invited. There must be over two hundred here tonight, she thought.

She had just sat down in her chair, a little flustered by all the lights and cameras pointed in her direction, when Jeri Swinger came over and grabbed her hand. He planted a wet kiss on the back of it.

"Ah the famous Leticia Zamforia! What a sight ... what a sight! Loved your new book; stayed up all night reading it and was shattered all the next day," he enthused with a twinkle in his watery blue eyes.

Leticia took a deep breath and did a small spell for composure. The cameras moved in and the interview began.

**

An hour later and feeling much relieved, Leticia headed towards the refreshment tables and bumped into Caitlyn, who had been Leticia's editor since her first book. Being the refined, educated fairy she was, she painstakingly removed every swear word and corrected Leticia's hit and miss grammar.

"How did it go, dearest? I hope you didn't fluff your lines!"

Leticia took a huge swig of poppy punch and shook her head. "Went like a dream, Caitlyn, I was so nervous!"

"Well, it's over now, dearest, come on, you have to sign your books. There's a queue a mile long in the library."

**

Leticia's hand was hurting. She had already signed a hundred signatures, and it was definitely time for a short break. There was a merry atmosphere in the adjoining lounge as the poppy punch started to take effect.

She stood up and stretched her wings, making her way to the refreshment tables. She could see Spellbound surrounded by young elf men and Drillian with a face like thunder as he couldn't get near her. Philip MacCavity made another bee-line for her and she frowned. She just wanted a little breather, not all this male attention. It had taken her twenty minutes to shake Jeri Swinger off as well, after the interview had finished.

"Leticia, you look stunning," Philip MacCavity said, as he went to take her hand. Clifford saw her plight and was at her side in an instant.

"I see you have the Rottweiler in residence," Philip hissed.

All of a sudden, there was there was a huge blast of lightening and a purple and scarlet explosion rocked the lounge to its foundation. Twenty of the fifty crystal chandeliers shattered and fell in shards at the guests' feet. Molten balls of fairy dust flew in all directions and some of the guests ducked as it headed their way.

Zamforia stepped out of the swirling green mist and the guests gasped. He looked stunning in a silver and black tunic, his emerald green eyes furious. His gaze swept over the room and fell on Leticia, who was rigid, her mouth agape. Clifford brought her closer into him, pulling himself up to his full height.

"Leticia ... COME HERE THIS INSTANT!" Zamforia roared at her.

She tossed her head in the air and spat out coldly, "I see you're back, Zamforia, but you will not get any welcome from me."

He strode towards her, his face thunderous. Immediately a pathway opened before him. He was still several steps away from her when Clifford stood in front of him, barring the way.

"And who, pray, are you, sir?" Zamforia bit out.

"Clifford Eyesaurus ... sir!"

"The Eyesaurus of the crystal ball?"

"The very same one."

Leticia pushed past Clifford and Zamforia's cold gaze scrutinized her from top to bottom. Grabbing her arm he started to march her towards the door, "You have a lot of explaining to do, madam."

"Get your hands off me, Zamforia. Everything you have endured is but your own fault, not mine. Now leave me be!" Leticia gasped as she struggled to free herself.

Clifford dragged Zamforia's grip from Leticia's arm, his hand on the dirk at his side. "Leave her, Zamforia. Do as she says."

"Unhand my wife, Eyesaurus, or you'll be sorry. Do you think you have some right to her or something?"

Clifford laughed softly and the throng watched in total fascination as the two stunningly handsome men squared up to each other.

"Maybe not yet but ... the future could be an entirely different matter."

At that moment, Spellbound ran like the wind across the room and threw her arms around Zamforia, kissing him all over his face. "Papa ... Papa ... Papa! I have missed you so much and I have so much to tell you. Have you missed me too? Promise me you will never go away again!"

Zamforia held her away from him and his eyes lit up. He kissed her on her little turned up nose. "Gosh! You're so beautiful, sweetheart, and grown up! Of course your Papa has missed you, more than you would ever know. I want to know everything, but let me talk to your mother first, darling," he said.

Leticia was standing near the door, her head held high. He had got his precious daughter and the quicker she had her own life and got a divorce, the better, she thought.

"LETICIA ... I SAID COME HERE! You have a great deal of explaining to do and I am not going to conduct my private life in front of the whole goddamn fairy kingdom!" he bellowed.

"Leticia, you must speak with him and get it over and done with," Clifford whispered urgently. "You'll get no peace until it is sorted out and he will not leave it, that is for sure."

He had barely finished speaking when there was another all mighty bang and flash and Tinky Bonk appeared in the middle of the room. She looked confused. Her skin was rather pale and soiled, her hair was mussed, and her famous wings were a dull grey and bent at the tips.

Leticia sniffed and glared at her disdainfully. "That's all we fookin' need, blewdy Tinky Bonk! Well, at least you won't have to go looking for each other." In a flash, she once again pointed her wand at the bedraggled fairy and turned her into a fat, slimy slug.

Zamforia grabbed Leticia's arm and frog-marched her out of the lounge, her feet nearly leaving the ground. He turned to the guests and announced formally with a stiff smile, "Thank you for your company but the party is over. Spellbound, please do me the honour of showing our guests out."

"Oh, and remove the slug from the carpet, dearest," Leticia shot over her shoulder.

Clifford sprang forward, "I will wait outside the door should you need me, Leticia."

She nodded and mouthed a silent thank you.

As she and Zamforia entered the library, Leticia prised her arm from his steely grip and rounded on him furiously.

"How dare you show me up in front of my friends! And take your fookin' hands off me!"

"I see we still have the language of a gutter snipe, that much hasn't changed, has it?" he snarled sarcastically.

"Now, start explaining. I want to know WHY you banished me to that desert island for three years and it had better be good."

Leticia rubbed her arm and saw a bruise appearing where he had gripped her.

"Well, I am waiting," he said, folding his arms and looking her over from top to toe.

She squirmed under his intense scrutiny and then bit out coldly, "If you had wanted an affair with Tinky Bonk then why did you not say? Why did you let me discover you both in the Cherub Pagoda, in the hot tub, fornicating like wild rabbits?"

Zamforia looked astounded. "Are you mad?" he asked. "What are you talking about?"

"I saw you with my own eyes, Zamforia, so don't bother lying to me. I was very angry and sending you away like that was perhaps wrong, but I was crazy and the pain was too hard to bear." Her eyes flashed violet and she looked down at the ground. "I paid for what I did and it nearly turned into the biggest nightmare you could imagine. It affected Spellbound terribly. She went into yearning for you and started to turn into a golden hare. It was truly awful. Oh yes, Zamforia, I wish I could turn the clock back because you weren't worth the energy I spent on getting you and your bit of crumpet banished."

Zamforia's nostrils flared, "I was not in the hot tub with Tinky Bonk," he said angrily. "Your eyes deceived you. It was you and I who were together that night Leticia. Were you so drunk that you were hallucinating? I don't care what you thought you saw, you are very wrong."

"Are you calling me a liar, are you telling me I don't know what I actually saw and then saying you think I was drunk? Make all the excuses you want Zamforia ... you are as guilty as hell and you know it!"

Suddenly she felt very tired. The recent shock of nearly losing her only child and then his unwelcome appearance in front of all of her guests; it was all too much to bear. She sighed and turned to gaze at him dispassionately, "What does it matter now? I have said sorry, I can do no more. I think I am right and you think you are right. I am sick of arguing. Now please leave, Zamforia. Tinky is waiting outside for you. She'll be back to her beautiful self in an hour ... just go."

He strode over to her and started to shake her violently by the shoulders. "You infuriating fairy, are you calling me a liar?"

"If the cap fits ... wear it!"

"You took three years of my life without a thought to how I would feel. If my magic was as powerful as yours, you'd be sitting on that blasted sand dune right now, do you hear me?"

She threw herself away from him and spat out angrily.

"I no longer love you and I want a divorce, Zamforia, and the quicker the better. I won't take a brass fettial from you; I have my own wealth and career now, so you can be as free as when we met. You belong with Tinky Bonk, not me. Our wedding was a miss-match, I see that now. I was a young foolish teenage fairy who was carried away with the romance of it all. Now go and claim the love of your life, she is waiting for you. I'll get my lawyers to draw up the papers tomorrow!"

His eyes were as cold as ice as he circled her like a wolf does its prey and he laughed softly.

"You'll have no divorce from me, madam. If it's Clifford Eyesaurus you want, then you'll have a very long wait! I bid you goodnight!" he said, and stormed out.

Chapter 18

Keep Your Distance

Leticia viewed the upheaval in her beautiful home. There were broken chandeliers everywhere and crimson and purple dust covered the alabaster furniture. She took her yew wand and with a flourish, she whipped it over her head. In an instant order was restored. Smoothing her dress down she turned to leave and saw Clifford leaning in the doorway. He clapped slowly and walked towards her.

"Clever little fairy. No-one would know we had a lightening storm in here last night," he smiled.

Leticia was still smarting over the way Zamforia had made a fool of her; the fairy phone hadn't stopped ringing all morning with her guests' curiosity. She was going to have to think up something extra special to stop the wagging tongues.

They walked into the dining room together and Clifford pulled her chair out before sitting opposite her. Three butlers placed food, piping hot chocolate and the fairy news on the table.

When they had gone, Clifford looked quizzically at Leticia. "Well, are you going to inform me of what happened between you and Zamforia last night, or do I have to guess?"

She shrugged irritably and bit delicately into a fairy cake. "He was adamant that he hadn't seduced that filthy creature and then had the audacity to say that I was mistaken. According to him, it was he and I who were making love. Any excuse. Does he think I have old timers' disease? Oh, and I asked him for a divorce too."

Clifford leaned forward and stared straight into her eyes.

"And what did he say about that? He must have agreed straight away."

She shook her head and took a sip of the delicious hot chocolate. Putting the cup with exaggerated care back into its saucer, she said flatly, "He refused, Clifford … point blank refused me and said

I would have to wait a long time. I think he wants to punish me for putting him on that island for three years."

"What!" Clifford expostulated. "Refused you?"

"The bastard!" she sniffed disdainfully.

***

Spellbound had spent the last week with her father in the family home. She had forgotten how beautiful it was. The grounds were spectacular and once Zamforia had returned, it was there in all its splendour, a fairy tale castle with turrets and arch shaped windows. She had the very top tower, which overlooked the rolling lawns. She could see the pale yellow elkies, which were very much like tiny deer. Zamforia had nearly three hundred in the herd and there were lots of green babies to play with.

She couldn't understand how her Papa kept denying being in the hot tub with Tinky Bonk. She didn't want to embarrass him by saying she had actually seen him there and so had kept quiet. Much of the time, he kept pacing up and down with his hands behind his back and it was plain to see he was still furious with Mamma. How she wished she could get them back together but she remembered what Mamma had said about how she'd interrupted his karma with Tinky and it could never be. She seemed not to care anyway and was busy trying to make peace with the guests who'd been present when Papa had returned. Spellbound sighed. She decided she would NEVER get married. It was all a load of rubbish anyway.

A few days after Zamforia's return, Leticia confessed to Lady Elf about the banishment and why she had done it. Esmee nodded and tutted in all the right places.

"I can't believe this of Zamforia, Leticia. Are you sure that is what you saw?"

Leticia nodded. "I saw the truth, but do you want to know something, Esmee? I no longer care. I am done with men, and the spaddy-whacker refused point blank to give me a divorce."

Esmee gulped, "You asked Zamforia for a divorce? Surely not, Leticia … not with his pedigree! Could you not overlook his one and only indiscretion, for Spellbound's sake at least?"

"Spellbound knows it all and she accepts my decision. She is free to go where she wants now. I have to cut the apron strings sooner or later. After all, she will soon be ten and seven. I will just have to concentrate on my career from now on," Leticia sighed.

***

Pavasnotty was performing at the Fairy Opera House and Leticia and Caitlyn had front row tickets. She needed a good night out now that the gossip had finally died down. They were a little late getting to the theatre and had to find their seats in the dark. Pavasnotty was already on stage and in full tenor voice. Trying to be as invisible as possible they sank down into the deep velvet rose upholstery and became immersed in the wonderful performance. As he sang the last cords of *Missing Korma*, Leticia grabbed her little lace hankie and dabbed it delicately at the corner of her eyes. He was truly awesome, she thought.

Sensing the person next to her was staring, she turned and met the ice green gaze of Zamforia.

"What the fooking hell are you doing here?" she exclaimed.

"I might ask you the same thing, dear," he bit out sarcastically.

"Shush, the whole place can hear you swearing," Caitlyn admonished nervously. She then saw Zamforia and sighed, "What is fate up to now?"

"That's it. I am leaving," said Leticia, gathering up her bag and stole.

"Quiet, Leticia, and sit down," Zamforia said as he pushed her firmly back into her seat. "Would you like another stand-up row, in front of a thousand people this time, because I sure as hell can arrange it?" he hissed.

Leticia knew that he had a will of iron and would do just as he said he would. She meekly sank back into the chair and she felt him relax. Caitlyn patted her arm and whispered to her softly, "Just be quiet, dearest, and watch the opera. Better that than cause another scene."

The lights soon went up and it was interval time. Leticia couldn't get out of her seat quickly enough. As she rose, she saw Lord and Lady Wizard waiting for her in the aisle. Zamforia grabbed her elbow and moved her towards them.

"Zamforia … Leticia! How nice to see you both. Are you enjoying Pavasnotty?"

Zamforia held onto Leticia's elbow with an iron grip. "Yes, he's wonderful, isn't he, Leticia?"

She was about to pull away when he leant over and whispered in her ear, "Just say one fooking word and we can have a ring-dinging scene!"

She nodded and smiled stiffly, a delicate flush stealing up her neck.

Lord Wizard smiled at Caitlyn. "Do join us for drinks, and Zamforia, we can't wait to hear about your visit to the Austrial Realm."

"Austrial Realm?" Zamforia cocked a jet black eyebrow at Leticia as they followed Lord and Lady Wizard to the bar.

"Umm ... Zamforia, just going to powder my wings," she said quickly.

"I think not, Leticia. You know very well how to do a pee spell." He laughed good-naturedly with Lord and Lady Wizard. Caitlyn looked bemused and quickly engaged Lady Wizard in conversation.

When Leticia got back to her seat, she was fuming. She'd had to pretend for thirty minutes to be the adoring wife. How she hated Zamforia. Staring wildly at the stage she tried to calm herself. "Deep breath ... deep breath ..."

Zamforia smiled cynically, sensing her discomfort.

"He is enjoying every minute of this, the bladderbart!" she seethed in frustration.

After the tenth encore, Pavasnotty bowed and left the stage, and the audience slowly started to leave the theatre. Leticia was exhausted, but there were at least thirty acquaintances who wanted to stop and talk to them. Zamforia held her hand tightly as he greeted friends and chatted amicably with them. He was really prolonging her punishment.

Leticia waved goodbye to Caitlyn and waited for her Damselfly to appear. Zamforia was idly chatting to the fairy Mariah and her son. His Locust swept up to the entrance causing quite a commotion, and Leticia breathed a sigh of relief. She could finally get rid of him and crawl into her bed and sleep off this nightmare of an evening. She turned and moved a few steps away from him, looking for her Damselfly, which was late. At this rate she was thinking of using her own wings to get herself home.

There was an admiring crowd around his car as it kept changing colour. It thrummed and vibrated with the most fantastic chords. How she missed that car, thought Leticia. It was so fantastic. It could fly, go under water and change shape, not to mention turn into the most comfy bed.

She spotted her Damselfly at last and walked towards it. Before she had moved three steps, she found herself propelled towards the Locust and pushed into the front seat. Zamforia grinned and waved to everyone as he changed the gears expertly and drove off.

"Okay Zamforia ... just what do you think you are doing?" Leticia gasped indignantly.

"You're my wife, Leticia, so try and behave as if you are. I'm taking you home right now."

"You are blewdy well not taking me home, buzzard face. I can't stand the sight of you and I can't wait to be free of you, you two-timing gigolo!"

He stopped the car with a screech of tyres and turned toward her angrily. Pulling her roughly to him, he forced her mouth onto his. After a while, his lips softened as he looked into her incredible violet eyes.

Leticia was so taken aback by his sudden kiss that for a moment she had surrendered to it. It seemed so natural to be in his arms and to be kissed so passionately by her husband, but then it all came flooding back and she did something she had never done before. She pushed him away.

Zamforia pulled her towards him again and once more, he kissed her passionately. But this time she stared at him coldly. There was a flash and a sparkle and a lingering smell of her intoxicating perfume. Suddenly his arms were empty and she was safely back in her new home.

***

Leticia swept into the grand hall and threw her stole and sequinned bag onto the ornate chest. She was still in a fury with Zamforia and his pig headed behaviour. She hated being controlled and he had controlled her life tonight, that was for sure. The anger she felt was so intense she wanted to banish him again, back to his coral isle where he belonged!

Clifford was waiting for her, looking resplendent in his olive green doublet. He seemed to favour the more sombre colours, which were virtually unheard of in Fairyland. The effect was all the more dazzling, as he stood out from the other folk.

"Leticia, is there something wrong? Your face is like a thunderous moon. Is everything all right, my dear?" he asked.

She beckoned him into the sumptuous lounge and threw herself on the sofa, spitting out bitterly, "It's blewdy Zamforia. He was at the opera tonight - in the seat next to me. Can you believe that? He took over the whole evening, threatening me with another scene if I didn't go along with him. He acted as if we were still married, the ginko!"

Clifford frowned, "But I don't understand this, Leticia. You did undo the love spell from him did you not?"

She nodded vehemently, "Of course I did. I made sure of that. When has a spell of mine ever not worked? No, he is punishing me for banishing him. He's always had a cruel streak in him and if he wanted his own way he always got it!"

"Perhaps it might be an idea to cast the spell again and make it more powerful this time. You were very confused and emotional the last time you performed it."

Leticia nodded and sighed. "Perhaps that is what happened. Oh Clifford, will this mess ever get sorted out?"

He came and knelt at her feet, gazing longingly into her eyes. "I will always be at your side, beloved. I will guard and watch over you." His lips were inches from hers, his hazel gaze mesmerising. Leticia mentally shook herself. His magic was so powerful and she felt herself being drawn into it. In his own way, he was as ruthless as Zamforia. As if sensing her mood, he stood up and pulled her with him.

"A hot tub and a good night's sleep will restore your spirits. Come."

***

The next morning Leticia once again placed the ingredients on the table to release Zamforia from the love spell. She would make sure this time that it was spot on and put in an added dose of everything she could think of. After a long hour of exacting detail and using three special wands, it was completed. She could do no more and that should be the end of it now, she thought.

She sat down, poured herself a shot of poppy juice and threw it to the back of her throat. Now at last she could get on with her life.

Clifford strode into the kitchen. "Poppy juice before twelve of the noon, Leticia?"

She half smiled, her mind on other things. "Don't worry, Clifford, I don't make a habit of drinking in the day. The spell is finished now." She had barely finished speaking when she heard the well know screech of tyres outside. It was Zamforia, and the Locust was jet black today. Her eyes flew to Clifford in alarm and she silently mouthed, "What now?"

Zamforia strode straight into the house without an invitation, his green gaze flicking over Clifford in irritation. "Pack your bags, Leticia. You're coming home and I will not take no for an answer, now snap to it!"

Leticia threw him a look which would have killed an army of ants. "Get lost, Zamforia. Who do you think you are, ordering me around?"

"You are my wife and I want you where you belong. Come, I will help you to pack."

Leticia's mind was on overdrive; had she lost the ability to perform spells all of a sudden?

Clifford stepped forward and placed his arm around Leticia's waist, pulling her into him.

"Zamforia, Leticia does not wish to go with you, please honour her decision."

"If I were you I would remove your hand from my wife's waist right now," Zamforia said slowly.

Clifford spoke very coldly, "Your magic would be wasted on me, Zamforia, so don't bother trying. You must know that Leticia no longer loves you, please accept that and move on. Give her the divorce that she wants."

"Give her the divorce she wants … so that you can wed her, you mean? I am not a fool, Eyesawrus. It's obvious you are smitten with her, but she will never be yours. She is mine and will always be mine. Now pack your things, Leticia, or I will."

Zamforia turned his brilliant green gaze on Leticia and he held his hand out. "Now come," he said gently.

Leticia turned to Clifford. "I will speak with him, Clifford, just give me a minute," she said gently.

He nodded his head and gave a small bow before retreating.

Closing her eyes for a second, she took in a deep breath and turned to face Zamforia. "I will not come with you," she said quietly, mustering as much self-control as she could. "Please just accept that our marriage is over. Again I apologise for banishing you and I hope in time you will come to forgive me for that." She watched as his eyes glazed over, and for a moment, guilt swept through her entire fairy being. "Look Zamforia, there is something else you should know. This passion you have right now is not a real passion. It never was, even in the beginning. I have to admit that when you were engaged to Tinky all those years ago, I cast a powerful love spell on you. I wanted to humiliate her the way she did me, so I deliberately made you mine to punish her. You were programmed to love me for life, you see, and I know it was stupid and I know I shouldn't have done such a thing but I was young and reckless and filled with fury. I have since released you from the spell, so you are free now, and again I am sorry for being so impetuous." She looked down with shame in her eyes. "There ... I have abased myself. There are no more secrets. You have the truth."

He approached her and knelt at her feet kissing the hem of her chiffon gown. As he stood up, he placed both hands on her shoulders and looked deep into her violet eyes.

"Leticia, I fell in love with you from the very first moment I clapped eyes on you. You didn't need to spell for my love; it was always there. I have never stopped loving you and whatever you think you saw in the Cherub Pagoda ...you were mistaken. I did not have sex with Tinky Bonk. It was you and I, dearest, can you not remember?" he asked earnestly.

His lips gently took hers and his arms twined about her. "I forgive you for banishing me. Kiss me, Leticia ... please. Let's be friends, I hate fighting with you."

Leticia stood as cold as ice in his arms. "Zamforia, I no longer love you; please go."

With shock he stared down into her stony face and search as he might, he saw no response from her.

"I will prove to you that I was not with Tinky Bonk in the hot tub if it takes me the rest of my life and then you will love me again, Leticia. There will be no divorce and Clifford will NEVER have you."

He turned on his heel and with a flourish of green smoke, he was gone.

Chapter 19

I Quit!

Drillian looked across the lowly lit dining table at Spellbound as she pushed a prawn aimlessly around her bowl. She sighed a huge sigh.

"Why are you looking so downhearted, Spell?" he asked her. "You've barely spoken to me for three days. For goodness sake, if it's about the other day when we were at it like rabbits, I didn't hear you complaining much."

She glared at him balefully over her bluebellade and sighed again.

"I'm not sure whether I prefer you acting like a hyperactive berry sucker or sulking like a depressed dodibell. Just face facts that you had a great time and get over it!" he said, pushing a fork of food into his mouth angrily.

Spellbound was listening to every word he was saying but was beginning to feel frustrated with it all. She had given in and had had the hottest rumpy ever, completely and utterly defying Aunt Hester's genes. She had gone against everything she and her Mamma had stood for and for what? Some male tart that could happily have his pick of any fairy in the realm! Oh please, how blewdy sad was she! She knew he had to have her just because she was not yet a notch on his bedpost and she also knew that he couldn't give a gnat's fart about how she felt. He was a callous asshole who had used her, and she had let him.

In her heart, she used to believe that being the daughter of the renowned Leticia and the ever so great Zamforia made her somehow special, different from all the rest even. But she wasn't; she *was* just like the rest, she realized, she wasn't special at all.

Her heart was twanging but at least it wasn't as bad as the yearnings she had experienced with her father's absence. This time, the emotion was deep and confusing and tore away in the pit of her stomach; she even felt a little ashamed of herself, which was definitely a first. Why the hell had she leapt into this elf guy's bed when only a few hours before, she had had no interest in him whatsoever? Sure, he was the hottest sexiest thing on two legs, with his dark tousled hair and sparkling grey eyes, and how magnificently handsome he looked when he was asleep.

This was so confusing she thought, and for a second or two she was lost in her memories. Then the harsh reality struck; all the other fairies and the endless hot tub sessions. She knew deep down that this was the real reason he needed a PA. He wanted someone to coordinate his sexual calendar and probably expected her to slot herself into his schedule once or twice a week when he had a spare moment. No, she thought with determination; if Drillian thought that after everything that had happened, she would be running and chasing after his entourage of fairy gals, seeing to their every need and hopping around to find Camel fags for his floosies, he could think again! She may be only ten and six but she was nobody's fool!

"Y'know what, Drill?" She said quietly, standing up and casually tossing the napkin down, "I can't do this anymore." She bent down to find her cobweb purse and as she did, her wings went a frosty grey. "I quit," she said quietly. "This is so not me, Drill."

Drillian nearly choked on his food, his head shooting up in horror. For a moment he thought he'd misheard.

"I'm outta here … sorry, but I just can't do this!"

Drillian was so shocked at this that all he could do was sit there with his mouth half open.

Spellbound sauntered towards the door of the beautiful ornate restaurant, and then taking a deep breath she stretched her arms out and flew high into the sky as fast as her wings would carry her. She would start her own business, she thought, or maybe become a writer like her Mamma. Yes, that's what she would do. She would write a thousand fairy stories and become as famous as the witchy author I.M. BOWLING.

***

Drillian sat in stunned silence, staring at the books in his library but not taking anything in. Nobbie, his faithful and loyal butler, had brought him in a flute of the finest poppy punch an hour before but it still sat untouched on the small oak wood table. It had been four long days since Spellbound had walked out of the restaurant and out of his life. These had to have been the worst four days ever. He knew that Spellbound had a tendency to be fickle and even a little outrageous, but he never thought for one minute that she would pass up working as his PA and walk away so easily.

He was beginning to regret ever having gone to see the crone Fenella. If only he had waited a while, she may have come to his bed and into his arms willingly. She was young and foolish and didn't yet know her mind. Maybe if he had just waited, given her time to grow up and mature, maybe then it would all have been so different.

He raked his fingers through his thick dark hair and hung his head. If only he were magick or had some kind of power so that he could enchant her back. All he had was heaps and heaps of money to offer her but her family was even wealthier than his. What bad luck! He had thought that one night with the beautiful Spellbound would satisfy his passion for her but since that day, and that oh so lovely night, he was feeling ten times, if not twenty times worse!

Every single thought that entered into his head was about her; every song he heard playing on the fairy airwaves he related to her; and every time he walked past that big brass four poster bed in the guest room, the memories of that wonderful time they had spent together came flooding back. She was exciting, unpredictable and heady. The sex had been dynamic and sent him into an erotic daze. Yes, it was official; he was completely buggered and had to get back to Fenella quick!

***

"So you're back then?" Fenella asked guardedly as he entered the stinking cottage. A worried frown appeared across her face as she showed her broken blackened teeth in the semblance of a smile.

"If you've come for more of me potion, I'll 'appily sell it to ya, Milord, but not if it's for the Zamforian fairy, mind. No, I took enough of a risk already with that."

She motioned for him to sit down on the mushroom stool and he was glad that the toad wasn't in sight this time as he sat down apprehensively

By the hearth was a huge coiled snake warming itself. It started slowly to uncurl and Drillian swallowed nervously. He had always had a fear of snakes, mainly because they were always so much bigger than him. Why anyone wanted to keep one as a pet was a complete mystery! It slithered around Fenella's feet and she stroked its scales affectionately. Suddenly it spotted Drillian and it made its way over to him. The snake rose high into the air and its face came within a whisker to his. With a snap, its huge red hood flicked out menacingly and the forked tongue flashed quickly in and out of its yellow fangs. Drillian held his breath as Fenella spoke sharply to the beast. "Flicka, come to mummy, that's enough now!"

The snake stared into Drillian's petrified eyes, swaying backwards and forwards ready to strike.

"Flicka, I won't tell you again, NOW ... MOVE IT!"

The snake turned around and slithered back to the warmth of the hearth.

"He means no 'arm, sir, just a baby really. He's only four month old, y'see, and I'm still training him, so to speak." She casually picked up a small baby mouse that sat shaking in the corner of the room and threw it to the snake. Flicka's attention was immediately distracted as he proceeded to devour it greedily.

"Now, where were we, 'andsome man?" Fenella cackled and he could hear the phlegm in the back of her throat. "What sort of spell would you like today?"

"It is for the Zamforian fairy and I'll double the price," he said coldly. "But this time I need it to last for a week. The fairy in question is still preoccupying my every thought and I think I need to get her out of my system totally; one night was not enough and we had lots of interruptions." Drillian knew that in order to get Fenella to agree to giving him more of the potion, he would have to pay her a handsome fee. This was a year's wages in one go, which, in her circumstances, would keep her in comfort for the rest of her days. Fenella scratched her whiskered chin in agitation.

"Double the price, eh? You must be very keen, sir!" she said in a high-pitched voice. Her eyes began darting about the cottage in a shifty manner. When she thought about money or touched it, she would almost have an instant orgasm. She was already spending the cash in her mind and Drillian could see her scouring her brain for a decision. She stopped suddenly and stared at him with a sickly grin. "Treble it and you have a deal." Drillian had a feeling she was going to say that and had already counted the exact amount of coins into another brown cloth bag. He tossed it at her.

"Done!" he said. "Now hurry with the potion, you grasping old faggot."

What was he doing, he thought to himself, as he picked his way carefully away from the cottage. He used to be able to control his emotions, so why had he become so obsessed with the fairy that was clearly out of bounds? He had never ever felt this way about anyone. He had even tried to bed the pretty Jasmine Flower the night before but the image of Spellbound had entered his brain and suddenly his elfhood had failed to respond and he had felt a real pullock! Seducing one fairy and thinking of another just wasn't his style. Hopefully, spending one week with his beloved Spelly ... fook! Did he just say beloved? He stopped walking and slapped the palm of his hand to his head.

"I said beloved," he muttered out loud. "What is wrong with me?"

A grasshopper hopped nonchalantly past him and then spoke in a deep Toncaster accent, "Ehh up, chavvie. I think yer in love mate!"

***

The spell phone was yet again darting in front of Spellbound's nose. With a quick flick, she tossed it towards her Mamma, who caught it expertly in her right hand.

"Tell him I'm out, Mamma, would you? I am sick to death of him asking me to come back to work."

Leticia tutted and pressed the receive call button.

"Drillian," she said icily. "Spellbound is not here I'm afraid. She is out at the Mushroom Mall with some friends and forgot to take her phone. I'll make sure she gets the message as soon as she returns." She was getting a dab hand at lying for her daughter and had done it four times already this week, and it was only Wednesday. Surely by now Spellbound should be able to conduct her own affairs, she thought.

"That's funny," said Drillian in a low drawl. "Has Spellbound managed to magically shape-shift herself into two places at the same time? I am peering through your kitchen window and I can see her sitting on the chair reading the *Fairy Mail* with her feet on the table!"

Leticia's gaze shot towards the kitchen window and she snapped the phone shut with a click. "Spellbound, get your fooking feet down right now and go and let Drillian in. He's standing outside watching you through the window and he knows that I have been covering for you." She began wagging her pointed finger vigorously. "This is completely ridiculous, Spellbound, and the last time that you get me to do your dirty work for you, do you hear? If you've had a lovers' spat then deal with it and do it pronto! Lordy lord, kids, who'd have them?" she hissed through her teeth and flounced out of the room, slamming the door behind her.

Spellbound's wings shot northwards as she glanced up from the paper and saw Drillian's dazzling smile through the glass. He waved at her and she threw him an exasperated look and slowly stood up to let him in.

"What the hell do you want, pervy, can't you take a hint? You've got a skin as thick as a rhinobug!" she spat out, with her hands resting on her hips. She was wearing a lacy black crop top and her black, leather hipster jeans revealed a cute sapphire navel jewel.

He pushed past her and entered the kitchen. "We need to talk," he said in a business-like voice.

"Oh we do, do we?" she replied haughtily. "Listen Drill, I have nothing to say. I don't wanna work for you anymore. It's a stupid job anyway and I'm tired of playing the whore house Madam. I think I can aspire to so much more, given half the chance. In fact," she added, sounding a little more enthused, "I am thinking of becoming a writer like Mamma. I have already whizzed up ten chapters of my new book and I intend to be a famous author."

Drillian turned to face her. "Well that's nice, Spellbound, really it is and I wish you well but you see, I really need you to come back to work." He was thinking fast on his feet, "And if I promised that you wouldn't have to play the ... er ... Madam anymore," he stopped and thought again, "and if I doubled your salary, would you please consider it? Just until I can get someone to take your place. It shouldn't take me long. You have left me a bit in the lurch you know, Spell. I can't get into the files on your computer and the system's really clogged up." He sounded desperate and Spellbound was beginning to bend a little to his pleas.

No, she thought determinedly, I am not gonna get drawn in to all of this, but he does look ever so gorgeous today. Drillian was wearing baggy black trousers and a tight black see through t-shirt. His hair was combed back revealing his cute, pointy elfin ears. She did like him really, just a little bit, she admitted to herself. His eyes became tender and then he gave her a cheeky smile with a doggy-eyed expression. Getting down on both knees, he shuffled up to her with his tongue hanging out and his hands in prayer mode.

"Pwease?" he asked sweetly. "Pwetty pwease ... I weally need you ..."

Spellbound started to giggle at the silly voice he was making and threw her arms in the air. "Get up, Drill. You look ridiculous. And you sound just like Eddie, who is a twit. Okay then. But I'm warning you. No funny business, you hear? I ain't falling for your charms anymore so this will be strictly work, got it?"

He saluted her, jumping to his feet and smiling.

"Absolutely, Miss Spellbound. Strictly business it is." He stopped and fumbled in his pocket for a second, pulling out a large green glass bottle.

"Oh, I nearly forgot," he said quickly. "I've brought you a present. I know you raved on and on about the flavour changing juice so I bought you a bottle. Drink it all at once though, because it turns sour after a day and then tastes like pond water." He placed it on the table before walking towards the door. "See you this afternoon at 1 p.m. sharp or," he said with a sly grin, "... maybe sooner!"

Spellbound sat at the table after watching Drillian whiz off on Jock Strap. It might not be that bad working for Drillian again, especially if she didn't have to entertain the entourage of fairies in the process, she thought. No, she would work for him as usual until a replacement was found and keep him at arm's length, and then in her spare time, continue to work on her new book. Mamma had been ever so proud that she had wanted to follow in her fairy footsteps. She had even bought her a top of the range Pentagram computer with an Elfish Pressme screen saver.

Spellbound leaned over and poured the flavour-changing juice that Drillian had brought into a glass. MMMMM ... this was lovely tasting stuff, she thought, as she drank the contents appreciatively. She must find out where he got it from so that she could ... oooooh, she thought suddenly, as a fizzy feeling started to work it's way through her veins ... ooooooh ... hic! She held her hand to her stomach and let out a little belch.

"Drilly," she shouted as she ran towards the door. "Drilly ... wait for me!!"

Leticia watched Spellbound hurtle out of the house in a flurry.

"What is that child up to now?" she said to Clifford as she entered the kitchen. "She is always in such a hurry these days."

"Well, thank the heavens that her mood has calmed down a little." Clifford replied, as he gazed at her adoringly. "I was beginning to wonder if we would have to cast a spell on her permanently to quieten down her temperament."

They both chuckled, and as Leticia approached the kitchen table, she picked up the green glass bottle and inspected the few drops of liquid left in the bottom. This must be the drink Spellbound was raving about. Without thinking, and hating waste, she uncorked it and drank the remaining drops. Suddenly, she felt a little zip and a fizzle in her nether regions. Clifford looked so handsome. He really was a real hunk, all muscle and brawn and those sturdy legs and that sexy cod piece ... or maybe it wasn't a cod piece after all! Coorrrrrr!!!

"Leticia, why are you looking at me like that?" he asked in amazement.

She sauntered over to him and began to walk her fingers coyly up his big broad chest and then walked them down to the top of his breeches.

He gulped and stepped back a few feet. "Madam ... have you gone mad?!"

She crooked her little finger at him and giggled, "Leticia would like an itsy bitsy lickle kiss, Cliffy."

Clifford shook his head. "You are playing with fire," he grated out passionately. "Are you sure?"

She ran her tongue seductively over her pearly pink lips and blew him an imaginary kiss. Suddenly she stepped forward and pulled his mouth onto hers. His response was instant and he devoured her lips, his hands running over her body hungrily.

"How long is it since you've had sex, Cliffy ... over four hundred years? Well now is the time to make up for it, lover boy." She started to undo the buttons of his doublet as his eyes blazed down into hers.

"Are you sure this is what you want, Leticia?" he asked in a tormented whisper.

She responded with another passionate kiss. With that, he scooped her up in his arms and in a flash of purple and silver fairy dust, he magicked them both to her bedchamber.

Chapter 20

Zamforia's Quest

Clifford gazed down in amazement at Leticia's face. His wildest dream had come true and he could not believe she had been with him for a whole day and night, lost in his arms, eager to please and be pleased ... in *every* way. She was everything he had imagined her to be and more, but his happiness had been brought to an unexpected and immediate halt. Just when he'd found her, he had to tell her that he must leave for *Trevania,* where his huge estates were located in the Caledonial Realm.

Now that he was free from the ball, the fairy law insisted that he reclaim his land, otherwise it would automatically be passed on to his descendants. He had dallied too long because of his need to be near her and now there was no more time. If he didn't claim back his estates, all would be lost. Once he put his affairs in order, he could return to Leticia and after the love and emotion she had shown him last night, who knows what their future would be.

Leticia looked sadly at him as he broke the news. In all her life, he had never been away from her and she would miss him terribly.

"If you want me at all, sweet fairy, I will be at your side," he said tenderly as she started to cry. "Just meet me in dream sleep on the Astral to connect and soon we will be together again. But for now, I must go." He bent his head forward. "Kiss me one last time before I go, Leticia." The kiss was brief and then suddenly, in a shower of bright red shooting sparks, he was gone.

She picked up the small silver star he had left for her from the pillow and smiled sadly. She would really miss him. And why did she have this rush of emotion for Clifford all of a sudden? Maybe she was falling in love with him, she wondered. After all, he was so gallant and reliable and made her feel safe and cherished. Lordy lord, she thought!

***

Later that morning, Spellbound was sitting impatiently at the kitchen table with Leticia. Her mother had decided it was high time for them to sort out what they were going to wear to Edward's seventeenth birthday ball, which was in a week's time. Leticia had summoned her daughter back to her, much to Spellbound's annoyance because she and Drillian were getting ready to go on a romantic picnic. Just as they were about to hop onto Jock Strap, with the wicker basket saddled and secured to the bird, Spellbound had disappeared in a puff of smoke and was found seated, facing her mother, in the kitchen, who was browsing through that month's *Rogue* fashion magazine and ticking off the dresses they would consider ordering. Now that money was no object, they didn't have to worry about the cost, and their wardrobes were bursting at the seams.

Leticia was enjoying her third cup of hot chocolate that morning and as she glanced through the pages, she stopped as one gown caught her eye. "Why don't we get you this dress?" she asked Spellbound, and spun the magazine around to show her the most stunning diamond encrusted ball gown. The sleeves were long and came to a point at the end and the basque was nipped in to show a flurry of cream silk skirts spilling from the hips. "I think Eddie would think you looked marvellous in that, my dear," she added.

"Fook Eddie," Spellbound sniffed, "Thank the goddess I haven't heard from him in a while."

"I still think you should consider Edward as a potential suitor, dear. He is to be a lord after all, and they say he has become even more handsome in the last few months. In fact, rumour has it that he has become positively dashing!"

"Well, he can positively dash right up his fairy arse. I only have eyes for Drilly," Spellbound said, going all gooey. "Oh Mamma, he is such a hunky elf and his todger, Mamma, I tell you, what a whopper!"

"Enough, Spellbound," said Leticia, spitting some of her hot chocolate all over the pages of the magazine. "There are some things even a Mamma doesn't wish to know!" She drew in a deep breath, re-positioned her spectacles back on her nose and peered over the top of them curiously.

"Er.....just how big exactly?" she asked with a slight grin.

Suddenly there was a mammoth commotion outside and both fairies sprang to their feet to see what was happening. Spellbound raced forwards and threw open the patio windows. Almost instantaneously her mouth dropped opened in surprise.

Zamforia was on his snow-white stallion, resplendent in red and gold, his black hair shining in the sun. Behind him were twelve coaches. His entire entourage of servants were hauling cases and trunks to the front entrance and Whitford, his secretary, was barking out orders to the stable boys to get the race horses and Damselflies into the coral. Fifteen goblin shepherds were herding the green elkies and the forty elkin babies towards the pasture land around the palace. Overhead, Zamforia's *Swirleybird* was circling the property, just as the famous Lotus car screeched to the gates in a shower of silver gravel. Leticia joined Spellbound in open-mouthed wonder and gawped in amazement at the spectacle.

Zamforia jumped off his horse with a flourish and strode towards them purposefully.

"Good morning, Leticia, and my darling Spellbound, how are you?" He hugged his daughter and encouraged the entourage to hurry up.

"Just what do you think you are doing, Zamforia?" Leticia spat out.

He stared at her coldly and barked, "Ah, my sweet wife, that is an easy question to answer. As you won't come home where you belong, I have decided to move in here for the time being; until you see sense, that is," he added.

"You are not blewdy well moving in here, Zamforia," she screeched. "Now get your household together and piss off my land!"

He sighed patiently, tapping his shiny booted foot on the cobbles. "Now, now, dear, you know very well by the laws of Fairyland that wedded couples have total access to each other's properties and dwell where they wish to. So don't think of moving elsewhere, for I will just repeat the process. And after all, this place is big enough to hold three hundred people, so don't think of coming up with any excuses, like there's no room. I intend to reside here indefinitely and that is that, and *you* my sweet fairy are going to have to live with it!"

Leticia was purple in the face and spluttering, completely furious and lost for words.

Zamforia looked at his daughter and grinned, "Ooh look, your poor little Mamma's in a really, really bad temper. Perhaps I should kiss her better," he said, as he yanked Leticia over to him and ravished her with his lips. Everyone started to laugh, including Spellbound. Dragging herself out of his arms Leticia slapped him so hard across the face it nearly knocked his head off his shoulders. But not one to be phased by a wild cat like Leticia, he roughly picked her up and threw her over his shoulder, marching her into the house, to a chorus of cheers and more laughter.

"Put me down right this instant, you spaddy- whacking shit head!" she wailed, as she beat his buttocks with her small clenched fists. "I mean it, Zamforia, I swear it, when I get away from you and find my wand, you're in deep, deep trouble."

Spellbound laughed out loud. She really had the utmost respect for her Papa and he certainly knew how to handle her Mamma, that was for sure.

The hours that followed were chaotic as Zamforia's household settled in. Leticia sat at the dining room table and sobbed so much her face was unrecognisable. Spellbound kept placing cold compresses on her eyes, but after a whole hour of trying to reduce the swelling, she waved her wand over her face when she wasn't looking and returned her back to her former glory.

Zamforia disappeared to find a wing of the palace that suited him, eventually settling on the East side, with the views that overlooked the lake. After three hours, everything went quiet and order was restored. Zamforia's servants were squirreled away to their respective rooms, as the cooks and gardeners frantically began collecting and preparing produce for the evening meal.

Spellbound had gone to her wing and just as Leticia decided she would go to hers, Zamforia appeared. She lifted her skirts and brushed past him angrily, but as quick as a flash, his arm shot out and she was pushed down into the armchair. He promptly dragged another chair over to her and sat down, facing her with determination.

"You won't beat me, Leticia. I aim to win this game, even if it takes me forever. If you banish me away once more, you know Spellbound will suffer again and go into the yearning, so your back is right up against the wall. Do you understand?"

She stared at him, completely lost for words. The unhappiness and desolation in her eyes were plain to see. She quivered on a huge sob.

"Zamforia, please end this madness and accept that our marriage is over. I really don't love you or want you anymore." Her voiced raised an octave. "I had a teenage crush on you, that's all! Why can't you see this and leave me in peace?"

He sat back and his eyes became hooded. This was a Leticia he had not encountered before. He was really becoming confused as to what to do or how to handle her. Her beautiful violet eyes drifted over him impersonally and he could see there was not an ounce of love in her gaze. She was convinced he had been unfaithful with Tinky Bonk and he had to prove to her that he hadn't. He had to make her love him again.

"And where is your protector, Clifford Eyesaurus? These days he seems to think he owns you," he snapped irritably.

Leticia sighed again, remembering the wonderful time she had spent with Clifford and her eyes grew slightly dreamy.

"You may as well know, Clifford and I are recent lovers," she said quietly. "There you are, Zamforia; I have also been disloyal to this sham of a marriage. Maybe that will ease your conscience and lessen your guilt a little!"

She turned her head away from him, thinking about Clifford for a moment. The rush of emotion she had felt earlier had somehow subsided, leaving her usual fondness for him but not the intensity she had encountered in the bedroom. How odd, she thought.

"Clifford has returned to his lands in the Caledonial Realm for a while, but he will come back and is urging me to marry him. I would like it if you would give me a divorce. At least if I marry Clifford, I can be sure of his loyalty and know that he truly loves me without any magical intervention." She glanced downwards, looking a little ashamed again.

Zamforia sprang to his feet and started to pace up and down. "You are lovers? I can't believe it; you have cuckolded me, Madam!"

She shrugged. "So divorce me," she said, scowling at him.

He came back over to her, staring down into her face. His eyes were tormented as he took in her every feature. "What's happened to you, Leticia?" he asked in a desperate tone. "You are not yourself, I can see that. You have Hester's genes and can only love one man, and I am that man. I have always been that man, not Eyesaurus!"

She placed her hand tight to her chest and interrupted him, "Our marriage is a charade, Zamforia, it was never real; can't you see that? The only good that came out of all this is Spellbound and she loves you so much. Take comfort from that."

He sat down again, his mind buzzing. "No … something is not right. I can sense it," he said determinedly. "You are not getting rid of me that easily, Leticia. Accept the fact that we are a couple once more and when Eyesaurus returns … there will be war, believe me! You my dear, belong to me and only me!"

Chapter 21

Desperate Drillian

Spellbound was reclining on the plush cream rug in front of a roaring fire in one of the many rooms in Cumalot Castle. Nestling behind her and stroking her wings was Drillian. To any onlooker they would have looked like the perfect couple, entwined in each other's arms, him gazing down at her, her gently stroking his knee with her dainty hand. They were a vision, completely caught up in the moment and oblivious to everything, other than each other.

Drillian was on cloud ten. Spellbound had been madly in love with him for six whole days and had spent nearly every waking moment by his side. He had organised his staff at Molars Inc. to deal with every eventuality and had given strict instructions that he was not to be disturbed all week. She had lovingly responded to every touch, every smile and had willingly gone to his bed at least four times a day. Who needed a harem of fairies when he had her, he thought to himself. She was just the most perfect thing he had ever laid his slate grey eyes on.

Unbeknown to him, his fervent need to have her near him had escalated beyond his wildest dreams. He laughed at her jokes with enthusiasm, combed her hair into the small hours of the night and even let her beat him at billiards. One thing was for sure, he didn't have any control over his emotions anymore and he was definitely in danger of becoming seriously fooked up once the spell wore off!

"Oh Drilly, what would I ever have done without you," Spellbound said in a soft lazy voice, "I just can't imagine my life without you in it, you know."

Drillian smiled contentedly before the usual heavy feelings of guilt engulfed his body. Just how was he going to cope tomorrow when she no longer gave him a second glance, he asked himself. He mentally shook off the question but it popped right back into his head again. He would be fine, he reassured himself resolutely. His wish had been granted and he had spent enough time with her for his needs to have been met. He would be perfectly okay tomorrow, for sure he would! He returned his attention back to Spellbound. For now, nothing was going to spoil their time together and he would just have to savour the few precious moments he had left with her before the potion lost its potency.

"Shall we have a holiday, Drill?" Spellbound said all dreamily. "We could go to the Avilion Realm for a month and pretend to be Lords and Ladies. I hear it's great fun there."

Drillian chuckled and snuggled his face into her hair. "You know, you are seriously the loveliest fairy I have ever had the pleasure of meeting, Miss Spellbound, and if your desire is to go to Avilion, then we shall make haste, sweet maiden."

Spellbound giggled at his mimicking and turned around to face him. She was fiddling with the button on his shirt, her eyes laughing and dancing before she kissed him gently.

"I wanted to ask you where you got the flavour changing juice, Drill," she said once the kiss had ended. "It's really tasty stuff and like nothing I have ever had before. Mamma rang my spell phone yesterday and said that after she tasted it, she went to the market to see if she could get some."

Drillian's heart started pounding. Her Mamma? The great Leticia Zamforia had tasted the potion?

"She said she scoured every corner of the market but no one had ever heard of it! I told her you probably got it from Toncaster or somewhere but I said I'd ask you anyway."

"Yes, Toncaster," he replied cautiously. "I got it from an *elf food* shop somewhere up there."

This wasn't meant to happen, he thought to himself nervously. Spellbound was meant to drink the entire potion, not just some of it. And what had happened to Leticia afterwards? He pushed that thought to the back of his mind before Spellbound pulled his mouth down to hers again.

"Oh Drill, I do lurve you, really I do," she said with a sigh. "You make me the happiest fairy in the realm, you do. I lurve you so much that I think I will hold a ball in your honour." With that, she giggled and rolled him over onto his back, straddling him. With her wings stiff in the air she began tickling him.

Drillian wasn't paying much attention to Spellbound's face because he was laughing so hard. He failed to notice the confusion appear in her eyes. Very slowly, she stopped tickling him and the look he so desperately didn't want to see was once again there. Carefully rising to her feet, she slowly smoothed her hands down her pink lace dress.

"I'm so sorry, Drill," she said in a small confused voice, "I don't know why I did that! In fact, come to mention it, my behaviour has been completely out of order these last few days. It's like I don't know my own mind anymore. I feel awful. I've led you on in so many ways. Oh my goodness, Drill, you must forgive me," she said, running towards the door. "I have to get on home now, Mamma will be wondering where I am and … and … I've hardly seen Papa. I'll phone you perhaps sometime next week." Her wings began to flick. "Oh my goodness, I am so sorry," she apologised and within a nanosecond, she had flitted through the large ornate door and out into the night skies.

Drillian sat on the floor with his head in his hands. The potion had worn off early. What was he going to do now?

***

Drillian approached Fenella's cottage with trepidation. The widder spiders were in breeding season and were on every bush, tree and blade of grass. The carcasses of the male spiders littered the webs to be savoured later. Thankfully, he had long riding boots on and he walked as quickly as he could to the cottage door, which was slightly ajar.

With a brief knock, he strode in uninvited and stood rooted to the spot. Fenella was right in the middle of having mad passionate sex with Gordon Zola, the ugliest troll he had ever seen. Flicka the snake, who was now twice the size he had been before, spotted him immediately and slithered over.

Suddenly a heavy gust of wind blew the door shut. Drillian raced over and tried hard to open the door and make his escape but the rusty latch was stuck fast and wouldn't budge.

Fenella lifted her head and stared over the troll's shoulder at him. "You'll have to wait a minute, dearie, I'm just having me whiskers parted and I'm nearly there. Make yerself comfortable," she leered.

They continued to groan and moan and the bed springs were clanking and cranking in rhythm. Drillian was more preoccupied with Flicka, who by this time had coiled his tail around his left boot and was slowly dragging him to the floor. The hood was wide and engorged to a deep magenta and the snake swayed backwards and forwards in a sinister manner, his golden eyes riveted on Drillian's face.

Fenella let out a screeching wail as she reached her orgasm and Gordon the troll rolled off in exhaustion. Drillian was dragged to the side of the bed as the snake coiled around his body, squeezing the life out of him. Suddenly the troll lifted one buttock and farted. The stench was so incredible it filled the cottage with its poisonous vapours, making Flicka reel and release his grip. Drillian coughed and threw open one of the filthy windows gasping for air, thankful that the snake had now slithered back to the warmth of the fireplace.

When he finally got his breath back, he looked around and saw Fenella pushing a wad of bank notes into the troll's grubby hands. "See you next week then, trollie boy," she sang, "And bring the whip, oh ... and a pair of Wellington boots."

Gordon Zola lumbered past Drillian, counting the money carefully and as he looked back at her. Sporting a toothless grin, Fenella began pushing her long pendulous breasts into her bodice. She shot a line of phlegm into the fire again before turning to face him.

"And what can I do for you this time, Milord?" she asked, wiping her mouth on her forearm.

"More potions please, Fenella," he said, fixing his eyes on the snake, "and make it quick."

"The potion shouldn't have worn off yet, it's supposed to last another day," she wheezed.

"Umm, yes I know ... but it's a long story," he said impatiently. "Miss Zamforia left it lying around and someone else drank the rest of it."

The smell in the cottage was so bad that Drillian wanted to throw up. Was one fairy worth all this, he wondered as he gazed around the damp, stinking room, now filled with more cobwebs that he had ever seen. The image of Spellbound entered his mind again and he recalled her gazing into his eyes lovingly. Oh, how he needed to have that gaze back.

"And who would that someone be?" Fenella enquired suspiciously.

"Er ... I would rather not say, Ma'am ... bit embarrassing if you know what I mean."

"Tell me now or you are in big trouble," she hissed, "and you'll get no more potions from me and that's a fact. If you try and lie to me, elfman, I will know and I just might make YOU drink the potion. I could do with a younger, more reliable model!" She let out a shriek of laughter as she poked the fire.

Drillian shifted nervously and ran his finger around the collar of his doublet. If he told Fenella that it was Leticia Zamforia that had drunk the last of the potion, she would surely never give him anymore.

"Well?" she shrieked, looking over her shoulder, "out with it!"

"Umm ... Madam Zamforia," he ended lamely.

"Leticia Zamforia? Fookin' hell, I'm really in big shit now, you brainless, brainless TWOT!" Fenella spun round, her hideous face aghast at the news.

"No ... no ... I promise you, nothing came from it; all is well there," he said earnestly.

Fenella was shaking as she hobbled up and down the cottage, wringing her hands into her filthy dress. She shot him a terrified look. "I'm done for and that's for sure," she yowled. "And YOU ... you're nothing but trouble. I knew I was stupid getting into all of this with those Zamforian fairies. Get out of here straight away and don't ever come back, d'ya hear? Now begone!"

Drillian went pale and swallowed nervously. "I'll give you five years wages, Fenella, please reconsider."

He threw the money onto the table but she turned her back on him. "Take yer rotten stinking money and get out of my cottage or I'll set me snake onto you," she ordered.

The door mysteriously opened and she pushed him out with the strength of ten men.

Chapter 22

Eddie's Bash

Leticia and Spellbound joined the throng in the Crystal Ballroom at Elf Hall. The place was heaving with hundreds of guests, all resplendent in their finery. Spellbound looked a dream in cream taffeta and her wings tonight were pale turquoise and rose. Her long dark hair was straight and hanging in a glossy curtain down to her waist; she had looped a dusky dog rose behind her ear and looked positively adorable. Zamforia had presented her with his grandmother's diamond necklace, which was glittering and flashing as she moved.

It was Edwards's seventeenth birthday party and the whole fairy kingdom seemed to be there. Lady Elf rushed up to Leticia, kissing her on both cheeks.

"You have all come … how wonderful … wonderful! And Zamforia, so nice to see you again," she gushed and thought that by having him there, it made the party terribly elite.

"And Spellbound … you look divine! Edward has been trying to find you but got waylaid. Come … come… you must have some refreshments."

Spellbound spotted Pumpkin and waved, "Mamma, Papa, I'm going to speak with Pumpkin if that's okay."

They nodded their approval as she flitted excitedly over to Pumpkin. Because she had been so wrapped up with Drillian over the past weeks, she hadn't seen her fairy gal pals for ages and she was looking forward to hearing all the local gossip and catching up with them all. She was sure she was really going to enjoy herself tonight. Of course, she didn't relish having to come to Eddie's birthday bash but it was nice to meet up with her friends again. These days she would have chosen a fairy rave over a formal event like this but even she had to admit, a birthday ball was definitely a good opportunity to get dressed up and she did look sensational in her gown.

They jostled to the drinks table and decided on the punch, which was a luminous green colour with a purple and orange mist trailing over the edges of the huge punch bowl.

"Hello, you gorgeous sexy fairy." said a deep voice.

Spellbound's gaze travelled up a pristine white satin doublet and collided with brilliant blue eyes.

"Eddie!" she exclaimed in amazement. Mamma had said he had become incredibly handsome, and he had. In fact, he wasn't just handsome, he was drop dead gorgeous!

"Hiya Eddie," simpered Taffeta. She remembered the sexy night they'd had together a few weeks ago. He had been red hot in the bedroom department and she wouldn't mind another session with him given half the chance. He winked and gave her a saucy grin before turning back to Spellbound.

"Fancy a dance, Spell? Come on, let's see if all those dancing classes you had when you were a kid have come to anything."

He grabbed her hand and spun her onto the crystal dance floor, giving her an impressive twirl. Suddenly the music changed to a waltz and the lights overhead dimmed to a luminous haze.

"God, you look divine, Spell, is there a more beautiful fairy here? I think not," he complimented her, "And where have you been these past months?"

"Working ... oh and working," she smiled, as he pulled her closer.

Where had slimy Eddie gone, she mused silently. And who was this red hot replacement? Eddie waltzed gently with Spellbound and for a while, she felt quite carried away by the moment. Maybe he wasn't so bad after all; maybe he had just needed to grow up and turn into a man elf. After all, she had known him from being very young and they'd both grown up together. He really was quite handsome, she thought to herself, and very charming with it. Sensing her relax into his arms, Eddie lowered his head and began whispering compliments into her pointy little ear. Spellbound giggled as they continued to dance.

"Oh Leticia, just look at them, don't they look wonderful together," Lady Elf drooled, "Such a dashing couple!"

Leticia nodded contentedly as their children circled around the floor together.

"Totally lost in each other and chattering away ... ah just look at them!"

As the dance ended, Edward bowed and led Spellbound to a private corner of the room.

"I am so pleased she's ditched Drillian and come to her senses at last," Leticia confided to Esmee, "He was far too dodgy in my opinion."

She was just about to say more when Philip MacCavity bowed formally and asked Leticia for a dance. Before she could refuse, he grabbed her by the hand and marched her onto the dance floor for a polka. He swept her into the crowd and whirled her around and around until she was dizzy.

"Ah, sweet Leticia, can you remember the last time we danced? What fun we had!"

She stared at him reprovingly. "Now Philip, we had both had a little too much punch, so you mustn't read too much into it."

"But how could I forget you dancing in my arms all night long, sweet fairy?"

Leticia pulled away from him and marched off the dance floor, straight into Zamforia, who looked furious, his green eyes flashing with jealousy.

"And pray who is this gentleman that is so familiar with you, Madam? Not another lover, surely?"

Leticia shifted from one foot to another and wished for a second that the ground would swallow her up.

"Philip MacCavity is my name, sir, and you must be the great Zamforia, the one who *everyone* has heard of." He gave a slight bow, glancing at Leticia's bright scarlet dress and creamy cleavage.

"Sir, are you ogling my wife?" Zamforia bit out.

Philip's eyes twinkled down at Leticia knowingly and she fanned herself in exasperation.

"One cannot help but ogle her, sir, such a vision and all. Perhaps we will dance later, Leticia," he said quietly in her ear, before spinning on his heel and heading straight for the refreshment tables.

Zamforia glared down at her impotently, "Just what have you been up to since I have been away?"

"Oh piss off, Zamforia. You don't own me. And for your information, that elf is the head of Molars Inc. and has employed your daughter for the past few months. Just take your hands off me and go and see a solicitor. I want a divorce and the quicker the better!"

***

When Drillian arrived, the ball was already in full swing. His eyes scanned the room for Spellbound but he couldn't see her anywhere. He had missed her so much this last week that he had drunk himself into a stupor every night. She had refused to come into work on Monday saying that she had a headache and hadn't returned any of his calls since.

Normally, he wouldn't have bothered attending this sort of ball but because he was so desperate to see her and because he had somehow to try and make her see that they belonged together, a swarm of wild dragonflies wouldn't have kept him away tonight.

Having made an extra effort with his appearance, he looked incredibly dashing and debonair in his dark green velvet doublet slashed with black satin. His ebony hair was tied in a Prince's plait and entwined with real gold thread.

As he entered the ballroom, five fairies encircled him, laughing, joking and trying their best to be the one chosen for that evening. He noted dryly that he had bedded each and every one of them at some point. Lily pulled his mouth down and kissed him whole-heartedly and Maybelle, feeling rather pushed out, dragged him off her to take her turn.

Spellbound and Eddie watched Drillian's entrance from across the room and Spellbound hung her head in shame. She was no better than any of them, she thought; if only she could just turn the clock back. To think she had been to bed with that male whore-bag. She shuddered as disgust swept over her once again.

"You okay, Spell … not cold or anything?" Eddie asked, a little concerned for her. He took his doublet off and draped it around her shoulders lovingly, being careful not to squash her wings.

Drillian saw Eddie bend forward and drop a light kiss onto Spellbound's cheek. She peeped coquettishly into Eddie's eyes as he looped a stray tendril of hair behind her ear. This made a red-hot flame of jealousy rock through Drillian, something he had never felt before in his life. He stood open mouthed, his heart beating wildly, and then, before he could catch his breath, Willow had claimed a French kiss of her own.

Holding hands, Spellbound and Eddie walked towards their beaming parents and Eddie was at last formally introduced to Zamforia. They were chatting amiably when Philip MacCavity approached the group again and bowed to the females. His gaze rested on Leticia warmly and in his most formal voice he said, "Madam, can I claim this dance?"

Leticia looked uneasy but knew there was no reason, as far as the present company was concerned, that she should refuse. Philip offered his arm and took her to the dance floor, making Zamforia frown deeply and clench his fists in an effort to control himself.

"And Spellbound," Drillian said, stepping up to them and holding out his hand, "Could I claim the next dance with you?" He had shaken off the fairy gals and decided to take action at last.

Spellbound was on the point of refusal and Eddie stiffened at her side. With a quick flick of her wrist, she was tugged abruptly onto the crystal floor and Drillian's slate grey eyes blazed down at her. "What the hell are you doing holding hands with him and letting him kiss you?"

"Me kissing him and holding hands with him? Ha … you are a fine one to talk! What about your simpering fairy entourage … you were making a real spectacle of yourself there. You are nothing but a bladderbart rat and you disgust me!"

She tried to break away from him but he held her fast. Eddie and Taffeta were dancing in earshot and Eddie voiced his concern.

"You having trouble there, Spelly? Just say the word and I'll clock him one."

Drillian gave him a withering glance and steered her into the middle of the throng.

"Spellbound," he said in a strained voice, "I have really missed you this last week, please say you've felt the same or at least that you regard me as something other than an enemy. I don't know how much longer I can go on like this, Spell. One minute we are lovers, the next you don't even return my calls!"

Spellbound did feel guilty about that. Her behaviour had been very unusual. Leticia had said that her hormones must be to blame and that everyone was entitled to make mistakes.

"Look Drill, I am sorry about all that, really I am. It's not that I don't like you or anything, I do. You're really not that bad as far as elves go. But let's face it, you can have any fairy you want and you do *have* them most of the time. No, when I settle down, I wanna settle with someone who I know will be loyal to me, and with the best will in the world Drill, you couldn't keep your todger in your breeches if your life depended on it!" she chuckled.

The music ended and Drillian led her into the same alcove that she had occupied with Eddie earlier. He looked down longingly at her sugar pink lips and lowered his head. Spellbound turned her face away and although she would have loved to have boxed his ears, she somehow managed to refrain from doing so.

"I said I didn't want anymore of that sex thing with you, Drillian," she said coldly. "You are really quite spoilt, do you know that? The only reason you want me is because I am not interested and you can't have me. You need to leave me alone, Drill. Go some place to pamper your ego and go and service the rest of the fairy kingdom while you are at it!" With a flick of her long black hair, she half walked and half flitted to the other end of the ballroom.

Drillian ran his fingers through his hair in agitation. He really, really must try and persuade Fenella to part with some more of the flavour changing love potion, he thought, or he'd go truly mad.

He sauntered over to the refreshments table and took a schooner of punch, downing the contents of the glass in one go. Then he filled it again and did the same. His mind was going into overdrive. This obsession was far more than just mere lust or a simple crush, he mused. It had to be more. I am usually one 'in control' guy, he thought, as the punch hit his stomach in a red hot ball of heat. He hadn't eaten much at all for two days and the poppy punch was working in double quick time. "How can one female leave a guy feeling this way?" he muttered under his breath. He threw another glass of punch down his throat and thankfully felt the edges of the anguish blur. He had to have her and that was that, he told himself. He had to have her and not just for one night or for one week; he had to have her by his side for always and forever, or he just couldn't live a normal life again.

He suddenly felt very tipsy and his head began to swim. Normally he could hold his booze and he should have remembered that poppy punch was lethal. I *will* have her, he decided, even if it means going against everything that is right and proper. She is mine and ONLY mine!

***

Leticia was trying hard to get away from Philip, who insisted on keeping her in conversation, even though the music had stopped five minutes ago. He was trying to pin her down for a date for supper and she could feel the noose tightening. She tried to explain that Zamforia was back now and it would cause all sorts of difficulties but he just wasn't having any of it. And then, as if by magic, Zamforia was at her side, looking more annoyed than ever.

"Leticia, we were wondering where you had got to. Esmee wishes to speak to you … come," he said, holding his hand out and glaring at Philip MacCavity as he led Leticia away.

"Does every man in the goddamn place have to ogle you? What is it with you, Leticia? You're no better than an alley cat," he spat out in a jealous rage.

She tore her hand out of his and hissed under her breath, "Me an alley cat? Question your own morals before mine, Zamforia!"

They both fell silent as Lady Elf approached them.

"Ah, there you are, Leticia, we are all going to make our way out to the gardens for the dragon display. Eddie is so excited as he has never seen a dragon before, so this is our gift to him," Esmee said happily.

The gardens were beautiful, with marble pagodas and lakes dotted around the grounds. Romantic statues, that looked very life-like, were lit up for the occasion and there was even a love seat for two.

A fanfare of trumpets blared out across the grass to signal the start of the show, and with a gasp, everyone looked up into the night sky. Twelve gargantuan dragons with their wings outstretched were looping and diving in synchronicity, fire shooting out of their mouths. Spellbound watched enraptured as the creatures performed their amazing feats. Two of them swooped over the crowd so low that she could count their purple scales. Everyone ducked as the other ten followed. The air smelt of brimstone and fire, voluminous plumes of green and orange making magical patterns in the air. They flew off to one side and there, where they had been, were the words 'Happy Birthday Edward' in fifty-foot letters, as if hanging from the stars.

To end the spectacle, a thousand fireworks shimmered in the sky above them. The crowd went mad, clapping and cheering as the dragons disappeared over the horizon. Spellbound walked towards the lake nearest to her, pushing her way through the dense crowd. Before she knew it, Eddie was at her side and looking kindly into her face.

"Did you enjoy the display, Spell?" he asked.

Spellbound looked up and smiled back. "It was amazing, Eddie, truly amazing. Your Ma and Pa really know how to put on a show, that's for sure."

"Listen, Spell," said Eddie, "I know you've always regarded me with contempt and I admit, before I became a man elf, I was a bit smarmy. Put it down to callow youth. But I'm really not so bad, you know," he continued, "and I have been in your life for as long as I can remember. I've always had a soft spot for you, Spell, and lately, well, I got to thinking that our parents' idea of you and I being together properly could actually be a good thing."

Spellbound giggled trying to hide her embarrassment.

"Look, I know you have a bit longer before you reach ten and seven but when you do and if you like, you and I could maybe try having a grown up relationship. What do you think?"

Suddenly there was a sarcastic laugh. "She's already had a very grown up relationship ... with me. Haven't you, Spellbound?"

Spellbound spun around and saw Drillian leaning nonchalantly against a nearby tree. He straightened and walked towards them.

Eddie looked down at Spellbound in amazement, "But you have Hester's genes, which means ..." His voice trailed off.

"I am NOT in love with him!" she spat vigorously. "I must have some of my Papa's genes as well!"

Drillian dropped his arm casually around her shoulders and gave Eddie a 'get lost' look. In an instant, she threw his arm away and turned her back on him. "Come on, Eddie, let's get some poppy punch."

"Take one step towards her and you're dead meat, elf man." Drillian said, slurring slightly. Spellbound shot him a venomous glare.

Eddie leaned towards her and held out his hand, "Come on, babe, it's my birthday and we've got more dancing to do. Leave this inferior specimen to sober up."

As Edward's arm encircled Spellbound's waist, his jaw suddenly connected with a fist of iron. He staggered backwards, seeing more stars than the fireworks a few moments ago.

"Get your filthy hands off her," Drillian said desperately, rubbing his fist.

Spellbound was so outraged that she grabbed Drillian's prince's plait and spun him around like a roundabout. With a left hook, she sent him sprawling to the ground. By now, a crowd had started to gather as Spellbound, realising what she had done, began screaming for help.

"Stop it you morons, both of you leave me alone!" she bellowed.

Drillian was up in an instant, his arm shooting out and knocking Eddie clean off his feet. Seconds later, the two were slugging it out like prize fighters.

Leticia rushed up and shouted to her daughter, "Come away, Spellbound, get away from these crazed males for goodness sake. Lordy lord, what is all of this about?"

Philip MacCavity saw his son collapse on the grass and Edward dive onto him; with no more ado, he waded in and tried to prise them apart, only to be pulled to the ground by Drillian. Lord Elf saw the kafuffle and tried to pull his son away by the pants of his backside, but this made Eddie's blow miss Drillian and end up on his jaw instead. Eddie turned and looked at his Papa, stopping dead in his tracks.

Leticia screamed at Zamforia, "Do something, for goodness sakes, before they all kill each other!"

Zamforia grinned and like a swallow, he nosedived into the mob, his fists pounding at Leticia's annoying admirer relentlessly.

"I didn't mean for you to fight, Zamforia," Leticia shouted. "Futtle-shucks you're as bad as they are!"

Esmee was crying and shredding her lace hanky to ribbons; her beautiful party was ruined. Looking at her downcast face, Leticia tutted and took her wand from the pocket of her gown. She waved it over the men, who all froze like statues in an instant.

"That will have to do for the minute," Leticia thought, "until I can think of something better."

She started to chant in Gaelic and a huge white cloud engulfed the frozen fighters. When it had cleared, the space was empty.

"The show's over folks," she grimaced. "They've all been returned to their homes and will be tucked up in bed by now, fast asleep, the spaddy whackers!"

Chapter 23

Tinky Bonk

Spellbound slept very late the morning after Edward's party. Lady Elf's spirits had been revived as the merrymakers had decided to stay well into the small hours and when leaving had congratulated her on the most fantastic party ever.

Mamma was still sleeping, so she thought she would venture to the west wing and see how her Papa was. She was sure that he'd be surprised to find himself tucked up in bed after the rumpus with Eddie, Drillian and Lord Elf, and he really shouldn't have fought with Philip MacCavity because of his jealousy. It was such a sorry mess and her thoughts were scattered all over the place.

She pushed the door to her father's study open quietly and found him with his head in his hands, looking awfully depressed. Immediately Spellbound ran over to him gave him a huge hug.

"Papa, what on earth is the matter with you?" she asked with deep concern.

He looked up at her with strain in his eyes and shrugging his shoulders despondently, he whispered, "I really don't know what to do, Spellbound. Your mother doesn't love me anymore; she's so cold and unfeeling. She has admirers everywhere I look. Thank god Eyesaurus is out of the frame for the moment because I know for a fact that she is seriously fond of him."

Spellbound looked at the torment in her Papa's eyes and stroked his back with her hand.

"Your mother is convinced I had sexual relations with Tinky Bonk and no matter how much I try to defend myself, she just won't believe me. I swear to you, Spellbound, I never touched her!"

Spellbound looked down at her silver slippers and sighed. "Papa, I hate to go against you in any way, you know that. You know that I love you and all, but," she paused for a moment and then looked him directly in the eye. "You are lying, Papa, and I know you are lying.

I saw it with my own eyes when Clifford was in the ball. I saw it all and I mean everything, Papa ... all the gory details ... the lot!"

His head shot up and his brilliant green eyes blazed into hers angrily. "I DID NOT HAVE ANY RELATIONS WITH TINKY BONK WHATSOEVER!" he shouted, "Why the hell won't anyone believe me?"

Spellbound looked at her father and coughed in embarrassment.

"Please say you believe me, Spellbound. I don't care what you saw, it was a pack of lies, I tell you. I was banished by Leticia for three years and now our marriage is a sham. Even my only child thinks I'm a philandering liar."

"I still love you, Papa, whatever you've done," she told him. "I missed you so much. It was awful but it doesn't matter to me what you did. I am just so pleased that you are back and we can be together again, Papa."

Zamforia's eyes were filled with anguish and for a moment she thought he was going to cry with frustration. "Go to your room, Spellbound," he clipped dismissively.

This was just awful, thought Spellbound, as she sat on her bed contemplating what to do next. Her Papa wouldn't even talk to her. He had ordered her out of his room and that had never happened before. Spellbound started to look for a solution and after a half an hour decided to go against all the rules and try to contact Moonflower. She would know what to do; she was wise and had told her that she would always be there for her. Now she was out of yearning her powers had increased thrice fold and although she wasn't allowed to visit the astral planes until she was ten and eight, she knew she could do it easily ... and it was an emergency after all!

No sooner had she laid flat on her bed and began to concentrate than Moonflower appeared like a flash of brilliance and smiled down at her charge.

"Spellbound ... how lovely to see you, although you shouldn't really be venturing onto the astral, dear; well, not yet anyway!"

Spellbound gazed around at the familiar pink clouds and the beautiful wheat-haired vision of her fairy godmother.

"I need you," Spellbound said sadly. "I don't know what else to do and I figured that you might help me."

"Well my dear, I will try my best but you know that there are only certain things I can help with, don't you? I may be your guardian and can intervene in life or death situations but my assistance is limited to a certain extent."

Spellbound wasted no time in relating the entire tale of woe about her parents and Tinky Bonk.

"I know Papa is lying, 'cause I saw them in Clifford's ball as plain as day and he *still* keeps insisting he didn't do it with Tinky Bonk," she added lamely. "Mamma doesn't love him anymore and he is so depressed, it's just all crap, Mooney, all crap, I tell you!"

A secret smile flickered over Moonflower's face. As much as she had evolved into the perfect guardian, pure of mind and pure of soul, she did love Spellbound's raw energy and found her quite hilarious at times.

"Do you think that you would be able to find out the truth, huh? You know, tell me exactly what happened that night?" Spellbound pleaded with Moonflower.

Moonflower drew her over to a small pool and motioned for her to sit beside her.

"Well dear, I suppose we could try," she said hesitantly. "I am not really supposed to interfere with these kinds of matters; it may affect your karma, you see, but I can't see the harm in having a sneaky peek, just this once."

Spellbound's face immediately broke out into a smile as she positioned herself to take a deeper look into the pool.

"Now, be patient, dear. I have not done this for many years, so I may be a little rusty."

Moonflower removed the crystal pendulum from her neck and waved it over the water in the pool. Small bubbles started appearing on the surface and a thin mist trailed over the edges and then deepened in the centre until the water was completely obscured. Suddenly it changed into a crystal-clear screen and the pictures of Zamforia and Tinky Bonk were brought to life on the surface. Spellbound quickly turned away in embarrassment and started fiddling with the pearl ring on her finger.

"I hate this bit," she said, screwing up her face. "It makes me feel sick, it does. It's really not natural to see your parents having nookie ... ooooh ... makes all the hairs on the back of my neck stand up ... yuk!"

"It's all right, dear," Moonflower said, "you can look up now."

The images had disappeared and the water in the pool continued to lap against the bright turquoise reeds. Moonflower spoke apprehensively, with a slight frown puckering her forehead. "Spellbound, it seems we have somewhat of a problem. Have you ever heard of *Fairy Glamour*?"

Spellbound frowned and shook her head.

"No, perhaps you haven't. It was banned four hundred years ago by the Elders because it caused so much mayhem. I need to explain this to you, dear, so it will finally end all of this confusion."

Spellbound looked worriedly at Moonflower's face and signalled with her hands, urging her to speak.

"Fairy Glamour was used for many generations to captivate humans and also entrap unwilling fairies into love matches. If you like, it's a form of shape shifting. A fairy could change how they looked at the drop of a hat, just like the human witches were supposed to do in medieval times. They could be whoever they wanted to be. A regular fairy could change shape and become a goblin, a troll, a beautiful queen, a dodibell or a swannikin, whoever and whatever they wanted to be. Many fae folk used this power to spy on a loved one or find out information that was secret to them. Spellbound, I think your father had this spell cast upon him. Now, I want you to try to be brave and look into the pool again."

Reluctantly, Spellbound let her eyes drift over the crystal surface and gasped in surprise as she now saw her father passionately kissing her mother.

"You see, your father believed that he was in fact making love to your mother, Spellbound. It seems he is innocent in all of this and has been telling the truth all along, although what the Elders will say when they hear that someone has resurrected Fairy Glamour is another thing!" Moonflower was seriously concerned and began repositioning her diamond crown.

"Oh poor Papa, he really thought that it was Mamma he was kissing!" Spellbound exclaimed. "He kept saying it was, over and over again and no one believed him. Tinky Bonk used Fairy Glamour to look like my Mamma, the fooking bitch! I tell you, Mooney, I am gonna seek her out and zap her up the arse with my wand and give her serious haemorrhoids, I am. Just you see, she is gonna be dead meat after this ... dead meat ... nasty fooking fairy ... nasty, nasty ..."

"Language, Spellbound!" Moonflower remonstrated with her gently. "You really must try and act more fairy-like, dear. Your tongue does not reflect your inner beauty."

"But I just don't get it," Spellbound went on frantically. "Why couldn't Mamma see what Papa saw? Why couldn't she see that Tinky was impersonating her? My Mamma is the most powerful fairy in all the realms, why didn't she clock the truth?"

Moonflower held her hand and smiled down at her tenderly.

"Fairy Glamour is the most disruptive of all spells, dear. It plays havoc with the mind and will only bewitch the one that has the spell put upon them. Your mother saw the truth; she saw Tinky making love with your father but your dear father was affected by the spell and truly believed that he was making love to his wife."

"Awwww Mooney, what should I do now?"

"You must tell your father what has happened," she explained. "He will know how to deal with Tinky Bonk after that, and he must do it as soon as possible. It would be best not to tell your mother for the moment, not until he has sorted it all out. Now, you must return, Spellbound," she added, and quicker than a cat's whisker could twitch, Spellbound was back in her room with the fairy duvet neatly tucked up to her chin.

Her eyes flew open. She must speak with her Papa and right this minute, she thought. She flew down the stairs and crashed into his study, frightening the life out of him. Throwing herself into his arms, she kissed him all over his face.

"Papa, I have some wonderful news to cheer you up. I know it's wrong and I'm not supposed to do it but I've just whooshed up to the Astral and been to see Mooney. She's my fairy godmother by the way, and oh, Papa ... you're never gonna believe this; she just showed me something that is gonna change everything and I mean EVERYTHING!"

He prised her fingers from around his neck and laughed into her earnest little face. Without pausing for breath, she related the story. His eyes flashed fire and his lips formed a thin line.

"So Tinky Bonk used Fairy Glamour? No one this side of the human realm dare use that kind of magic and go against the will of the Elders. The consequences are too great." Zamforia raked his hand through his hair, a look of consternation washing over his features. "Come to mention it, how on earth could Tinky cast such a spell? Her magic was never that superior. Her spell-casting was only ever considered average."

Spellbound shrugged, and waited for her father to speak.

He thought for a few seconds then stood up, placing his hands on her shoulders and looking down into her green eyes reassuringly. "Don't worry, Spellbound, I think I know what to do about Tinky Bonk now, and you can be as sure as hell I will be beating a path to her door. I want this mess cleared up once and for all and my wife back in my arms where she belongs!"

***

Zamforia switched his top-of-the-range computer on and waited for the information to load. He would *Poogle* Tinky Bonk's address and then the sparks would really fly. Clutching the printout, he summoned the Locust and went to the part of the forest that Tinky dwelt in. The beautiful contraption got him there in three minutes flat and as it glided down into a clearing, he could see her humble cottage set back in a small copse of trees.

He marched to the door and rapped on it loudly. Eventually it opened and Tinky Bonk stood staring back at him, open mouthed. He pushed straight past her into her small parlour and turned his furious green eyes on her. She reeled back in alarm, putting a nervous hand to her throat.

"Zamforia, what do you want?" she croaked.

He pushed his face close up to hers and spat out, "I want an explanation from you and it had better be good or I'll snap your wings straight off your back, do you hear?"

He knew by the look on her face that she was already guilty.

"Start talking NOW!" he yelled.

She shrank away from him and put a chair between them for safety.

"Do the words *Fairy Glamour* mean anything to you, Tinky?" he asked, slowly sidling towards her. She went a deathly white and her eyes slid around the room like a trapped animal seeking an escape.

"You have broken a four hundred year rule that was set in place by the Elders. You made me think I was making love with my wife when all along it was you! You had better tell me the whole sordid tale, Tinky, because I am not leaving here until you do!"

She sank weakly into a tulip chair, her mouth working, but no sound coming out. Zamforia dragged another chair over and sat down, his eyes fixed furiously on her face. Eventually she found her voice. "She stole you from me. We were to be married ... or had you forgotten that, Zamforia?" she sobbed. "She set out to take what was mine and used witchcraft unashamedly to get you. All is fair in love and war, they say, and I fought fire with fire, especially after she turned me into a slug. TWICE! I will never forgive her for that!" Tears pricked her eyes as she recalled the memory with a shudder of repulsion.

"How did you get such a powerful spell put on me, especially one that has been banned for so long?" he asked, eyeing her venomously.

"Oh, I was left a very large inheritance by my Grandpapa in the Nether Realm," Tinky continued desperately. "As much as I hate the place, I had to go there to receive it and it was there I met the dark Arch Lord, Kazar Khan. He was the one who provided the Fairy Glamour."

Zamforia stiffened at the mention of that name and disgust swept across his face. He had heard of this beastly magician and knew well of his reputation.

"He is renowned for being the most immoral of Lords," he spat. "What did you give him in return for this favour?"

Tinky shifted uncomfortably in her chair. "He has been intrigued with Leticia and her magic for many years and has watched her closely from afar. He admires her power."

Zamforia stood up suddenly and approached the quivering fairy. Tinky leapt up and ran behind her seat in the hope that it might give her some protection. She spoke quickly. "He ... he ... knew that Leticia had performed magic to get you. He senses all great magic that is cast in all the realms and he is also very interested in gold bullion. He approached me at an underworld ball and he said that he could help me seek my revenge for a fee. He knew I had inherited a great amount of gold and so we struck a deal. I slipped the potion into your drink that night and the rest is history. It cost me the whole of my inheritance, a small fortune. I stayed down by the lake and watched you go into the Cherub Pagoda. I thought that once she had thrown you out, you would come back to me and we could begin again."

Her eyes pleaded with him for understanding but his gaze was as cold as ice. "I was banished for three years because of you and missed my daughter growing up," he hissed.

"I was banished too!" she screamed back at him. "You weren't the only victim, Zamforia! And can't you see ... I still love you. I have always loved you. You were meant to be mine."

She paused. Catching her breath, the anger suddenly began to rise in her throat. "And if you have forgotten, let me remind you that YOU loved ME too, before that witch did her magic on you!" she screeched.

She watched the pained expression on Zamforia's face and immediately fell quiet. "Look, forget Leticia," she said, moving towards him. "I hear she wants Eyesaurus now anyway. We can be together like it was originally planned. I will somehow try to accept your daughter and make her part of my life. Let us forget the past and try again."

He reached out abruptly and grabbed her by both arms, his eyes boring coldly into hers.

"I will never forgive you, Tinky. And you are lucky that I haven't sought my revenge and turned you in to a slug myself. I will let the Elders decide what they want to do with you and may the gods help you!"

He spun on his heel and left her in a crumpled heap on the floor.

***

"Yes, she admitted it all, Spellbound, she never tried to hide it," said Zamforia, running his fingers in agitation through his thick black hair, as he paced up and down the room.

"Everything that has happened has been bad enough but one thing that really worries me is that Kazar has been watching your mother closely. I don't like that, not for a minute!"

"Who is this Kazar anyway?" Spellbound asked with curiosity.

"Oh, you don't want to know, child," he replied with concern. "Kazar is the most unscrupulous, dark scoundrel that ever inhabited these realms. Many centuries ago, he stumbled upon a spell to strip fairies of their magic and take it for himself. This in turn made him all powerful. He is untouchable, unstoppable. No amount of magic could stand up to his. It worries me greatly."

"So why would he be watching my Mamma? You don't think ..." Spellbound's eyes widened.

"There's only one reason why he would take such an interest," Zamforia butted in, "and that is because Leticia is the most powerful fairy in this realm. To have her magic would make him unconquerable.

"But at least we know the truth now, Papa, and you can tell Mamma and she will have to believe you ... won't she?" asked Spellbound.

Zamforia was still looking perturbed and scratching his chin uneasily.

"We can tackle the nasty bladderbart Lord if we have to," said Spellbound. "With your magic, Mamma's magic and mine, we can zap him in his nuts and stop him from ever taking her powers. He doesn't scare me, Papa."

"What are you two plotting?" Leticia said from the doorway. Both looked at her guiltily and then Spellbound turned and faced her Mamma with determination.

"Mamma ... Papa has something to tell you."

"He's leaving? Oh good and about time too," Leticia said bitterly.

"Won't you just hear him out and stop being so nasty all of the time? Honestly, sometimes you can be a real pain in the arse."

"Oh thank you, daughter," Leticia said sarcastically. "And we certainly know where your loyalties lie, don't we?"

"Just listen, Mamma, would you?"

Leticia relented, and a few moments later, they were all sitting in front of the log fire, watching the flames snap and crackle. Leticia sat in complete silence as first Spellbound told her about Moonflower and then Zamforia related his story of his visit to Tinky Bonk.

"But this is unbelievable. Fairy Glamour has been banned for hundreds of years; how could she have got someone to resurrect it? Even Clifford and I do not have that power! Who is this Arch Lord Kazar anyway? I must meet with him and remonstrate with him for causing such pandemonium. In fact, I'll turn him into a gnat on the arse of an elkie, just watch me!"

"You mustn't concern yourself with him right now, Leticia. I don't want you anywhere near him. He's totally evil." Zamforia said gently. "Spellbound will talk with Moonflower about him. The Elders will vanquish him for sure."

"Mamma, do you know what this means?" asked Spellbound excitedly. "This means that you and Papa can finally be reunited and we can all be happy again. Oh, I am so, so bleedin' happy at last, I really am! This is just the greatest day and I love you both so much …"

Leticia held her hands out in front of her and shook her head.

"Zamforia, I am truly sorry that I caused such trouble when you were innocent all along. Really, I apologise from the bottom of my heart."

"You are forgiven, sweet angel," he replied with a smile, "I have never stopped loving you, not from the first moment I met you on the dance floor."

"Awww! Ain't it all so romantic?" Spellbound gushed, as she rose into the air, her wings flapping madly.

Leticia looked at them absently and then said in a matter of fact voice.

"But this doesn't change anything. Too much water has gone under the bridge for that. Maybe this all happened for a reason. Our marriage cannot come back from this, Zamforia. Too many spells, too much time apart, too many painful memories. No, I'm sorry. We need to face the fact once and for all that it's over."

Chapter 24

Decisions, Decisions, Decisions

Drillian woke up with the sunlight streaming through the curtains and a throbbing pain in his chin. Rubbing it lightly, he began to recall the events of the previous evening and just then that all familiar longing started to erupt in his soul at the thought of Spellbound. Slowly rising from the bed, he found that it was not only his chin that was aching. His back and left knee, not to mention his heart, were extremely sore as well. As he went to look in the mirror, he let out a disgruntled moan. His top lip was the size of an acorn and his right eye was virtually closed. That must have been some fight, he thought. But he would have slain the darkest demons just to have her by his side again, he mused, and without anymore ado he threw on his clothes and headed out of the door, knowing exactly where he had to go and what he now had to do.

***

"Spellbound, just consider the possibilities," Zamforia said to his daughter. "Edward is a decent and noble fellow with a fortune greater than most, not to mention a title. Although we are wealthy, it is only right and proper that you marry your equal."

"Awww, Papa, I am too young to get hitched and as nice as Eddie seems to have turned out, I don't love him, not even a little bit!" she replied.

"Spellbound, you may not love him now but love is something that can grow, child," he told her gently. "You are only a babe in arms right now but blossoming by the day and a long betrothal to Edward wouldn't be such a bad thing now, would it?"

"For once, I think I have to agree with your father," said Leticia, chiming in. "Although how you can sit there preaching to your daughter with a face that looks like it's been in the ring with Mike

Python, I'll never know! Honestly, Zamforia, you made such a spectacle of yourself last night, jumping in and punching our acquaintances. I will have to keep apologising for you until next year!"

Zamforia turned and looked at his wife. How could she not love him, he wondered. What had gone wrong? Surely now that she knew the truth about Tinky, all could be forgiven and things go back to normal.

"But Mamma, I'm always being told that I have Aunt Hester's genes and that I can't commit to a guy unless I love him and now you're suggesting I marry someone I do not love. What happens when we have a fook, huh? I'll be cold stone frigid, lying there like a plank, I will! You really do confuse me, you know!" Spellbound was becoming exasperated.

Her comment made Zamforia raise his hand to his face to hide his grin from his wife.

"Don't laugh at her swearing, Zamforia, you're just encouraging her! Now, daughter," Leticia replied in a strictly 'no nonsense' way, "You have to face the facts that not every fairy in these lands is destined to fall in love. The things I write about in my *Spells and Swoon* books very rarely happen. Some folk never find happiness; they just spend their entire lives looking for the right elf, wasting time and valuable energy. You'll never be guaranteed your soul mate, dear, so maybe it's time to get these romantic notions out of your head and just do what needs to be done to get a secure life."

Zamforia glared at his wife. The way she was talking was beginning to make him very irritated.

"Is that what you did, Leticia?" he spat out. "The right thing. Was that why you wanted me? Money, position ... my lands...? Yes, it all makes sense now. Well, you certainly made sure you got the whole package, didn't you? Got me to fall in love with you, casting your spells and messing around with my emotions and then you got bored and coldly detached yourself. Do you ever think about anything or anyone but yourself Leticia, do you?"

"Oh shut up, Zamforia, this isn't about us. This is about Spellbound and securing her future."

"Like you secured yours, you mean?" he sneered, "You must have been pig sick when you banished me and all the money left with me."

"Spellbound and I managed very well without you, Zamforia, and now I am rich in my own right."

"The only reason I am back from your banishment is because OUR daughter went into yearning. God forbid, if she hadn't, I would still be a thousand miles away living in solitude! You really can be a dark wicked fairy at times. You don't think about the consequences and worst of all, you don't care. And now I am back and you know the truth, you still don't love me, so what am I to do now, Leticia, eh? What next, or don't you care about that either?"

"OH FOOKING SHUT UP, THE PAIR OF YOU!" Spellbound shouted at the top of her lungs.

Both parents shot their heads up and echoed the words simultaneously, "STOP SWEARING, Spellbound!"

"Well, he's got a point Mamma. You did cast a love spell on him to make him yours. It's no wonder he's pissed off now."

"Yes, but I undid the spell, TWICE actually, and you know very well I did. If your father is still in love with me then it's not my fault. Hell's teeth, why are the pair of you always ganging up on me?"

"Are you dense? Have you already forgotten what I told you, Leticia? I was in love with you long before you cast any spell on me. Your magical meddling would have had no affect on me whatsoever. And as much as it pains you to hear this, I will never go away and if you think that I will stand back and allow another elf, or warlock for that matter, to step into my shoes, you can think again, because it will never happen."

Spellbound looked towards her Mamma and nodded knowingly at her father's comment. "He won't either, Mamma, you know he won't!"

"Oh Spellbound, you always did take your father's side and after everything I have given up over the years. Honestly child!"

Leticia felt a pang of guilt rise in her heart. After all, Zamforia was innocent; he never did make love with Tinky intentionally. It must be an agony for him ... loving her and not having it reciprocated. She sighed. Even now that the whole truth about what had happened was out in the open, their problems still hadn't gone away. If anything, things had become even worse.

**

Drillian approached the main doors to Spellbound's house and was greeted by Biff the butler, who formally took his coat. He was shown into the library, where he paced the floor waiting for her entrance. After what seemed like an age, he decided to take a book off a shelf and sit down in one of the chairs placed in the corners of the room. He casually glanced at the title, 'Money for Love' by Leticia Zamforia, and began flicking through the pages. His attention was immediately distracted when he started to read the book. He whistled through his teeth and laughed out loud at the sexy portrayal of the heroine's antics. Spellbound's Mamma could certainly teach him a thing or too, he mused.

Suddenly he heard tiny footsteps approaching and he stuffed the book hastily back on the shelf. Spellbound was muttering some obscenity at having been disturbed. She threw open the doors with a flourish and with her hands planted firmly on her hips, she glared at him, her eyes blazing.

"What do you want? And just look at the bleedin' state of your face!" she said, shaking her head, obviously irritated by his presence. Drillian sprang to his feet and in three short strides, he was standing in front of her.

"Spell, this isn't easy," he said with sheer determination and adulation in his eyes. "I never imagined that I would be here saying this but ... but ..."

"Oh Drill, spit it out will you, I'm having a massive bitch fight with Mamma and I was winning for once. You've got three seconds."

"Forget that," he said. "I need to speak to you urgently and I need you to listen to me."

She was just about to argue with him when he clasped her hand in his and fell to his knees. Spellbound stood open mouthed and gawped at him.

"There's no other way of saying this, Spell," he said softly, "but I think I have fallen in love with you. Massively even. You are in my thoughts from the morning till the night and I know I cannot live unless I have you with me. I go to sleep dreaming about you and I wake up dreaming about you. I can't work; I can't even function normally anymore. Marry me, Spell," he said with tears in his eyes. "Make me the happiest of all elves and agree to be my wife."

Spellbound still had her mouth wide open with her finger pointing to the door and no matter how much she tried to make a word appear from her lips, nothing would come out.

"Don't answer me now," he said, taking a beautiful Tanzanite ring from a silver jewelled box. "Just take this betrothal ring and promise me you will consider it."

She held the ring up to the light and stared at its beauty. It had to be the most enchanting thing she had ever seen. The deep royal blue crystal shimmered in the centre of a cluster of diamonds and the sparks of magic could be seen dancing inside the stone like sprites on a still pond. It must have cost him a small fortune. Drillian stood up again and gently kissed her cheek, and for the first time ever, at least when she was not under the influence of a spell, she failed to clock him on the jaw for doing so.

Regaining her composure for a moment, she took her wand out of the back pocket of her little denim jeans and waved the staff under his nose. His handsome features were restored immediately. Gazing down into her incredible green eyes he asked quietly, "Promise me you will think about it?"

***

Spellbound sat in stunned silence while Pumpkin and Taffeta probed her with endless questions.

"Marry the great Drillian MacCavity? The best catch in all the realms and what a screw he is as well! You gotta be mad not to even consider it, Spelly!" exclaimed Pumpkin.

"He's obviously got it bad," Taffeta giggled. "Prepared to change his ways and settle down, stop shagging all the other fairies and all. I'd snap his wand off if I were you, hun."

Spellbound looked at them in exasperation. When Drillian had asked her to marry him, her first instinct was to laugh in his face, but over the past twenty-four hours, she had actually begun warming to the idea. Her parents wanted her security and were keen for an engagement. He did love her after all, and he had sent her five huge bunches of bluebells every hour, on the hour, since their meeting the day before, knowing they were her favourite flowers. Mamma was sneezing so much that every time another bunch arrived, she zapped it away in the greenhouse before Spellbound could read the note.

Her Papa had received a visit from Drillian that morning and was quite impressed at the elf's determination.

"I'll say one thing to you, my lad," Zamforia said with his hands tucked stylishly behind his back. "It's obvious that you hold Spellbound in high regard and I have no doubt that you would lavish your worldly goods on her. But if my daughter does accept you, and you so much as step one foot out of line, I will use every ounce of my magic to see to it that you never see the light of fairyland again!"

Drillian stood his ground and bowed like the true elf he was. "I would expect nothing less, sir," he said with sincerity.

The three fairies sipped their Zimpto and giggled.

"But what about Eddie?" Spellbound said suddenly. "It was only yesterday that Mamma and Papa wanted me to settle down with him! And now Drillian wants me to marry him and ... oh hells bells, I am so confused!"

"What does yer heart tell you to do, Spell?" Pumpkin said with concern. "My Mammy always tells me to go wiv whatever me heart says."

Spellbound fell silent for a moment and began listening to her heart. "I dunno girls, I really don't know! My heart's not telling me anything," she said in despair.

***

Leticia was pacing the kitchen surrounded by bunches and bunches of bluebells.

"Spellbound, this is getting silly now. There are so many flowers that I've had to start magicking up vases; we have the whole of Bluebell Forest in here, not to mention in the greenhouse. I'll get cook to take them to the kitchen and make a few vats of bluebellade. It's a lovely morning drink as you know and its better when the vintage is older and so good for one's skin. This lot will set us up for life!"

She leaned forward and inspected her flawless complexion in the wall mirror. "I don't know about using spells to get rid of the wrinkles ... ACHOOOOOOO!" She let out a loud sneeze, "but maybe something to stop your suitor from being so generous with his gifts might help. Hay-fever is all I need!"

Spellbound giggled. "Oh Mamma, you are so funny," she said with a twinkle in her eye. "And I totally agree with you, no more bouquets; it's gone beyond a joke."

"This Drillian fellow, he's certainly not one to be ignored," Leticia remarked. And Clifford said I wasn't to interfere with your karma, so whatever you decide to do is fine with me and Papa."

Spellbound's thoughts drifted to Drillian; his handsome face, his beautiful slate grey eyes. His passion for her was infinite and unbelievable and whether he knew it or not, he certainly had made her wings flap and on more than one occasion recently! Spellbound's dreamy eyes turned to a slight frown.

"Mamma, would you do something for me?" she asked earnestly. "Before I really decide, I need to make sure that he truly does love me and that he will be faithful. Will you ask the Tarot cards for me?"

Leticia smiled a cheeky smile and drew an ornate box from her apron pocket.

"I already did, my darling," she said. "I already did!"

***

Spellbound whizzed in and out of the trees, her sylph-like body gliding with perfect precision, not even knocking one leaf off a branch. The Tarot cards had said that Drillian really did love her and her Mamma's readings were always fairy accurate. She approached Drillian's castle and hovered in the sky, taking in the splendour of the building. Cumalot Castle was really magnificent, not perhaps as grand as Papa's or Mamma's but its stunning light stonework spoke of wealth and nobility, and the four large phallic-shaped turrets stood proud and superior. She raced towards the main entrance and before she could even greet the guardsmen, they threw open the door, letting her fly straight inside.

Drillian was waiting in the 'blue room'. It had been recently redecorated and had now become his favourite of all the rooms. Heavy ornate tapestries were hung on the walls, each one embroidered with full length images of Spellbound in flight, Spellbound laughing, Spellbound waving, Spellbound winking, Spellbound cuddled up in bed surrounded by dodibells, and Spellbound hopping on one foot and balancing her wand on her nose. He immediately rose to his feet as she approached him.

"I hoped you would come," he said in a strained voice, and she noticed he looked pale and a bit on the skinny side. With a laugh, she hurtled towards him, leaping in to his arms and wrapping her legs around his waist.

"The answer's YES!" she said.

Chapter 25

Tears and Tantrums

Leticia sat back in her chair and closed her eyes. She had not slept well the night before and felt shattered. It was still quite early in the morning, but the house was unusually quiet for a Friday, so much so that she stood for a while near the window to see if there was any activity outside. Returning to her chair, her thoughts turned to Zamforia and strong feelings of guilt washed over her as she thought of him incarcerated on the island she had banished him to for three long years. He had been innocent all along. She shook her head in despair. Poor Zamforia, he didn't deserve that, and after all she had done to him, he still loved her and had forgiven her so readily. In the last few days her heart had softened towards him and her eyes had started to light up when he came into the room. Maybe she had been too harsh, she thought.

Her mind then drifted to Spellbound and the upcoming nuptials. It was to be a huge event and money was being lavished on the very best of everything for the couple. Their golden carriage was to be drawn by four snowy white unicorns, which were rumoured to be the only four in all of the realms. Leticia had a strong bond with animals and had visited the outer Astral to confer with them. She was over the moon that they had agreed to attend the wedding and draw Spellbound's crystal coach.

Leticia was still unsure about the match, but Spellbound seemed to be happily and madly in love and Zamforia approved wholeheartedly of Drillian. He kept reminding her that Spellbound had secured the richest elf in all the realms, after himself of course, and the whole forest was alive with the gossip. She knew she should be the proudest Mamma, but why did she feel so uneasy about it all?

She sighed and rubbed her finger in between her eyebrows. The last thing she wanted was a headache. She closed her eyes wearily.

Perhaps she would just have a little nap and try and catch up with some sleep.

Some time later, she awoke with a jolt. The unusually quiet house was now a hive of activity. She stretched her arms above her head, flapped her wings a couple of times to remove the creases and glanced over at the clock. It was well past noon.

"What is all that noise about?" she muttered to herself, putting on her dressing gown and going out into the corridor. She looked down into the hall from the landing at the top of the stairs. She saw two maids and three elves carrying boxes and cases out of the front door and there, with his back to her, was Zamforia. He glanced up and signalled to one of his gardeners, beckoning him over.

Leticia stood watching the hustle and bustle through sleepy eyes, not awake enough yet to realize what was happening. Next, she saw Spellbound appear from one of the rooms downstairs. What a vision, she thought to herself, her tired eyes failing to notice the sad expression on her face. The once little fairy was now blossoming into an exotic beauty. Her sweet tiny figure was changing shape and curves were appearing in all the right places. Very soon she would be married and … her thoughts were interrupted by shouting.

"But Papa, why are you leaving? This is so stupid. I've never seen you walk away from anything in your life, so why are you running away now? I just don't get it!"

"Spellbound, my sweet child," he said softly. "Try to understand that sometimes there are things in life that just aren't worth pursuing."

Leticia sped down the stairs and into the commotion, her eyes full of concern. "What is all this?" she asked in alarm.

Zamforia turned to face her, a cold expression in his eyes. She searched his features but the love and adoration she usually saw when she was in his presence had been replaced with an empty expression of indifference.

"You have your wish, Leticia," he said, whilst directing one of the valets to a chest sitting in the corner of the grand hall. "I am going to relieve you of your wifely duties and leave you in peace to marry whoever it is you wish to marry. I have spoken with my lawyer and the papers you so desperately want in order to divorce me will be on your mail mat as soon as he can draw them up, ready for you to sign. Please do not tarry with them. The sooner you sign them, the quicker we can go our separate ways."

Her lips tightened and her back went stiff.

"This is your entire fault, Mamma," shouted Spellbound. "See what you went and did?" Tears sprang into her eyes as she looked at her mother with disdain.

"Now stop it, Spellbound," Zamforia said. "All is fair in love and war, just like your mother said. If her feelings have changed then who am I to stand in her way? She knows that I am innocent of any infidelity yet still she regards me with scant care. No, it is best this way and then we can all get on with our lives."

Spellbound turned towards each of her parents desperately and let out an ear-piercing wail of total grief. Leticia shuddered in her shoes, as her only daughter dashed out of the house, crying heart rending sobs.

"Zamforia," Leticia said gently, but he was walking away now and rounding the rest of his entourage up to vacate the palace.

They left a deathly quiet behind them. All that could be heard in the sumptuous hall was the ticking of the grandfather clock. Leticia walked in and out of the empty rooms and glanced around, at a loss as to what to do. What was happening to her, she wondered. Somehow everything seemed to be going haywire and she was making all the wrong decisions, but what she did know was that now Zamforia had left and Spellbound had sped out of the house seeking comfort in the arms of Drillian, she was all alone in her contemplation. And that didn't feel good at all.

***

"There, there, sweets," Drillian crooned whilst cradling Spellbound. She had somehow managed to wrap her legs and her arms around him so tightly that he was having severe difficulty in breathing.

"I just can't stand it," she sobbed into his neck. "Mamma can be such a stubborn frog at times. You don't think I'm gonna go into the yearning again, Drilly, do you? Oh blewdy hell, what if I yearn again … oh no!"

"You're not gonna go into the yearning again, sweetness," Drillian reassured her as if he she was a child. "I'll make sure that nothing bad will ever happen to you again, I promise." Drillian's shirt was drenched in tears as she pulled back to look at her future husband.

"Prr … promise?" she gulped gently.

"I promise, now come and tell me the story from beginning to end."

***

It was no good, thought Leticia. I will have to go and speak with Zamforia. He had been gone from the house for two hours and the more she thought about it the worse she felt. Who was she kidding? It wasn't Clifford she loved, although he was the sweetest of warlocks and a life-long friend. No, she had loved Zamforia for over half her life and whether he had bonked the wicked Tinky even though he was under a spell, she couldn't deny that deep in her heart she would always love him.

She sped through the trees in the direction of his palace, her heart beating as fast as bat wings. As she approached she stopped and smoothed down her dress, making sure she looked perfect.

Zamforia was sitting in the library, hunched over with his head planted firmly between his hands, when he heard Leticia enter the room. Lifting his head, he looked into her eyes and as she gazed back, all she could detect was pain.

"What do you want, Leticia?" he asked bitterly. "Leave me be so I can heal myself."

"We need to talk, dear," she said softly. "This just won't do, we need to discuss our marriage and which way forward we are going."

He looked at her with disbelief. "Have you not played enough games with me, Leticia?" he spat. "Is this some kind of sick joke? What's the matter with you, can you not bear to lose your infantile game? Is that what all this is about?"

The venom in his voice shocked Leticia and as she approached, he shot out his hand as if to warn her not to come any closer.

"Now get out of my house and don't come here again."

"But Zamforia!"

"I said go! There will be no more negotiations except with our lawyers."

He quickly stood up and left the room, leaving Leticia alone again.

***

As sure as daisies were daisies, and just like he had promised, one morning the dreaded divorce papers fell like an axe onto her mail mat. Leticia felt wretched as her eyes scanned the document. Zamforia had offered her half his fortune on the condition that she never make contact with him again. He really meant it. She panicked and then she chastised herself for pushing him away these last few months.

In desperation, she reached for her spell phone, which was lying on the kitchen table, and called Larissa.

"My dear, you have always been so wilful and contrary," she told Leticia. "What did you expect? First you cast your spells to make him love you, then you magically banish his sorry ass, then you cast a spell on him to make him not love you, then you spell cast to bring him back. It makes my head spin! No, no, sweet child. In my opinion, it's about time you realised that using magic to solve your problems often makes them worse. You have got yourself into this mess and I'm afraid I have a hot date with a fairy horny Pixie in half an hour so you will have to figure this one out all by yourself. What you sow is what you reap, and after all, Zamforia is a very fine elf."

Suddenly Larissa put the phone down and Leticia sat motionless at the kitchen table. Of course Larissa was right. She did use magic all of the time and in this instance, it had backfired dramatically. She reached for the phone again and tapped in Caitlyn's number.

"Oh dearest, you sound so very sad," Caitlyn said gently, "but it was bound to happen sooner or later. You do have this habit of making sure you get exactly what you want. Dearest, I am your best friend so I know that you won't take this personally, but you have always wanted to avoid the real issues in your life. As soon as something emotional or dramatic starts to surface, you whip out your wand and magic it all better. Sometimes I guess even you have to face the fact that waving that special little wand of yours doesn't always get you exactly what you want. Maybe just for once you should try and sort things out the right and proper way." Then Caitlyn, whispered her usual 'I love you, dearest' and hung up.

Spellbound walked into the kitchen and gave her mother a steely stare. "Mamma, I'm off to stay with Papa for a while. He needs me. I don't know when I'll be back."

"Huh? But I need you too, Spellbound. This isn't easy for me either, you know!"

"Mamma, I love you so much, but Papa is unhappy right now and I need to try and sort him out before my wedding. In less than six weeks I am saying 'I do' to Drilly on the same day as my seventeenth birthday and Papa has sunk into a deep depression and we all know why, don't we Mamma?"

Leticia saw a young, responsible, grown up fairy instead of the childish sprite her daughter once was.

"When you think of just what you have put poor Papa through, Mamma, you should be thinking more about him and less of yourself. You cast love spells on him, you twice turned Tinky into a slug, you banished the pair of them for three years, and then you really go and rub his nose in the fox shit by taking a lover ... the list goes on, Mamma. You know, all your meddling made me go into yearning and I can't even begin to explain how crappy that felt. No, Papa really needs me right now and I have to go to him."

Spellbound shot out of the front door and into Drillian's Roller Royce. In no time, they had driven away, leaving Leticia all alone again.

Chapter 26

Trevania

In the two weeks that followed, Spellbound divided most of her time between visiting her father and being with her future husband, leaving Leticia to make a difficult decision. She made up her mind to leave Bluebell Forest behind for a while and spend some time with Clifford in Trevania. Larissa, Caitlyn and Spellbound were told of her forthcoming departure and she promised Spellbound faithfully that she would return for her wedding.

Deep in her heart she knew that Clifford would know what to say and do and as he had always been there to advise her, it was only right that she seek his wisdom now. He patiently accepted her moods and understood her thirst for magic.

Yes, Clifford would help her to heal and put this behind her, she hoped.

That night, she connected with him on the Astral and in less than two hours their combined spell craft would have her transported to his huge granite and pearl castle in the deepest part of the Caledonial Realm. She worked tirelessly and finally her gaze flicked over the huge wooden table littered with the potions and herbs for the spell. Placing the moldavite crystal carefully in the middle of the table, she tapped it three times with her citrine wand and watched in total awe as Clifford suddenly materialised in the room.

He looked charming in deep magenta silk and was grinning delightedly from ear to ear. With two strides he was drawing her up in his arms and breathing in the familiar aroma of her perfumed hair.

"My sweet, sweet Leticia. Come, we have but a few moments."

He gathered his huge purple cloak around them both and in a flurry of silver stars they were gone.

Leticia's head was spinning as they whizzed through thousands of miles in less than a second, and true to fairy form, she rotated around for the last time and delicately fainted into Clifford's arms.

"My dear, are you all right?" he asked her, fanning her cheek gently with a swannikin feather as he leant over her on his huge fur-strewn bed.

Leticia's eyes fluttered opened and she gazed up into Clifford's beautiful hazel eyes.

"Oh Clifford, it is so good to see you. I have missed you so, so much, dear friend," she said. She wrapped her arms around his neck and couldn't help herself from sobbing like a child for the best part of twenty minutes.

"Come Leticia, what is all this about?" he asked, a little confused. "Why are you so unhappy? When I left you, you had your life together and were determined to be happy."

Leticia choked back a sob and tried to gain some self control. Gradually she managed to tell him the whole story as he watched her changing expressions, totally absorbed.

Her journey to Trevania had already been late at night, and it was nearly dawn when she finished her tale. He could see how exhausted she was from all the stress and needed to rest. Gently he took her hand to his lips and clicked his fingers. Instantly, Leticia was in a deep sleep, and he lifted her to the room he had prepared for her earlier.

In all that he had heard, something was not quite right, he thought. Some piece of this puzzle did not quite fit, but he just could not put his finger on exactly what it was. Taking his crystal ball, he threw it in the air and it slowly hovered over Leticia's sleeping form, crackling and sending out electrical sparks, which showered all over her. He summoned the ball back to him and with a slight frown, looked deep within its depths.

Staring for what seemed like an age, Clifford had the answers he needed. She seemed to have some form of enchantment over her, he mused. Had she been given something in liquid form?

He frowned again as he lovingly pushed back a stray lock of her raven black hair. For the next hour Clifford worked tirelessly restoring her energy patterns and lifting any negative vibrations that she had encountered in the past few months. When she awoke she would be cleansed, refreshed and positive once more.

For three whole weeks, Leticia spent every waking moment with her mentor Clifford. After never being away from him for more than a few days in her entire life, she realised just how much she had come to miss her dear and trusted friend. Her heart ached deeply for Zamforia though, so much so that at one point she felt that she had connected with the yearning that Spellbound had felt when she herself was separated from her Papa.

Zamforia was one of the five in their soul group so there was no denying that in her heart she would pine for him. The situation was hopeless. She had caused all of this pain and unhappiness and just like the great goddess always said, "What one sows, one always tends to blewdy well reap!"

Clifford had once more offered to cast a love removing spell on her, but she had remembered Caitlyn's words and sadly declined again. She must face her pain head on even though it did hurt like hell, and for probably the first time in her life she wasn't going to resort to spell craft to solve her emotional problems.

On the last evening, she looked fondly at him and placed her small hands in his. His sorrow and longing was apparent and his beautiful hazel eyes held a dignity that no other warlock could portray. As he spoke, he gave her a wistful smile.

"You know that I will always love you, Milady," he said sincerely. Leticia gazed back at his face and nodded shyly. "Last week I took it upon myself to look into the Akashic records," he continued, "and it seems that we have been united in many of our previous lives." Leticia gazed up at him dreamily. "We have been lovers, companions and even husband and wife ... but always friends, my princess, we have always been that."

"I felt that there must be something very special between us," Leticia whispered.

Clifford sighed and suddenly got to his feet. He stood like an Adonis in front of the huge baronial fireplace.

"I also know that as much as saddens me, we cannot be together this time, Leticia. Whilst reading through the Akashic records, I was visited by an Elder and told that in this life it was my role and duty to protect you but not lay with you. I also have something else to relate," he said, looking down at his feet. "After our magical night together, one which I will carry close to my heart forever," he said with intensity, "and also on the first night you came to stay here, I sensed something that I could not identify, and chose to ignore it. A few days ago, I looked into the Nordic Runes to see what would become of our future and was shocked to see that you had been enchanted in some way. Regrettably, you did not come to my bed with free will, for something paranormal had intervened. I have to seek out what happened but so far I am at a loss and keep slamming up against brick walls."

Leticia was shocked and put her hand to her throat.

"I will get to the bottom of this, I promise you that, and when I find out the person that has done this to you ... then woe betide them," he said with a vengeance.

"Ditto," she hissed vehemently.

She joined him in front of the fire and placed her arms around his waist, laying her head on his chest. "Clifford, if I did have some kind of spell cast upon me, I don't regret it," she told him. "You have a very important place in my heart and you always will. You are my best friend and my salvation and I love you dearly." For a moment both fairy and warlock stood locked in a silent embrace and without speaking, they both felt the strange familiarity in being united together.

"Leticia, you must return soon," he said as he stroked her hair. "I still have essential business to attend to here regarding my estate, and your daughter's wedding is approaching fast."

She looked up at him adoringly, her heart visible in her beautiful violet eyes.

"As much as it pains me to say this, you belong to Zamforia this time."

Leticia thought she saw a tear prick his eyes and then suddenly his voice cracked.

"We will have another life, dearest heart, this I know; the Elders promised me that much, and until then, I will be here waiting for you, your friend, your confidante and your servant. Being in the ball has taught me one thing and that is infinite patience."

***

"Mamma ... Mamma ... you are back and I have missed you sooooo much!"

Spellbound flew into the hall, scattering fairy dust everywhere. She had never been away from her Mamma for this long and was relieved she was home again. Leticia waved her wand over by the door and her luggage immediately appeared and then ascended the giant staircase. Spellbound spun her around and around until she was dizzy.

"Now Mamma, I want you to come and look at my dress, oh and tell me the names of the four Unicorns so I can have their bridles engraved in gold and could you do a special spell so that they will stay for at least a week before they have to go back? And do you think I could actually hitch a ride on one of them?" Spellbound was nattering on as usual but this time it was clear that she was giddy with happiness.

It was less than a week before her wedding, the preparations were in full swing, and Leticia's home was in a flurry. Over a hundred guests would be staying with her and at least two hundred with Zamforia. The rest would be occupying every fairy motel in the realm, and every seamstress, caterer and maid had been summoned to attend on the masses.

The whole place was having a spring clean and extra food was being prepared for the uninvited guests as well. The uniformed flunkies were whizzing in and out of the Grand Hall with golden platters of fruit and delicacies and twenty goblins were high up on ladders hanging golden sun spheres from the ceiling.

Spellbound was still chattering on with Leticia when she was tapped cheekily on the bottom.

"Drilly, oh Drilly!" She spun around and hugged him with as much strength as she could muster.

"Hello gorgeous bride to be," he replied, winking at Leticia over her shoulder.

Leticia gave him a frosty smile, still not quite sure about the uneasiness that she felt in his presence, but seeing her daughter so happy couldn't be such a bad thing, surely, she told herself. And she kept reminding herself that Spellbound did have Aunt Hester's genes, so if the coupling wasn't meant to be then her darling daughter wouldn't be giving him a second look!

Drillian pulled Spellbound towards him and kissed her passionately on the mouth. Leticia's left eyebrow shot northwards and she turned her head discretely away to give them some privacy. The kiss seemed to go on much longer than she had anticipated and as she quickly glanced back at the couple they were still locked in a firm embrace.

Spellbound was letting out little giggles of pleasure and Drillian's hands were sliding up and down her bottom. Leticia sighed irritably and zapped her wand at them; they sprung apart in surprise.

"That's quite enough of that, Spellbound. There is a time and a place for such things, dear, and the hall isn't that place. And you, sir," she said, giving Drillian a withering look, "Stop showing my daughter up in public. Surely your parents have taught you some decorum?"

She motioned to Spellbound to come closer and when she was in front of her she took a snowy white hankie from her gown. She spat on it and rubbed furiously at her daughter's smudged lipstick. "If you are to continue with the kissing thing, daughter, it might be an idea for you to whiz up some of that magic lip gloss, dear. You know ... the stuff that doesn't smudge?"

Drillian gazed lovingly at Spellbound and reached out his hand, linking his finger in hers. Leticia took a silver comb out of her pocket and brushed Spellbound's hair back into place. "And Drillian, please don't mess her hair up again, we can't have her anything but perfect. Now you two run along and let Mamma get her breath back. We will catch up later when I've bathed and rested, though lordy lord, how one can rest with such a commotion going on around here, one will never know!"

She flitted up the spiral staircase leaving Drillian and Spellbound staring after her. As she disappeared out of sight they threw their arms passionately around each other and locked lips once more.

***

Zamforia stared into the fire moodily and threw a glass of poppy punch to the back of his throat. Leticia had run straight into Clifford's arms, he mused bitterly as he poured himself another shot of the golden liquid. Spellbound had decided that she wanted to marry her beloved on her seventeenth birthday and tomorrow was the big day. His little fairy girl was not only becoming a young woman but also someone's wife, and he had not seen his own wife since he ordered her out of his house almost seven weeks before. It was going to be very hard for him to act normally around her tomorrow.

News of their divorce proceedings were being held back until after the wedding. This was Spellbound's time and he felt as a father, he must not distract any attention away from her. The gossiping would be rife soon enough; at least he must let her have her day. Besides, Leticia had not even signed or returned the papers. What was she playing at?

Suddenly there was a huge flash and a spray of electrical sparks showered and cascaded in the corner of his study. The smoke was a hazy pale green and Zamforia coughed and waved his hand from side to side to see who had intruded in such a way.

Clifford emerged from the magical fog and bowed formally before walking towards Zamforia, who rose to his feet in anger.

"I come in peace, Zamforia and all I ask of you is that you hear me out."

Zamforia shrugged and turned his back and stared out of the window to the lakelet beyond. "What do you want, Eyesaurus? Don't you think you have ruined enough of my life already? It is you she wants, not me. Take her and be done with it."

"Zamforia, it's you she loves not I. You must understand I have loved and protected her from birth. Before she visited me everyone had turned against her; she had no one to go to except me."

"You've slept with my wife. She told me that herself, and you've probably been enjoying her every night since." Zamforia bit out tiredly. "You cannot deny that, Eyesaurus."

"I will not lie to you. Yes, I did share her bed once and it was the most wonderful experience of my life. But whether you care to believe it or not, we did not lie together when she visited me recently."

"Oh spare me the lies."

"But Zamforia," Clifford continued, "I have since found out that the reason she gave herself to me so willingly was that she was under some sort of enchantment spell. You must help me to get to the bottom of this and find out who had done this to her."

Zamforia's eyes suddenly lit up incredulously. "A love spell? But who would have the power to do this to Leticia. Who would even dare?"

"I will find a way soon to clear up the mystery," Clifford promised. "But can't you see? She would never have gone to the bedchamber with me under normal conditions, as you would never have laid with Tinky Bonk in the Cherub Pagoda. Leticia has always been besotted by you, even when she was ten and five. I should know, I had to sit in the ball and listen to her drone on and on about you till I fear, I nearly fell asleep. Even when she banished you, she talked incessantly about you and made me find you in the ball, so that she could look at you on your desert island. It all got rather tedious for me, I must say."

Clifford smiled kindly and his face lit up the room. "Zamforia, put an end to this nonsense and reunite with her. She truly loves you. I will always adore the very ground she walks upon, but alas, this is not my time. Come, let's be friends. We both love her but she is yours, you must know that."

Zamforia's heart lifted. She really did love him and not Eyesaurus. They could be happy again. They WOULD be happy again! He crossed the room to where Clifford was standing and grasped his hand. "Clifford, would you do me the honour of being my guest tonight and attending my daughter's wedding tomorrow?"

Clifford bowed slightly. "I would be more than delighted, Sir."

***

Leticia combed her long black hair into a shimmering curtain. She was ready to retire to her rooms when she heard muffled voices in the hall. The butler opened the door and Zamforia sprang into the room, his emerald eyes ablaze. She put a nervous hand to her throat. The last thing she wanted was a row on the eve of Spellbound's wedding. He would be demanding she sign the divorce papers and that was for sure. As he approached her she stepped back a few paces and braced herself for his harsh words.

In three strides he was in front of her and then he sank to one knee and lifted her hand to his lips. She gazed down at him in astonishment and he laughed outright.

"Leticia, I love you and I cannot live without you," he said urgently. Leticia's mouth dropped open as she listened to him intently.

"Your warlock has been to see me and told me everything."

"W..w..what did he say?" she asked.

"Well, let's just say that I have it on good authority from Clifford that you love me too. Is that right, sweet fae?"

Rising, he gathered her into his arms and whispered ardently, "I love you, Leticia, I always have and I always will."

She gazed into his eyes and nodded, stroking her trembling hand down his handsome cheek. He laughed again, lifting her in the air and then, as he brought her down, he kissed her passionately. Leticia clung onto him, her head spinning madly, her long fingers running through his thick black hair. There was a flash of pale lavender smoke and in the wink of an eye they were transported to her sumptuous bedroom.

Chapter 27

Do you take this Elf?

"I'M GETTING MARRIED, I'M GETTING MARRIED," shouted Spellbound from the top of the stairs. "Mamma! Where are you? Come here and hug me right now! ... HA HA HA! MAMMA ... MAMMA ... YOU NEED TO GET UP HERE AND WISH THIS CUTE FAIRY A HAPPY BIRTHDAY AND MAKE ME LOOK AWESOME FOR MY BIG DAY!"

Leticia opened her left eye with a start and pointed her toe high in the air.

"Why has she always been so loud and excitable?" Zamforia asked, taking a pillow and stuffing it tightly over his head to drown out the noise.

"She certainly must have got it from your side of the family, dear," Leticia replied, half asleep. "Our side are all very refined and polite. Quiet is our middle name."

Zamforia grinned and rolled over to kiss his wife. "Lies, all lies, Leticia, I'm sure that you would have me believe anything you say." He had to be the most happiest of elves, he thought to himself. Here he was, in the most luxurious of all beds, snuggled in tight with the most beautiful fairy. His fairy, his wife. "You know, we could always just try and ignore her for half an hour or you could take that wand you have hidden under your pillow and zap her lips shut!" He nestled in closer in the hope that she would respond to the gentle kisses he was feathering on the side of her neck. Leticia shivered and wound her arms around him.

"MAMMA!" Spellbound shouted, storming into the bed chamber like a hurricane, all eager and excited, only to witness her father's head sticking out from the top of the covers.

"Blewdy hell!" she said, giggling. "And about time too! My parents in bed at last, does this mean you two are an item again?"

"She might be nearly full grown and soon to be wed, Leticia, but her vocabulary is still way down in the gutter!"

"I tell you Zamforia, I don't know where she fooking gets it from," Leticia laughed.

She popped her head from out of the covers and smiled at her daughter. "Happy birthday, darling."

Zamforia repeated the greeting and then snapped his fingers in a swift movement, making three cups of sweet tea magically appear on a little silver tray on the small table next to the bed. Spellbound plonked down onto the rose petal bed and began chatting incessantly about her upcoming nuptials. Both parents sat upright listening patiently.

"And Drilly is so handsome, Mamma, he really is. You know, I think I picked the most perfect of husbands. He is gallant and kind and rich and ... sexy." She winked at Leticia. "And he has a SUPER ... DUPER big ..."

"Erm ... it's a little early in the day to be discussing the elfin anatomy, dear." said Leticia, nearly spitting her tea all over the bed covers. "But one thing does bother me, child. Are you that certain you love him? I mean, you haven't known him that long and ... well, you still seem so young and childlike." Her attention had now switched to her sugar pink nail polish. "I'm really not so sure about him, dearest. You know, if you did want to change your mind and postpone it for a decade or two, your Papa and I can stand the shame, can't we, dear?"

"Oh darling, leave her alone, she's young and in love, and I can still recall quite clearly that very same look in her eye that you had in yours the day I married you," he said with a laugh.

"Yes, well ... that may be so. But seriously, Spellbound, I worry that you haven't thought it through. Then again, I suppose you can always divorce him if it doesn't work out. I know it would cause a scandal, but what the heck, we've created far worse scandals in this family."

"Your mother is right, but is also being VERY negative," Zamforia butted in. "Now don't let her words ruin your day, dear girl. Just enjoy it and know that whatever happens, we both love you very much."

Leticia nodded with a slight frown.

"Just as long as you don't go having any faebies straight away. Then, if need be, you can get a quickie divorce within a day or two."

"Faebies?" Spellbound asked suddenly. "Why do you say that, Mamma?"

"You do know the rule about the suckling fae, don't you, dearest?" Leticia asked. Spellbound's face went blank. "No Mamma, what's that?"

"Zamforia!" she said, giving him a gentle smack on the arm. "Didn't you tell her about the faeby law?"

"I seem to remember that I have been away for a considerable amount of time, dear," he said, tickling her in the ribs and making her giggle. "SOMEONE, had a hissy fit and banished me for three years!"

"Oh Zamforia, do stop it," she said, catching her breath. "What your Papa should have told you is that when a married fairy has a faeby, whatever the circumstances, the couple must stay together to raise the suckling for one year and a day. This is because it is the most important year in the young one's life. Should the married couple break up before the faeby is a year old, then sadly the Elders can take it back to the heavenly realm."

Spellbound looked shocked. "You mean, they kill off the poor little bleeder?" she said aghast.

"Not in so many words, dear," Leticia said with a tender smile. "More like, they send the little sprite back to where it came from and then its soul awaits for a more united set of parents. The child always comes first. That is the law of the Elders."

***

"Oh Spellbound, didn't I tell you not to eat all that chocca-choc that your future husband keeps stuffing down your throat? I knew it. I just knew when I saw you eating that big bar of Toad-la-roam the other day that we'd have trouble fitting you in your gown.

Leticia was trying frantically to cram Spellbound into her wedding dress but as hard as she tried, the seams were just not meeting. "Just how many of those bars did you thrust into your greedy mush anyway?" she asked, getting all red faced and flustered.

"Erm ... not sure, Mamma, one, may be two ... a day even?"

"Oh lordy lord, Spellbound! Why did you have to go and eat so many? I really didn't want to use magic, today of all days. I wanted everything to be perfect without any kind of wand intervention and now you leave me no choice. And all because you insisted this dress was made with ten thousand diamonds. No magic in the world is going to make it bigger. Typical bleedin' Taurean ... always thinking about the next meal, they all eat like pigs!"

"Excuse me, Mamma," Spellbound snapped. "Just who did a body transformation spell recently? Have you forgotten that already?"

"I am going to have to go downstairs and get out the figure reducing potion and try and resize you for this creation!" Leticia retorted and marched out of the room.

When she returned with the phial concoction, she caught sight of the most peculiar expression on her daughter's face.

"What's with the sour look, Spellbound?" she asked, tapping her little booted foot on the floor irritably. "Why do you look like you've just stepped in some elkie dung that hasn't dried yet?"

Spellbound gave her mother a worried look.

"What ... what will that potion do to me, Mamma?" she asked.

"Well, it will make you a size smaller, dear. Now don't worry. You know Mamma drinks it all the time. How am I supposed to stay looking this good and still eat all those cream buns, eh? Answer me that!"

"Mamma, I can't drink the potion!" Spellbound said reluctantly.

"Yes you can, dear, now just throw it to the back of your throat. It stings a bit on the way down but after a couple of seconds you'll feel fine." Leticia pushed the blue glass flume towards her, encouraging her to drink it.

"No Mamma, I really can't drink it, I'm afraid to!"

"Afraid? What of, dear? Oh come now, you silly fairy, hold your nose if it makes you feel better but for fook's sake, drink it up, we can't stand here arguing. We have a really busy day ahead."

"Mamma, I can't drink the potion because ... because ... well ..."

"Spit it out, dear."

"Well, you know those faebies you were talking about earlier?"

"Yes dear."

"Erm ... well ..."

"Well?"

"Well ... I'm ... I'm ... I'm gonna have one!" There, she had finally said it. She'd been trying to tell Leticia all weekend but the timing just hadn't been right.

"YOU'RE BLEWDY WHAT?" Leticia bellowed for the entire palace to hear.

"I'm gonna have a faeby!" Spellbound answered with a sickly grin. "I decided a few weeks ago ... once I realised just how much I loved Drillian ... I thought that it would just be the most romantic wedding present for him. Oh, but Mamma," she went on, wide-eyed, "you mustn't tell him, he doesn't know yet. I thought I would announce it at the wedding reception."

Leticia was swooning on the spot and reached over quickly for her glass of sweet cherry sherry, which she swallowed in one gulp.

"And were you going to inform your own Mamma of this news, Spellbound, or were you just going to make my fairy heart faint in front of hundreds of guests?"

"Oh Mamma," Spellbound said, moving over and putting her arms around her mother. "Of course I was. I was just trying to find the right *way* to tell you, that's all!"

Leticia looked down at her daughter's exceptionally happy face. "Well, don't expect me to be changing any hankies, Spellbound. I never did do yours. Most of the time I just zapped you a few times with the birch twig wand and you would clean yourself up, but I hear that the Elders put a ban on those kinds of spells saying that lazy parents make for lazy children. Load of codswallop in my opinion but I will not do it, dear, take my word for it! No poopey hankies for me, is that understood?"

Spellbound laughed and hugged her mother even tighter. "I won't ask you to change any hankies or do any of the feeding, Mamma. Just be there to support me if I need it, and help me choose out a name for him."

"Oh HIM! You decided on a son! Oh that's just great that is! Another male to populate this pitiful realm. That's all we need and gawd help us if he turns out to be anything like his father. I think I need to sit down!" Snatching a swannikin feather, she fanned herself madly.

Spellbound pulled a chair up for Leticia and chuckled at her mother's reaction.

"You're nothing but a child yourself," Leticia said, looking a little forlorn. "I just hope that you are doing the right thing, because whether you are or you're not, you have to marry Drillian now and you *have* to make it work!"

"Mamma," Spellbound said, taking her hand and holding it to her cheek. "You were my age when you had me and you are just the best Mamma in every realm this side of the universe. If I can be anything like you then I will be just as terrific."

"What a load of crap, Spellbound, you know Mamma has done many things wrong and perhaps been a little strict with you."

Spellbound shrugged her shoulders and giggled. "It's all in the past and you did what you thought was right and I am going to be SO happy. Would you do just one thing for me, Mamma?" she asked excitedly.

"Anything, child," Leticia replied with a tender smile.

"Zap me up a new wedding dress, please?"

***

The palace and grounds were buzzing with activity and guests were starting to arrive. Cascading rainbows fell from the sky and hit the eight hundred-acre lawns in unison. The trees were all dripping with glitter dust and the palace was spelled to change colour every six minutes. Zamforia had been demonstrating his magical talents all morning and even he was proud of his expert spell casting.

Spellbound was a vision. Her dress was shimmering ivory, embellished with thousands of sparkling diamonds and pink pearls. The neckline sunk to expose the tiniest amount of swell and the back plunged down to the base of her spine leaving her pale pink, iridescent wings in full view. The train of the dress spilled behind her for what seemed like a mile, but under the circumstances, Leticia had been sure to make it as light as a feather so that she didn't have any difficulty pulling it. Spellbound's girl friends were in attendance as hand maidens and every one of them looked a vision.

Leticia stood in front of her daughter in her bedroom, arranging the gossamer veil around her diamond crown. A tear pricked her eyes as she said with a lump in her throat, "Oh darling, you look just perfect. Your eyes are sparkling and your hair is as glossy as satin and this dress, even though I say so myself, is the most stunning thing I have ever created ... even better than your birthday gown!"

Zamforia stood silently at the door observing the two most important females in his life. He loved them both so much, no words could ever explain the feelings he was experiencing right at this moment. The last three miserable years were forgotten and his heart was singing with happiness.

"You both look truly beautiful," he said. Both fairies turned to look at him. He walked up to his daughter and let out a sigh. "Oh Spellbound, what can I say!"

***

Drillian was standing in front of the stone altar, dressed in a spectacular ivory satin doublet encrusted with tiny diamantes and amethyst crystals. A snowy white ruff around his throat accentuated his dark handsome looks. His black leather breeches were skin tight, and on his feet he wore elkie full length black boots with silver flashing buckles. His hair had grown a little longer and was tied behind in a prince's plait, making him the most handsome elf in all of the land.

Every single female fairy held her breath as she looked across at him, and most were sad that he was no longer available. He hadn't noticed any of the delightful fairies enter the wedding circle because his mind was totally fixed on the fairy he was about to marry. This was his day, the day he had imagined. Finally he would have Spellbound by his side, wearing his ring, to be united for life.

Drillian's heart was beating fast as his eyes scanned the hundreds of guests all seated in the pink marble pews. Many were smiling and others glanced in his direction and gave him a respectful nod. His father stood up and bowed to him and the whole of Molars Inc. smiled and waved.

Glancing to the right, he could see Spellbound's family and friends already seated and he espied Aunt Hester, whose gaze travelled over him frostily. She was still a beauty and must have captivated many admirers in her youth. What good it did them, he thought smugly, with her being frigid and all!

Just as he began to try and see who else was present, Leticia graciously swept down the aisle. Even he had to admit that she was a vision of loveliness. She was dressed in a lavender ball gown with silver tips to her deep purple wings. Her raven black hair was swept up into a chignon, with the magnificent Zamforian emerald tiara placed perfectly amongst the curls. She elegantly arranged her skirts and took her seat, waiting patiently as she fanned herself with a huge swannikin feather. Daughters were supposed to take after their mothers, he thought to himself, and if Spellbound looked as stunning as that in a few years from now, he would be one happy elf.

The energy in the chapel swiftly changed as twelve elfin musicians took their golden trumpets and blasted out the fanfare for the beginning of the service. Drillian's heart started to beat faster and faster as everyone turned their heads to see Spellbound standing at the far end of the aisle. Zamforia, dressed in a silver doublet, stood proudly with his daughter, her hand lightly on his arm. Gasps filled the grand hall as she proceeded down the aisle carrying a perfect bouquet of pink and blue jonnikans, which had never before been seen in their realm.

Moonflower had left these flowers on Spellbound's pillow that morning. They were enchanted and had a powerful aroma that made everyone who smelt them supremely happy. Spellbound had encouraged Leticia to smell them whilst she was getting into her bridal gown and was sure that their magic had toned down Mamma's mood about the surprise grand-child.

Spellbound's train was carried by the airborne fairies Pumpkin, Taffeta and Trumpet. They all looked stunning in little soft pink tulip dresses with crystal pointed stilettos and pale green satin headbands. As they all reached the foot of the altar, the fairies dropped the train and it settled like a cloud around the bride.

Drillian gazed at Spellbound's veil and saw her sweet smile through the gossamer lace. The assembly were suddenly quiet as the High Priest stepped forward to begin the handfasting. For a moment, you could hear a pin drop until a loud "Blinding, hey hey!" from Steffan Hogsbeer broke the silence. Half way through the service, she passed her bouquet to Pumpkin, and Drillian slowly lifted the veil from around her face. She was glorious, he thought, and all his ... for ever and ever. How could he ever be as happy again as he was right now?

The High Priest asked both fairy and elf to repeat after him their vows, and once the rings were exchanged and the silken ribbons entwined about their wrists those magical words were finally spoken.

"Do you, Drillian MacCavity, take thee, Spellbound Elspeth Zamforia, to be your lawful wife in wedlock?"

He turned to his bride with immense pride in his heart and said solemnly, "I do."

"And do you, Spellbound Elspeth Zamforia, take thee, Drillian MacCavity, to be your lawful husband in wedlock?"

She looked over briefly at her parents and witnessed her father giving her a slight nod of encouragement, but Leticia's face was expressionless as she muttered under her breath *"This is it, dear, if you want to call it off just say 'I fooking don't' instead of 'I do' right now! No-one will be offended. All will be well, trust me on this, daughter!"*

Spellbound turned back to Drillian and smiled. "I do," she said triumphantly.

"Then with the power vested in me, I now pronounce you husband and wife in matrimony. Mr. MacCavity, you may now kiss your bride."

He did, and the congregation erupted with cheers of joy.

***

Once the ceremony was over, it was time for the reception back at the palace. The grand hall was bustling with noise and fae folk from every realm were chattering and gossiping about the wedding. An orchestra of fifty elves sat on a huge raised dais and were playing continuous romantic tunes. Long tables were weighed down with a king's feast of every meat, fruit and insect you could imagine. Poppy punch was poured by smartly dressed pixie waiters, all resplendent in bright scarlet and golden tunics. The bride and groom sat at the top table, hand in hand, gazing adoringly into each other's eyes.

Clifford Eyesaurus was standing at the back of the hall and hadn't enjoyed the ceremony at all. He was anxious and uneasy. Since his return to the Brittanic Realm three days before, his warlock senses had been warning him that something was definitely amiss. He carefully observed the hundreds of guests all busy talking and dancing, and with a swirl of his cloak, he swiftly made himself invisible. This would be a much easier way to eavesdrop on the ensemble and see if he could fathom out his feeling of unease.

"Spell, you look just yummy," said Eddie as he came over to plant a kiss on the bride's hand, "although if I'd tried just a little bit harder, mate, it might have been me sitting in your seat right now." He grinned at Drillian, who still made it obvious that he couldn't stand to be in the same vicinity as the soon to be Lord.

"This time, Spellbound is all mine," he said proudly, as he gazed lovingly at his new bride. Spellbound mischievously pinched his arm and then looked down at the brand new handfasting band on her finger, glinting in the candlelight.

"It's lovely to see you, Eddie," she said kindly, "and with your handsome face I'm sure you won't have any trouble finding a fairy that is willing to marry you. They will be queuing up around the block!"

Eddie turned around and a group of fairies, all donned in their finery, tittered and waved, trying to attract his attention. With a formal bow to the newlyweds, he quickly adjusted his cravat and smiling at the giggling fairies, made his way towards them.

Leticia had arranged for Lord and Lady Elf to be seated with her and Zamforia, and she and Esmee were now deeply engrossed in a conversation.

"Of course, her father approved wholeheartedly and who am I to object," Leticia whispered. "You know what Zamforia is like, Esmee, once he makes up his mind about someone he never goes back on it."

Lady Elf let out a little sigh. "Oh Leticia, I did so have my heart set on a coupling between Edward and Spellbound and although I am very happy for the bride and groom today, it really does sadden me."

Leticia patted Esmee's hand sympathetically and nodded, "Me too."

After all the speeches were made, there was a roar of applause when Spellbound announced the news that in three months from now, their faeby son would be born. Drillian's eyes filled with tears. He was overwhelmed with joy. Why hadn't she told him before? He had the fairy of his dreams and was going to be a father. He had never felt so happy in all his life, a feeling his father shared. Philip MacCavity slapped his son on the back and took out one of his revolting purple cigars from his waistcoat, offering it to Drillian. Turning to his wife, Drillian swept Spellbound up into his arms and carried her to the crystal dance floor where they had their first dance.

As the newlyweds swayed to the rhythm of the music, there sitting right at the back of the throng in a secluded corner of the ballroom were Fenella Phlegm and Carmella Cacklejuice. Fennella's old battered tiara was askew on her matted hair, which she had tried to comb into some semblance of order. Her dark purple ball gown looked quite presentable but when she smiled tipsily, her black toothless grin spoilt the whole effect.

"I can't quite understand how you did it, let alone why," Carmella whispered secretively behind her hand.

"The elf is a fool, but a rich fool," crowed Fenella, "and when he offered me Prince Fitzwilliam's baby tooth, how could I refuse? Do you know how much that tooth fetched on the Elfbay auction site before he bought it last year? Two million zigagons, can you believe it?"

Carmella's eyebrows shot upwards as she mouthed the amount in astonishment.

"I may be an old crone, my dear, but I'm a fooking wealthy one now!"

Fenella cleared her throat and swallowed the huge ball of phlegm with relish. She was a real lady now and wouldn't spit it out at such a fine function.

"So let me get this right," Carmella said with a wicked chuckle. "The great Drillian MacCavity gave you Prince Fitzwilliam's baby tooth for a love spell that would make the Zamforian fairy his for eternity? That is just brilliant! But how on this earth did you manage to whizz up that kind of spell?" Carmella asked in an amazed whisper.

Fenella looked around shiftily, making sure she wasn't overheard. "I laced a hundred and fifty bunches of bluebells with a love potion I got from the Arch Lord Kazar Khan. I cleared the whole of the wood of every flower," she cackled. "The elf boy sent them to Spellbound, who of course, smelt every bunch. And I heard on the grapevine that the stupid Leticia Zamforia had her cook turn them all into bluebellade ... ha ha! That just enhanced the spell's potency even more. There's no way now that Spellbound will ever be able to reverse Kazar's powerful magic. It's just a shame that the stupid Leticia Zamforia hasn't drunk any of it yet. Kazar is losing patience and hopes she will do it soon. Don't ask me why, I have no idea what he is up to."

Fenella leant backwards and took a huge swig of poppy punch, wiping her mouth on the sleeve of her gown. She bent towards Carmella and whispered again. "I'll let you into another little secret. Leticia accidentally took a sip of one of my earlier love potions for Spellbound and bedded her warlock as a result! I was terrified at the time when the MacCavity boy told me about it, but I scanned the crystal ball after he had left and had a good look. Watching her running her sugary pink nails all over the naked, ancient Eyesaurus was just hilarious! Who knows, if she had drunk any of the bluebellade, it would have been a totally different story today!"

Both fairies shrieked with laughter.

Clifford Eyesaurus stood silently behind the pair of crones and his body stiffened. So this was how the farce of Spellbound's marriage had occurred. Within an instant, he transported himself to the peace and quiet of the library to contemplate his next course of action.

Chapter 28

Leticia's Fury

The muffled sounds from the departing guests began to fade and finally, after what seemed like an age, Clifford could hear Leticia and Zamforia approaching. Spellbound and Drillian had retired to their quarters earlier to change into something more suitable for their honeymoon. As a surprise, Zamforia had paid for them to have an all inclusive trip to the Barbadeous Realm and Spellbound had all but burst with joy when he presented his gift to them.

It had been at least two hours since Clifford had overheard the conversation between Fenella Phlegm and Carmella Cacklejuice. He paced up and down in agitation, his anger simmering beneath the surface. It was not often he lost his temper, but today he was seriously having difficulty in remaining calm. He heard Leticia breathe out a contented sigh from the hall and he rose from his seat and went to meet them.

"We need to talk," he said abruptly, "NOW." He stood near the doorway, running his hand through his mass of chestnut hair. Zamforia looked quizzically at him, wondering why the usually calm and urbane warlock seemed so agitated.

"Come," said Leticia. "We will retire to the drawing room and have a stiff drink. You look like you need one!" She turned on her heels and led the way. "Where have you been anyway, Clifford? We've hardly seen you all day," Arranging the skirts of her dress, she seated herself at the large oak table. Zamforia joined her and began pouring himself a large goblet of blackberry wine. He offered one to Clifford who shook his head absently.

"You haven't seen me because I chose to make myself invisible," he said quietly. "Whilst I was concealed from the crowd, I found out some very disturbing information."

Zamforia glanced worriedly at the warlock and then at Leticia.

Quickly Clifford related the story from beginning to end and watched as the colour began to drain from Zamforia's face.

"You mean to tell me the entire wedding was a mockery and this Fenella creature was behind the whole thing?" he rasped.

Leticia moved uneasily in her chair, trying to gather her scattered thoughts together. "I knew it, I knew something was wrong," she gasped. "I had a feeling within my very being that something wasn't right."

"Have you made an enemy of this fairy in the past, Leticia?" Zamforia asked.

"No, this is not the case, Zamforia," Clifford interrupted. "As far as I could gather, her motives seem to be entirely related to money and nothing more."

"But where did she get such a spell?" Zamforia shot back. "Everyone knows that love enchantment spells and potions are not that easy to concoct."

"The Arch Lord Kazar Khan is behind it all," Clifford replied with steel in his eyes. "He has many fae folk who work for him here. Fenella must be one of his creatures."

"For pity's sake," Leticia hissed. "This fooking Kazar is going to be on the end of my stiletto shoe when I catch up with him - no, better still, I am going to wear his mushrooms for earrings, that's what I'm going to do!" She stood up and began pacing the kitchen floor, realisation suddenly hitting her.

"First he goes against the Elders and resurrects the fairy glamour spell which makes my husband think he is making love with me when all along it's that trollop Tinky Bonk! I then go and banish HIM for three years, which just happens to result in my daughter going into the yearning and nearly turning her into a blewdy golden hare. Then, he gives Fenella Phlegm another love spell so Drillian can bed Spellbound and *I* drink the remains of the spell and end up in the sack with dear Clifford. Then more spells to let Drillian marry our girl. He is an unscrupulous, controlling, sex-mad rogue who has no morals whatsoever. Now Spellbound is so blewdy loved up, she has ordered a faeby from the Elders and she is only ten and seven!" she spat out, taking a huge gulp of air. Leticia's wings were waving frantically and her anger was visible for all to see as she shook with fury from top to toe.

"Listen," said Clifford quietly. "Whilst I have been sitting here, I have had time to gather my thoughts and regardless of all that has happened, the one thing that concerns me most is Spellbound's child and the consequences of what will happen to him should she find out about all of this."

Zamforia placed his head in his hands for a brief moment and then looked up at his wife in utter despair. "What a mess this is," he groaned.

Leticia couldn't think straight. Her head was spinning madly; her whole being was consumed with raging anger. How dare this Arch Lord ruin her family and change the karma of her beloved daughter. How dare HE mess with Leticia Zamforia and give that creature Fenella Phlegm power over HER!

She looked wildly around the room for her spell book. "I need to find a potion quickly and free my daughter from this magical crap. And I need her here ... NOW! Zamforia, help me look for my spell book!"

Clifford took her gently by the shoulders and looked down into her eyes with deep concern. "Leticia, *listen to me*. We CANNOT remove the love spell that Spellbound is under. Don't you see? This would automatically cause a rift between her and Drillian and because of how the fae law stands, the child, YOUR GRANDSON, would have to return to the heavenly realm. No, she has to remain under this enchantment for the full year and one day, and only then can we remove it."

"He is right, Leticia," Zamforia agreed, sounding deflated. "She is our daughter and this child is a part of us, part of this family. We have a duty to him now!"

Leticia sank to the ground, her lavender skirts spilling out all over the floor and she began to weep hysterically. She knew Clifford and Zamforia were speaking sense. As much as she didn't want to admit it, she was secretly thrilled at the prospect of meeting this new child and had day-dreamed all afternoon about the fact that she might *even* change his hankies. She dashed the tears from her eyes, trying to regain her composure.

"I swear this to the goddess above. The moment I get that bastard Drillian on his own I am going to toss him around the room like a rag-doll for doing this to us. He will be turned into a newt and live at the bottom of the lake forever. I might even send his father there for his company!" she ground out menacingly.

"So what is the plan now?" Zamforia asked, looking towards Clifford for some kind of inspiration.

"I tell you what the plan is. Fenella Phlegm is dead meat!" Leticia screeched. And in the blink of a cat's eye, she conjured her silver broomstick, which automatically positioned itself for flight.

Clifford and Zamforia watched in horror as Leticia waved her hand across the palace door and it crashed open within an instant, as her broomstick took her speedily through it and onwards into the night.

"Oh that's just great!" Zamforia said as he watched Leticia disappear from view, "now what are we going to do?"

"Kazar's magic is very powerful," Clifford said worriedly. "We must be cautious. He has robbed many fairies of their magic over the centuries and will not stop until he has the ultimate power. I fear that even our combined efforts will not be enough to conquer him. We must follow her, Zamforia. She could be in grave danger."

***

Leticia was so angry nothing would stop her. Her faithful broom, which she only brought out on hay-days and holidays, was programmed so precisely that she only had to think of a person or a destination and it would take her there at the speed of light. Seconds later, she was at the edge of the dank forest, hovering over the putrid space. Her swift arrival and explosive energy had caused many of the creatures and insects to scatter into their homes and huddle together for fear of straying into her path.

Leticia's beautiful hair had become loosened from the chignon and was flying behind her like a black curtain whipping in the wind. Her skirts rippled behind her. She paused for a second to push her hair out of her eyes and to get her bearings.

"Leticia dearest, we need to think this through," said a voice to her left. She turned and looked in amazement at Zamforia, then turned and saw Clifford to her right. Both were hovering in the air next to her.

"How the hell did you two get here so quickly?" she gasped in amazement.

"Your warlock has this knack of knowing exactly where you are, my dearest!" Zamforia told her. "And although I hate to say it, this time, I am ... well ... grateful for his second vision!"

Clifford pulled out a small crystal ball from a secret pouch. "My faithful friend never fails me," he grinned and then promptly waved his hand over the ball so that it disappeared. "Now come, Leticia. Before you go charging in, we need to discuss our next move."

Leticia was in no mood for discussions. She had been wronged and she would take her revenge. If nothing else, it would make her feel better and help her to rectify the injustice.

"There is nothing to discuss, Clifford," she snapped. "I know exactly what I am going to do!"

Both warlock and elf watched as the distraught fairy suddenly lurched forward and sped deeper into the dank forest.

"My guess is that she'll use the slug spell," Zamforia said, as he raced to keep up with her. "She always does that when she is seriously pissed off."

Clifford raised his eyebrows. "No Zamforia, this time Leticia will have blood on her hands. I fear she will kill this witch. Make speed, we need to find out!"

***

Leticia stood before Fenella's cottage, her eyes wild with fury and her heart beating fast. She paused for a moment, catching her breath at the stench of the forest and then fumbled inside her skirts for her abalone wand. Slowly, she pointed the staff at the door and it flew open with a crash. A wizened old fairy emerged, holding her hand slightly over her eyes to shade them from the blinding light of Leticia's wand. With a terrified wail, she recognised Leticia immediately and scuttled back inside, closing and bolting the door frantically behind her. Leticia aimed her wand at the door again, this time taking it clean off its hinges.

As the door flew high into the night, Clifford and Zamforia arrived and came to a stop directly behind the incensed fairy, both ready to fight with whoever was present.

"Face me, you filthy, wretched hag … let's see how powerful your magic is now!" Leticia screeched. "Show yourself to me so that I can scatter your flesh and bones all over the forest and send your sorry ass into an eternity of hell!"

Fenella huddled in the corner of her decomposing cottage, shaking uncontrollably. With fire in her eyes, Leticia strode into the room, followed by her two guardians. Her wings were dark red and twitching in a sinister fashion and the air turned icily cold as she viewed the sorry excuse of a witch. Fenella was still wearing her crown and was a little worse for wear with the copious amounts of poppy punch she had consumed earlier that evening. Her eyes were darting around the room, looking for an escape.

"Flicka," she shouted at the curled up snake snoozing by the fire. "FLICKA," she howled frantically at the top of her lungs again. The snake began to stir and opened an amber eye menacingly. Leticia had never seen such a large monstrous snake before and it nearly took her breath away.

The reptile began to slither threateningly towards the three of them and then, realising his mistress was in danger, reared upwards towards the roof of the cottage and bared his fangs, moving his head back slightly, ready to strike. Leticia was fearless and pointed her wand at the venomous creature, which, in a blast of purple smoke, shrank down to the size of a worm. With the spiked heel of her shoe, she ground him deep into the dusty grooves of the cobbled floor, killing him instantly, before turning her attention back to the shaking crone.

Fenella screamed in anguish as her pet snake was no more. "You have killed my beloved Flicka," she groaned, wringing her hands together pitifully.

Leticia laughed quietly, "And now my dear, it is your turn."

"Don't kill me, oh, please don't kill me," Fenella begged. Zamforia and Clifford stood back and watched cautiously; both knew not to interfere. Zamforia had his hand positioned firmly on his dirk and Clifford had taken out his crystal ball again, in case it was needed in a hurry.

"Oh, but I am going to kill you, make no mistake about that," Leticia screamed, "and I am going to relish every moment of it, that's for sure! You will never interfere with the Zamforian fairies again, do you hear me? NEVER AGAIN, CRONE!"

Leticia raised her wand and began to chant slowly, as she recited the spell over and over again.

Suddenly a strong gust of wind flew round the cottage and sparks of scarlet and magenta fire scattered into the room. A purple fog made it almost impossible to see anything and everyone started to choke and waft the air around them with their hands.

"You'll be killing no-one, Madam Zamforia," a deep male voice cut in. "At least not tonight." A sinister laugh echoed throughout the cottage.

As the fog cleared, a tall striking wizard, with long flowing dark hair, appeared before them. He was dressed as a warrior with silver studs embossed on his shining breastplate. He leant on his huge sword, standing between them and Fenella, scanning the group with disdain.

"Oh, Master Kazar! Thank you, thank you! You came to me rescue," Fenella wailed pitifully.

"Silence, creature," he snorted, as both Zamforia and Clifford braced themselves for an attack.

Zamforia stepped forward and confronted him. "You bastard. You have caused havoc in my family. Explain yourself and your meddling," he commanded angrily.

Kazar laughed. "I don't have to explain anything to you, you pitiful elf. I am a law unto myself," he sneered.

Clifford was shooting the fireball from one hand to the other, ready to be hurled at the evil Lord. "That's where you are wrong, Kazar. Who do you think you are? You believe you are even above the Elders and the laws of the universe but when they find out about your antics, you will be vanquished for certain. You play a very dangerous game, Sir!"

"Ah, the famous Clifford Eyesaurus. The one who was encapsulated in the crystal ball for four hundred years! Your powers are wasted on me, warlock," Kazar said mockingly, "and I would imagine after four centuries of gazing out of a piece of glass, your magic would be a tad on the rusty side!" He tittered to himself and turned towards Fenella, who was cowering in a heap. "You did good, Miss Phlegm, luring the fairy witch here." He began inspecting his nails nonchalantly. "It's virtually impossible to enter into the more refined areas of the forest when you have a reputation like mine. No, this is perfect, a proper little party," he said cruelly, looking up and smiling.

Leticia had finally got her breath back and stared at the intruder. She pointed her wand towards his face, venom dripping from her tongue. "YOU ... YOU ..." she hurled at him. "YOU have much to answer for. How dare you use my family for your entertainment! You are an evil piece of shit, that's for sure!"

Kazar laughed and brushed her wand aside. He menacingly took a step forward, leaving hardly any space between them. "I don't think I have ever been called that before," he said in an amused tone, "but this is far more than entertainment, believe me." His face was so close to hers that she could feel the heat from his breath. "I've been watching you closely for a very long time and you have something I want," he spoke.

She raised her wand a second time, and positioned it under his nose, but he showed no fear at all. For a moment their eyes locked; his were wicked, yet tender, and hers tormented and swimming with angry tears.

"You are incredibly beautiful, Madam," he bit out softly with a wry smile. "I have only seen you through the crystal scryer, but here in the flesh ... yes, you are far more pleasing to the eye."

Leticia raised her arm even further, her wand now prodding hard into the side of Kazar's cheek. She twisted her mouth angrily and began to chant the spell again. Kazar started to laugh even louder and even more menacingly.

"Leticia, move aside," Zamforia said urgently, as he took a magical staff from his belt, sensing the danger she was in. Clifford levitated the fire ball in front of him, its colours now shifting from blood red to fiery blue.

Kazar caught Leticia's wrist, sending the sparks of magic sideways into the wall of the cottage and still looking intently into her eyes, he laughed again. "Let us stop this nonsense now," he snarled. "I have got what I came for and we must make haste. You and your magic belong to me now. Say goodbye to your lovers and your life with them," he chuckled, shooting a glance at Clifford and Zamforia.

They both stepped forward hastily in a bid to free Leticia. Clifford hurled the ball in his direction and Zamforia lunged towards them but in one quick motion, Kazar encircled her with his cloak and they were gone.

Crouched in the corner of the rancid room, Fenella shivered and blinked, while Zamforia and Clifford stood rooted to the spot.

"Clifford!" Zamforia said urgently. "Use your power like before and find out where he has taken her."

Clifford immediately waved his hand over the invisible crystal globe, bringing the object into view once again. Without hesitation, he stared into the depths of the glass, his eyes scouring and searching frantically for any information of her whereabouts. After what seemed like an eternity, he looked up.

"Well?" Zamforia asked hysterically.

Clifford stared into his eyes and all Zamforia could see was Clifford's ashen face. "For once in my life, M'lord, I have no idea!"

To be continued ...